James Bruce Earl of Elgin

Extracts from the Letters of James, Earl of Elgin

to Mary Louisa, Countess of Elgin, 1847-1862

James Bruce Earl of Elgin

Extracts from the Letters of James, Earl of Elgin
to Mary Louisa, Countess of Elgin, 1847-1862

ISBN/EAN: 9783744766012

Printed in Europe, USA, Canada, Australia, Japan

Cover: Foto ©ninafisch / pixelio.de

More available books at **www.hansebooks.com**

EXTRACTS FROM THE LETTERS

OF

JAMES EARL OF ELGIN.

EXTRACTS FROM THE LETTERS

OF

JAMES EARL OF ELGIN
ETC. ETC.

TO

MARY LOUISA COUNTESS OF ELGIN

1847-1862.

PRIVATELY PRINTED.
1864.

EDINBURGH : T. CONSTABLE,
PRINTER TO THE ... 'N, AND TO THE UNIVERSITY

CONTENTS.

CANADA, 1847-1854, .	1
MISSION TO CHINA, 1857-1859, .	11
SECOND MISSION TO CHINA, 1860-1861, .	173
VICEROYALTY OF INDIA, 1862, .	245

CANADA.

1847.

Monklands, Montreal. —January 31*st*, 1847.—I have already told you of the gratifying reception I met with at Boston. All the authorities vied with each other in showing me attention. . . . They wished that I should remain a day or two at Boston, and I believe some public mark of regard might have been the consequence. But I thought it my duty to proceed. We left therefore on the 26th for Canada, by railway to a place called Franklin, thence to Lebanon by sleigh. The following day we sleighed to Burlington on Lake Champlain; the next, to St. John's in Canada, and arrived at Montreal at about two P.M. on the 29th. Mr. Paine, formerly Governor of Vermont, and a person of very high consideration among his people, accompanied me from Boston to Montpelier, the chief town of his State. I found him a very intelligent, agreeable person. At Philipsburg, on my entrance to Canada, and at La Prairie on the St. Lawrence, I was met by addresses to which I returned *viva voce* replies. . . . Yesterday was my great day. I agreed to make my entrance to Montreal, for the purpose of being inaugurated. The morning was unpropitious. There had been a tremendous storm during the night, and the snow had drifted so much that it seemed doubtful whether a sleigh could go from hence to town (about four miles). I said that I had no notion of being deterred by weather. . . Accordingly, I got into a small machine, with very small runners, which conveyed me to the entrance of the town, where I was met by the Mayor and Corporation with an address. I then got into Lord Cathcart's carriage accompanied by the Mayor, and a long procession of carriages was formed. We drove slowly to the Government House (in the town), through a dense mass of people—all the societies, trades, etc., with their banners. Nothing could be more gratifying. After the swearing in, at which the public were present, the Mayor read another address from the inhabitants. To this I delivered a reply, which produced, I think, a considerable effect, and no little astonishment on some gentlemen who intended that I should say nothing. I have adopted frankly and unequivocally Lord Durham's view of government, and I think that I have done all that could be done to prevent its being perverted to vile purposes of faction. . . .

February 3d.— . . . I have been exceedingly busy since I reached the seat of government. There is a vast deal to do, and much to learn of what is of course quite new to me. To-day I received three deputations:—First, The Roman Catholic Bishop and Clergy, who were very civil, and to whom I made a little *viva voce* speech in French; next, the Justices of the Peace; and thirdly, the Board of Trade of Montreal, with whom I was able to indulge in a little free trade. . . .

February 8th.— . . . I think my influence is growing daily, and I do not much expect to be worsted in any encounter with my Ministers. . . . I should like the first report of my arrival here to be without a cloud. It will however embrace the history of nearly a month of my government, and that is a long period of sunshine in this naughty world. . . .

February 12th.— . . . On the 10th my first levee took place, and is allowed to have been better attended than any one ever seen in Canada. All the leaders of all the parties appeared. . . .

February 27th.—The French leaders have declined to join my administration, so that now I have a plain course before me to make my government as strong as I can without them. I think they have committed a mistake, but *nous verrons*. . . .

March 3d.— . . . I do not know when I shall be able to call my Parliament. I have not yet arranged my ministerial matters. The Opposition are beginning to be a little crusty, and I do not think that the next budget from here will contain such unqualified commendation of the Governor-General as the last did.

March 4th.— . . . I ought to be, and I am, very thankful that things have gone on so well with me hitherto. I certainly have some very delicate matters to handle here, but I think they *can* be managed. Yesterday *the Papineau* called upon me, and left his card, with a particular request that I should be informed that he had called. I believe that he has hitherto kept quite aloof. . . .

March 11th.— . . . I still adhere to my opinion, . . . that the real and effectual vindication of Lord Durham's memory and proceedings will be *the success of a Governor-General of Canada who works out his views of Government fairly.* Depend upon it, if this country is governed for a few years satisfactorily, Lord Durham's reputation as a statesman will be raised beyond the reach of cavil. . . . I told you formerly that I thought it ought to be possible (not easy) to govern Canada under the system introduced by Lord D., and that if it was found to be possible to carry on the Government under that system, his title to be considered a great benefactor to his country would no longer be disputed. I am fortified in these convictions by all that I have learnt since I came here. I do not indeed know whether I am to be the instrument to carry out this work, or be destined, like others who have gone before me, to break down in the attempt, but I am still of opinion that the thing may be done, though it requires some good-fortune and some qualities not of the lowest order. I find on my arrival here a very weak Government, almost as much abused by their friends as by their foes, no civil or private secretary, and an immense quantity of arrears of business. It is possible therefore that I may not be able to bear up against the difficulties of my situation, and that it may remain for some one else to effect that object, which many reasons would render me so desirous to achieve. Hitherto, however, I have not seen any cause for despondency. The French Canadians have declined to join the present Administration. I never very much expected that they would accede to my overtures, but I thought it well to take an early opportunity of putting on record my willingness to include them in my councils. I have now told my Ministers that they must strengthen themselves as they best can, and meet Parliament. They shall have all the support they are constitutionally entitled to from me, and so shall their successors, if they are forced upon me by the voice of the representatives of the people. . . .

March 14*th.*—Papineau dined with me last night, one of a party of twenty-four, and I made great friends with my rebel. I found him really a very well-bred, intelligent man. . . . Though the French Canadians will not act with my present Ministers, I think that I have succeeded in convincing them that I am really anxious to give them a fair share of the Government. . . .

March 23*d.*—. . . I have succeeded in persuading Major Campbell, who was military secretary to Lord Sydenham, and I believe without any exception the best man for the purpose in Canada, to act as my secretary, for a time at least. I believe that he is chiefly induced to do so by hearing my views as to how the government ought to be conducted. . . .

March 27*th.*—The mail is now going. I write from the

Government House, Montreal, to which I have walked through such a snow-storm that it was impossible for any four-footed animal to move, and I do not believe any biped except myself and my two companions have attempted it. . . .

April 10*th*.—We are now in a state of transition, passing from winter to summer, and suffering sundry discomforts. The roads are in such a state that they are with difficulty passable either in sleighs or on wheels. I do not know how a less active and walking Governor could have got on since I have been here, the road between this and Montreal has been so frequently out of order. My feat in walking into town the day the last English mail was despatched has been greatly commended. Snow however is not the only obstacle on the route, for we have no police, and a most daring set of villains infest it, who have been robbing everybody they met with for some time past. . . . My appointment of Major Campbell has given universal satisfaction. "The first appointment in Canada," say the newspapers, "which has pleased all parties." . . .

April 17*th*.—. . . The summons for calling my Parliament has at length been issued. The day of meeting is fixed for the 2d of June.

August 10*th*, 1848.—. . . We are still quiet here, and all attempts by the American Irish to stir disaffection have failed. It is impossible however to say what may be the effect of disturbances in Ireland on the population here, which consists so largely of Irish Catholics; our last news from England was alarming and produces considerable anxiety. . . . I was present the other day at an examination of the students at one of the Roman Catholic Colleges of Montreal. It is altogether under the direction of the priesthood, and it is curious to observe the course they steer. The young men declaimed for some hours on a theme composed by the superior, being a contrast between ancient and modern civilisation. The greater part of it was a sonorous exposition of ultra-liberal principles, "*Liberté, Egalité, Fraternité*," "*Vox populi, vox Dei*," a very liberal tribute to the vanity and to the prejudices of the classes who might be expected to send their children to the institution or to puff it—with an elaborate *pivot à la Lacordaire;* that the Church had achieved all that had been effected in this *genre* hitherto. *Au reste*, there was the wonderful mechanism which gives that Church such advantages: the fourteen professors receiving no salaries, working for their food and that of the homeliest; as a consequence, an education, board and lodging inclusive, costing only £15 a year. The youths subjected to a constant discipline under the eye of ecclesiastics day and night. I confess when I see both the elasticity and the machinery of this Church my wonder is not with Lacordaire that it should do so much, but that it should not do more. . . .

Monklands.—November 8th, 1848.— . . . We have on the whole been preserved from the evils from which you have been suffering in Europe : though my excellent neighbours, the Yankees —who, with true republican simplicity, look upon the rights and interests of adjoining states as so much stock-in-trade to be trafficked in with a view to their own internal electioneering objects—happened unfortunately to conceive that the affectation of a prodigious sympathy with Ireland, coupled with the promise of plunder in Canada, would be an excellent bait for certain sections of the sovereign people whose votes may go far to determine the election of the President of the Union. The inhabitants of this province have happily preserved a becoming attitude, which has thus far secured us against mischief. I am not, however, quite sure that we shall get through the winter quietly. General Cass is one of the candidates for the Presidency, and affects a bitter hostility to England. If he be elected, evil may ensue. . . .

Spencerwood, Quebec.—June 12th, 1854.- . . . Yesterday being Sunday I landed *incog.*, early in the morning, at the Coves, to prevent a turmoil in Quebec. As I drove along, the people put their heads out of the windows generally with a kindly nod of recognition, and one old lady whispered, "Welcome home again!" . . . I drove up the *côte* into the grounds, up to the house. Never since I left it, assuredly, have I seen anything half so lovely. It was a perfect morning. The trees clothed in the tenderest green. The ships with their flags hanging motionless on the masts, and standing fixed like statues on the burnished mirror in which they were reflected. Not a breath of wind, yet a delightful refreshing coolness in the air. The whole scene bathed in a perfect ocean of light. I went into the house; had a few hurried words about the state of the province, its unexampled prosperity, the prospects which my Washington treaty was opening up for it; I passed on. . . . And so I have with my own hand severed the tie which bound me to this spot, to the interests which have so long engrossed me, and where any trouble or anxiety I may have had has been so amply compensated in the abundance of the return for the seed sown. . . . But I know that the logic of the question is in favour of the course I have taken. I can argue it against all comers, and end with a Q. E. D., and that is some comfort. . . .

June 16th.—Quebec.— . . . The House met two days ago. They have only begun business to-day, and there are appearances of a good deal of ill-humour. It is probable that the Tories and Ultra-Radicals will join to condemn the postponement of the Clergy Reserves and Seigneurial Bills. If so, perhaps the Ministers may be beat.

June 24*th.*— . . . My Parliament has been trying to diminish my sentimentality for this country by behaving very badly, but I have sent them about their business. . . . My life has not been an idle one since I landed on this continent. A mission to Washington,—where a job was finished in a fortnight which has been on hand for seven years: a triumphal procession to Quebec: a meeting of Parliament; prorogation and dissolution of the same.

July 24*th.*— . . . Our Quebec election has ended in a majority of some 1300 (about 1200 to 2500) in favour of the Government candidate. This is satisfactory, and a curious illustration of things here. The Quebec press has been most blackguard for about a year, abusing me in the vulgarest and most absurd way, but when it comes to the test you find at once that it represents nothing but the opinions of a clique, who are abusive partly on the calculation that if enough dirt be thrown some will stick, and partly because they are conscious of their weakness. To enable a person, however, to understand how to estimate such a press aright is a matter which requires some experience, and I do not think that any one, however able, can be expected to have that appreciation by intuition. . . .

August 25*th.*—If I had allowed the last Parliament to deal with the Clergy Reserves no doubt they would have secularized them; but they would have done so under circumstances which would have enabled the friends of the endowment to say that the opinion of the province had not been fairly taken on the question, and this allegation would certainly have been very extensively believed in England. In the new Parliament, the fate of the endowment will be the same, but at any rate it will be impossible to say that the country was taken by surprise; and the divisions in the Provincial Parliament will probably show that its preservation was impossible. From all that I can learn, it would appear that, out of 130 members of which the new Parliament consists, not above about fifteen are pledged to support the endowment. It will therefore be obvious, here and at home, that the Clergy Reserves must go; and whether this be a disastrous result or not, one thing is certain, that it is better that a measure of this description, if it be adopted, should carry with it as much as possible the prestige of unanimity. If I thought (which I fortunately do not) that the fate of religion was bound up with the preservation of the endowment, I should not, of course, be reconciled to the measure by any amount of unanimity. But looking to the political and social consequences, it is of the utmost importance that it shall seem to be adopted by nearly general consent. I have no doubt but that when the heats of present controversy had subsided, I should have been able (had I remained here to point the moral of the tale) in this, as in former cases, to bring people round to the opinion that the course taken was the right one. . . .

September 8th.— . . . As I expected, Hincks arrived with his tender of resignation. I accepted, and sent for M'Nab, who is now engaged in ascertaining whether he can make an Administration. Should he fail, I have plenty of other shots in my locker. . . . I like this active *crise* a great deal better than the dull abuse of the last three months.

September 14th.—The new Ministry, Sir A. M'Nab at the head, will I suppose be able to get on well enough. . . . It is rather amusing for me to find myself abused for my partiality for Sir A. M'Nab, and my selection of him ascribed to personal feelings. I believe, indeed, that it would be difficult to do anything here which would not be attributed to some bad motive. . . .

September 22d.— . . . I have brought into office the gentlemen who made themselves for years most conspicuous and obnoxious for personal hostility to myself, thus giving the most complete negative to the allegation that I am swayed by personal motives in the selection of my advisers; and these gentlemen have accepted office on the understanding that they will carry out in all particulars the policy which I sketched out while my former Administration was in office, thus proving that the policy in question is the only one suited to the country, the only one which an Administration *can* adopt. I do not see how the blindest can fail to draw this inference from these facts. The first thing which my new Administration have had to do is to adopt and carry through the House the Address responsive to my speech from the throne. This is, certainly for me, and I hope for the country, the most fortunate wind-up of my connexion with Canada which could have been imagined. . . .

September 23d.—Both branches of my Parliament adopted yesterday, *unanimously,* the bill necessary to give effect to my Treaty, in so far as Canada is concerned, and I am now going down in state to give it the Royal Assent. This is a triumph for which I cannot be too grateful. . . .

Niagara Falls.—October 1st.— . . . I have had a very busy week, and have done some good work. Left Quebec on Monday; travelled by special train along the Richmond Railway and to Longueuil; got into a steamer to visit the Victoria Bridge, and by the merest accident arrived just as the first stone of the most important part of that stupendous work was being dropped into its place; got a trowel and mortar, and went through the ceremony of laying the stone. . . . Then joining the St. John Railway, I spent the night in a steamer on Lake Champlain, and reached Buffalo about nine P.M. on Tuesday, taking the same route as on my return to the Falls in 1851. This was the quickest journey ever made from Quebec to Buffalo. Next morning I was conveyed by railway to London, this point being the object of my trip, as here the great Provincial Agricultural Show was being held. I was hospitably received by Mr. John Wilson, and commenced proceedings by delivering an answer to an address presented to me. On Thursday, the great day of the show, I was occupied in seeing the sights, speechifying, etc., dining at Mrs. Harris's. Having heard that day that the Detroit Agricultural Show was taking place at the same time, I determined to take the opportunity to pay my friends in Michigan the compliment of a visit; and being provided again with a special train, went thither on Friday; was entertained at dinner, and went through the ordinary routine of such business very successfully. On Saturday, I came on from London to this point, spending some hours at Hamilton on the way. You remember how long it took me to return here from London in 1849; so this report of my tour will give you an idea of what a change the railways have made in this part of the world. I remain here to-morrow. . . . My reception during this tour has been, up to the present time, very satisfactory. . . .

October 7th.—On the St. Lawrence, off Beauharnais.— . . . We spent Monday at the Falls. I never saw them more lovely; the day was perfect. I spent nearly the whole of it on Goat Island. On Tuesday I went to Toronto; by rail to Niagara town, and thence in Captain Dick's new boat the Peerless. . . . There was an address on the wharf at Toronto, and addresses next morning at the Normal School, University, Mechanics' Institute, etc.; and on Tuesday evening a select party dined at Mr. Allan's, who has a very sumptuous kind of house, where we were comfortably lodged. On Wednesday, a little before twelve, I embarked in the Lake boat for Coburg, where we landed at about six. An address, and speech in reply there, after which we got into a carriage, and drove about twenty-six miles to the house of a respectable Methodist yeoman, and arrived at eleven, very cold and famished. By about one we got to bed, and pretty early next morning got under weigh for Belleville, which we reached at three, through a fire of addresses. There was a very warm reception there; addresses, public dinner, and a dance at the Mayor's,—all which combined kept us at work till twelve at night, my share in the day being ten speeches. On Friday we started, with most lovely weather, to sail down the Bay of Quinte, reaching Kingston at about five, after delaying half an hour to visit a little lake, curiously situated on the top of a hill. At Kingston there was a very grand reception, and six addresses were fired at me at the City Hall, where I was received pretty much in the same way as we were in 1847. Then a grand dinner, with every appearance of enthusiasm. At midnight I embarked on board this boat, on my way to Montreal, and hope to reach Quebec to-morrow morning. . . . This day, too, is perfection. We are at this moment nearing the "Cedar" Rapids, under a perfectly calm sky; a glowing sun sinking in the west, and casting a mantle of fresh gold over the wooded banks, which are already clothed in their most brilliant autumnal colours. Shall I own that it is with very mingled feelings that I have made this tour: gratification at the evidences of improvement which I have seen around me, and at the kindness of my reception, and sadness to think that it is a last visit. . . . I cannot without a pang bring myself to believe that henceforth all the interests of this great and thriving country are to be to me as a matter in which I have no concern. Notwithstanding the atrocities of the press, it is impossible for me to go through the country without feeling that I have a strong hold on the people of the country; that I occupy a place here which no one ever filled before. . . .

Quebec.---November 1st.— . . . I get on very smoothly with the new Administration, and of course the complete denial which has been given by its formation to the charge of partisanship on my part, strengthens my position here. . . .

November 11th.— . . . There is a strong feeling in favour of my passing the Clergy Reserves and Seigneurial Bills. There is every probability that the Legislature will adjourn for the winter in a few days, and I intend to remain in order to pass the obnoxious bills of the Session, and to hand over the government in a perfectly quiet condition to Sir E. Head, who is arrived. Three of the four colonies affected by the Reciprocity Treaty have passed the laws necessary for giving effect to it. Two of these by unanimous votes, the third with only four dissentient voices. There remains only Nova Scotia. . . .

November 15th.— . . . I am to get the Clergy Reserves settled with the consent of all parties, and I hope to get a good deal of unanimity on the Seigneurial Bill. . . .

November 25th.—I have succeeded with Nova Scotia. The Parliament is called for the 2d December on purpose to pass the Treaty. . . . Here, the Clergy Reserves and Seigneurial Bills have both passed the Assembly. It was inevitable, and is being done by the Tories themselves. . . . The Seigneurial Bill is the measure I have least satisfaction in of any in which I have been concerned. . . . I think, however, that it is my duty if possible to remove this stumbling-block from the way of my successor. . . .

December 3d.— . . . I have given my farewell ball, made my farewell speech . . . All augurs an early move. . . .

MISSION TO CHINA.

1857.

Thursday, April 30*th*, 1857.—*Off Corsica, on board H.M.S. Caradoc.*—We are now going on smoothly, with a bright, but not yet oppressive, Mediterranean sun and a calm sea. The snow-clad mountains of Corsica on our left, and the coast of Sardinia emerging on our right; in an hour or two we shall be in the Straits between the two islands. Both coasts seem entirely barren; the Sardinian, especially so; hardly a sign of cultivation. On the Corsican side there are a few villages. We began our journey more sadly, with heavy thoughts. . . . A cold north wind, and a gloomy sky overhead. We travelled from Paris to Lyons, and then to Marseilles. When we embarked the sea was rough; our vessel tossed and rolled not a little. I was obliged to beg the captain to excuse my non-appearance at the dinner-table. . . . It was a relief, as the hours of the night passed on, to feel that the sea was subsiding, and as morning broke, to perceive a bright sun streaming into the cabin. . . .

Friday, May 1*st.*—This morning the breeze is decided, though fair, and we are tossing and rolling considerably. The captain is in great spirits; says it is a good omen, as he expects to make the shortest passage to Malta he ever made. I tell him that I do not care how soon I give him an opportunity of boasting of the speed with which he can bring me back from Malta. We are now (noon) passing between the coast of Sicily and the island of Maritimo; one of those in which King Bomba retains his convicts; a lonely rock. The coast of Sicily is only slightly visible on the other side. We have frequent showers, which makes it disagreeable to be on deck. . . . We have had no heat to complain of yet, though the sun is a little powerful when he breaks through the clouds.

Two P.M.—I have been on deck looking at the coast of Sicily, and taking advantage of the temporary smoothness afforded by the protection of the island of Maritimo; and after passing it on the right, we passed another called Favignano on the left, and so on to Marsala, off which we are at this moment. To judge from appearances, there is much more industry and cultivation in the dominions of King Bomba than in Corsica or Sardinia. The latter, which we passed yesterday, seemed absolutely barren: but the coasts which we are now running along seem to be cultivated wherever cultivation is possible. . . . Our present captain is a pleasant man, and makes us very comfortable. The vessel is small, and, I daresay, if the sea was meeting us, we should suffer a good deal; as it is, we get on very fairly.

Nine P.M.—I have been standing for two hours on the paddle-box, looking at a bright starry sky, fringed with a few white breezy clouds along the horizon, and watching the opposite paddle-box dipping into the trough of the sea, and rising out of it again. The captain says he never went faster, or rolled more. Notwithstanding which, I have got through the day very tolerably well. But it is a sadly monotonous life, until one can settle down to one's book, which it is difficult to do at first. . . . We are to arrive at Malta at about two or three to-morrow morning. Lord Lyons is there, not to mention the Governor; and some dozen regiments, so I shall finish this to-night, in case I should be prevented from adding anything later.

Malta.—Six A.M.—A salute firing. I am going on shore.

H.M.S. Caradoc.—May 2d.—I have just returned to my ship after spending a few hours on shore, and visiting Lord Lyons in his magnificent Prince Albert. . . . How beautiful Malta is with its narrow streets, gorgeous churches, and impregnable fortifications. I landed at about six; and walked up to the Palace, and wrote my name in the Governor's book, who resides out of town. I then took a turn through the town, and went to the inn to breakfast. While I was there Sir W. Reid arrived, in great regret that he had not been there sooner to invite me to breakfast with him. . . . By way of conversation with the waiter, I asked who were in the house: "Only two families, one of them Lord Balgonie and his sisters." . . . I saw the ladies first, and at a later hour their brother, in his bed. Poor fellow! the hand of death is only too visibly upon him. There he lay; his arm, absolutely fleshless, stretched out. His large eyes gleaming from his pale face. I could not dare to offer to his broken-hearted sisters a word of comfort. These poor girls! how I felt for them; alone! with their brother in such a state. They go to Marseilles by the next opportunity. Probably by the packet which will convey to you this letter, and they hope that their mother will meet them there. What a tragedy! . . . I met some of the 71st. . . . This is not quite the end of my Malta adventures. As I was descending the stairs of the Palace, a man ran down after me, and claimed acquaintance

with me because he had been at Farrance's Hotel with us, before
I went to Canada in 1847! The particular incident in my
history which rested on his memory was that my servant left
my brushes behind at Farrance's.... Then again, I had been
incog. at the hotel till Sir W. Reid found me there. When
the innkeeper learned who I was, he was in despair at my
having been put into so small a room, and informed me that he
was the son of an old servant at Broomhall, Hood by name, and
that he had often played with me at cricket! How curious are
these strange *rencontres* in life! They put me in mind of
Heber's image, who says that we are like travellers journeying
through a dense wood intersected by innumerable paths. We
are constantly meeting in unexpected places, and plunging into
the forest again! We have now something of a tropical sun,
and Malta puts me in many ways in mind of my West Indian
experiences, but the weather is still delightful. . . .

Sunday, 3d.—. . . Our object is if possible to reach Alexandria during daylight on Tuesday. The Indus, with Oliphant on
board, has some twelve hours' start of us from Malta, and the
Euxine from Marseilles, three hours'. We expect to beat the
latter. . . . I have got fairly settled to my books, so that the
time will pass more lightly. Though blue-books about opium
are not lively reading, still they are an occupation, and do something towards filling a void. . . .

*Monday, 4th.—*Another lovely day. The temperature perfection and the sea smooth, with only ripple enough upon it to
show that we are not becalmed. Not that a calm is to be
dreaded, for it is the great blessing of steam that one not only
gets on in a calm, but that one creates by going through the air
a pleasant breeze for one's-self. However, to-day we have not a
calm but a gentle breeze nearly a-head of us. A few minutes
ago we saw a steamer a-head. It turns out to be a war-steamer
wending her way slowly back to Malta. We hoisted the red
flag to the fore, to let her know what we are, but she passed us
at a considerable distance, so I cannot say whether or not she
will report us as thus far on our way. . . .

*Tuesday, 5th.—*Another fine day but rather more rolling. No
wind, however, so if there has been a storm it has passed away
from this region. Last night was very pleasant and cool. The
sun is powerful to-day, but in the shade it is not oppressive,
and we make a good breeze by moving through the air at some
eleven knots an hour. . . . *Nine* P.M.— Alexandria in sight.

*Alexandria.—May 6th.—*I made up my letter last night, not
knowing how short the time of my sojourn at Alexandria might
be. But at about one in the morning I received a letter from
Frederick, telling me that the steamer due at Suez had not yet

arrived, that an official reception was to be given me, and that I had better not land too early. . . . Notwithstanding which, washing decks, the morning gun, and a bright sun, broke my slumbers at an early hour, and I got up and dressed soon after daybreak. At about 6.30 A.M. a boat of the Pacha's, with a dignitary (who turned out to be a very gentleman-like Frenchman), arrived, and from him I learnt that the Governor of Alexandria, with a cortège of dignitaries and a carriage and four, was already at the shore awaiting my arrival; but Frederick did not come till about half-past nine, and it was nearly ten before I landed. I was then conducted by the authorities to the palace in which I am now writing, consisting of suites of very handsome rooms, and commanding a magnificent view of the sea. I agreed to dine with the consul, Mr. Green, but consented to have here a slight repast by way of *déjeuner* or luncheon. This has been just served, and consisted of a series of about twenty dishes carried round in the Russian way, and a proportionate variety of wines. About a dozen attendants are loitering about and watching every movement, not curiously, but in order to supply any possible want. At this very moment a mild looking Turk is peeping into my bed-room where I am writing this letter, and supposing that I may wish to be undisturbed, has drawn a red cloth *portière* across the open doorway. This palace, which is set apart for the reception of distinguished strangers, is situated in the Turkish quarter of the town, and all the houses around are inhabited by Mussulmans. The windows are all covered with latticed wooden shutters, through which the wretched women may, I suppose, peer as they do through the grating at the House of Commons, but which are at least as impermeable to the mortal eye from without. The streets are very empty, as it is the Ramadan, during which devout Turks fast and sleep throughout the day, and indemnify themselves by eating, drinking, and amusing themselves all night. The Pacha is not here, but I am now going with F. to call on Mustapha Bey, his cousin. . . . I ought to have told you that we performed rather a feat last night;—coming into Alexandria, after nightfall and without a pilot, steaming up among all the ships in the clear moonlight was a very fine sight.

Cairo.—May 7th.— . . . Most of yesterday afternoon was spent in drinking coffee and smoking long pipes. Two ladies partaking of the latter enjoyment after dinner at Mr. Green's. One of them (Mrs. Green) told me that she had dined with the Princess (the Pacha's wife) a few days ago. She went at seven and left at half-past twelve, and with the exception of a half hour of dinner, all the rest of the time was spent in smoking and drinking coffee. After dinner, the mother of the Pacha's only child came in and joined the party. She was treated with a certain consideration as being the mother of this child, although she was not given a pipe. The Princess seemed on very good terms with her. This child (a boy three years old) has an English nurse, and this nurse has persuaded the Pacha to allow her to take the child to England on a visit. The mother, who has picked up a little English from the nurse, said to Mrs. Green, " I am very unhappy ; *young Pacha*" (her boy) " is going away." The mother is no more thought of in this arrangement than I am. What a strange system it is! During my drive yesterday afternoon I visited Mustapha Bey, the Swedish Consul-General (who had expected me at a great banquet he gave the day before), and then went to F.'s own house, about two miles in the country, and really very nice. I accomplished this drive in a carriage and four, with a mounted guard of *cavasses* and outrunners alongside of the horses. Whenever I descended, a Turk, with a scimitar and a stick like a footman's full dress stick, preceded me. To us who have lived among the free and easy gentlemen of the West, the importance which attaches to a position of authority in the East is quite astounding. . . . F. seems to have been doing good work here, and to have great influence. . . . We started at a very early hour this morning, and reached Cairo within four hours, travelling in a special train at the rate of forty miles an hour. Conceive this in Egypt! I am now writing to you in a hotel at Cairo, where I have just been summoned to the window by shouting, and find that it proceeds from a gang of donkey-boys contending for the honour of furnishing a *monture* to L. We passed through the wonderful Delta to-day, and certainly the people looked more comfortable than those of Alexandria. The beasts too, camels, oxen, donkeys, showed signs of the fertility of the soil in their sleekness. What might not be made of this country if it were wisely guided! We have just heard of the arrival of the Bentinck at Suez, without any news from China.

May 8th.—A further telegram informs us that the Bentinck cannot sail till to-morrow at night, so I shall stay over this day at Cairo, where there is a good deal to see. Last night I went to the mosque at the Citadel, illuminated for the evening service of the Ramadan. The interior of the mosque, with its central dome flanked by segments of domes, and the lines marked out by rows of lamps, had a fine effect. When we first went in, the service, which was going on, consisted in a very shrill intoning of something by the leader of the service, and a sort of responses by the congregation, accompanied by prostrating themselves at stated periods, and touching the ground with their foreheads. The movement was graceful and almost devotional; but a church without either priest or altar seems odd at first to us. After this ceremony was over, a set of queer-looking parties, seated on a bench, began to chant through their noses in honour of Mahomet and the Prophets, near the tomb of Mehemet Ali, which is in a sort of chapel at one end of the mosque. I was told that a hareem was behind the screen round the tomb saying their prayers. This seems to be the only way in which women are allowed to take part in church services in this country. They are sometimes permitted to be *parquées* in pens about the tombs of their lords and masters.

Steamer Bentinck.—Sunday, May 10*th.*— . . . I write to you from the neighbourhood of Mount Sinai, which we passed at an early hour this morning, gliding through a sea of most transparent glass, with so little motion that there is hardly an excuse for bad writing. . . . I am very comfortable in this vessel, although it is pretty hot. The Peninsular and Oriental Company is much more considerate than the Government, for while the latter only pays at the contract price for six places, the former, in point of fact, is giving us accommodation for sixteen. . . . I must, however, take you back to Cairo. We began to move at a very early hour, about three, on Saturday (yesterday) morning. We were actually in the railway carriages at half-past four. I was placed in a *coupé* before the engine, in order that I might see the road; and in this somewhat formidable position ran over about forty miles of the Desert in about an hour and a half. It is a wonderful sight this strange barren expanse of stone and gravel, with here and there a small encampment of railway labourers, after passing through the luxuriant Valley of the Nile, teeming with production, and life animal and vegetable. In the morning air there was a healthy freshness, which was very delightful. At the end of our hour and a half we reached the termination of the part of the railway which is already completed, and embarked in two-wheeled four-horse vans (such as you see in the *Illustrated News*), to pass over about five miles of trackless desert, lying between the said terminus and a station on the regular road across the Desert, at which we were to breakfast. This part of our journey was rough work, and took us some time to execute. Our station was really a very nice building; and while we were there a caravan of pilgrims to Mecca, some women in front and the men following, all mounted on their patient camels, passed by. After we were refreshed we started for Suez; and you will hardly believe me when I tell you that we travelled forty-seven miles over the Desert in a carriage as capacious and commodious as a London town coach, in four hours and a half, including seven changes of horses and a stoppage of half an hour. In short, we got over the ground in about three hours and three-fourths. We had six horses to our carriage, and a swarthy Nubian, with a capital seat on horseback, rode by us all the way, occasionally reminding our horses that it was intended they should go at a gallop. As might be supposed, we distanced our followers. . . . I shall not, I suppose, have so much to tell you henceforward as I have had during the past few days. There will be less variety in the ship-board life, although even here we have a curiously mixed world, not to mention the beauty of the coasts of the Red Sea, which are far more mountainous than I expected to find them. I never saw anything more lovely than the colouring both yesterday afternoon and this morning, so long as we had the mountain ranges in sight. The shores have now receded from our view, but no doubt we shall meet them again before long. . . . We had prayers in the morning; the purser officiating. . . .

May 11*th*.—The ship is not very full, so that we are comfortable. Most of the passengers are young officers and cadets for India; some with brides. There is also an A.D.C. of General Ashburnham's, etc. . . . *Au reste*, the weather still continues perfect; there is really no motion to inconvenience any one. They say that the thermometer in this cabin where I am writing stands at 90°; but it is not oppressive, as there is a gentle head-wind, enough to fan us without making a sea. I had a capital bath this morning; a canvas hut on the deck, with a shower-bath bucket on the top, through which salt-water was poured. . . . I am glad to have had two days in Egypt. It gave one an idea at least of that country; in some degree a painful one. I suppose that France and England, by their mutual jealousies, will be the means of perpetuating the abominations of the system under which that magnificent country is ruled. They say that the Pacha's revenue is about £4,000,000, and his expenses about £2,000,000, so that he has about £2,000,000 of pocket-money. Yet, I suppose that the Fellahs, owing to their own industry, and the incomparable fertility of the country, are not badly off as compared with the peasantry elsewhere. We passed, at one of our stopping places between Cairo and Suez, part of a Turkish regiment on their way to Jeddah. These men were dressed in a somewhat European costume, some of them with the Queen's medal on their breasts. There was a hareem, in a sort of omnibus, with them, containing the establishment of one of the officers. One of the ladies dropped her veil for a moment, and I saw rather a pretty face; almost the only Mahomedan female face I have seen since I have reached this continent. They are much more rigorous, it appears, with the ladies in Egypt than at Constantinople. There they wear a veil which is quite transparent, and go about shopping. But in Egypt they seem to go very little out, and their veil completely hides everything but the eyes. In the palace which I visited near Cairo (and which the Pacha offered, if we had chosen to take it), I looked through some of the grated windows allowed in the harcems, and I suppose that it must require a good deal of practice to see comfortably out of them. It appears that the persons who ascend to the top of the minarets to call to prayer at the appointed hours are blind men, and that the blind are selected for this office, lest they should be able to look down into the hareems. That is certainly carrying caution very far. Did I tell you before that on Friday afternoon I visited a very beautiful garden near Cairo, and a kiosque of a gorgeous character, surrounding a basin of water, where Mehemet Ali used to retire with his ladies; and that on my return, I had an opportunity of seeing some horsemen amusing themselves by throwing the *djereed?* Some of them rode well, and threw their lances skilfully, but there was nothing very wonderful in the performance. . . .

May 12*th*.—I hear that we sometimes communicate with the home-going steamer, if we happen to pass near it at sea, so that I must have this ready for the chance. Last night was really hot, rather seriously so; and to-day the official report at noon is 92°. The wind, too, which is still very light, has shifted, and become nearly a fair wind, which, of course, makes it much hotter. But so long as we are gliding through the water with so little motion that we can hardly remember that we are on board ship, it is impossible to complain. Another advantage in tropical travelling in calm weather is, that everything in the shape of windows, doors, and port-holes is left wide open, so one has much less of smell than in steamers elsewhere. Still I confess I feel the heat a little to-day; more particularly, in becoming sleepy when I take to my book. This may in some measure arise from the fact, that Mr. Meadows is now discussing Chinese religion and philosophy, and throwing light upon them down from German metaphysics. The passengers are almost all English. There is, I think, one French pair; but among the crew we have all sorts of Indians, and some Chinese. To look at, the latter are incomparably the finer race, and are capable, I apprehend, of double the work of the former. It is odd to see the Indians going through their toilette, eating their meals, and sleeping on the deck, which they never seem to leave; and the composure with which the ladies witness these proceedings. There is certainly great protection in a black skin.

May 13*th.*—I have just been told that we may meet the steamer to-day, and send our letters. I therefore close this for the moment. . . .

May 14*th.*—We met no steamer yesterday. . . . We expect to reach Aden to-morrow evening, and remain some hours to coal. . . . It is very oppressively hot to-day, although the thermometer only marks 90°. It is hung up in a cool place. I was on deck both the last mornings long before sunrise, and got my Red Sea bath just as that luminary was leaving his. There was nothing very striking in the sunrise; but the nights are beautiful. We are getting, evening after evening, more completely under the southern cross, and a very large and clear moon (nearly full) puts the stars out of countenance at successively later hours. To-night, if I wait for the moon, I must make up my mind to go to bed in the dark, as the lights are put out at half-past ten. . . . To-day we have passed some picturesque-looking islands, of the group which runs up to the Straits of Babelmandeb. There is a very narrow and interesting passage at the strait itself, but I fear we shall pass it in the night. We are building a lighthouse, and, I fancy, fortifying in a quiet way an island called Perim, which will give us a capital military position there. . . .

May 15*th.*—At about seven o'clock last night we met the homeward-bound steamer, and the captain came on board with newspapers, etc., for me. He took back with him our letters. . . . The only news of importance from China seems to be that the Rebels are making progress at Shanghai, and that the Chinese authorities are putting a duty on opium as a means of raising a revenue. This if true points to a solution of one of our greatest difficulties. Last night was a miserably hot one in the cabin, though it was breezy and comfortable on deck. I got up soon after four as usual, and saw the passage between the island of Perim and the coast of Babelmandeb. The former is a lowish island, but well situated to command the strait. The coast is rocky and mountainous, and we have never lost sight of it since we passed the straits. The colouring of the mountains is very beautiful, the sparkling white sandy sides capped with summits of a velvet blue, but they seem barren and fearfully hot, and I almost dread the prospect of landing at Aden. . . . There is more of a heaving motion in this Indian Ocean than in the Red Sea. . . . We have passed what is generally considered the worst part of our voyage for heat, but my cabin is on the wrong side for wind, and I do not expect to be very cool again for many a long day. They are coming to lay the tables for dinner, so I must say good-bye for the present. . . .

Steam-ship Bentinck, off Socotra.—*May* 19*th.*— . . . No

writing for these last three days; the heat was unbearable, upwards of 100°, and it was impossible to sit in the cabin. Yesterday we had a good deal of wind and sea, and most of the passengers were off work. . . . It is blowing and rolling still a good deal, but I am somewhat better. . . . This steam company is a monopoly, and the fruits are visible in the management. The feeding is very bad. Wine is, by way of, given by the Company; the consequence is that one can get nothing except what they choose to allow. There is not any champagne in the vessel, and save at the regular hours nothing can be got except on medical certificate. Of course they are not quite so strict with me, but the system is bad. . . . I left my last letter at Aden. We landed there at about four P.M., under a salute from an Indian man-of-war sloop and the fort, to which latter place I was conveyed in a carriage which the Governor sent for me. It was most fearfully hot. The hills are rugged and grand, but wholly barren; not a sign of vegetation, and the vertical rays of a tropical sun beating upon them. The whole place is comprised in a drive around the hills of some three or four miles, beyond which the inhabitants cannot stray without the risk of being seized by the Arabs. I cannot conceive a more dreary spot to dwell in, though the Governor assured me that the troops are healthy. He received me very civilly, and insisted that I should remain with him until the steamer sailed, which involved leaving his abode (the cantonment) at about half-past three in the morning. He took me to see some most extraordinary tanks which he has recently discovered, and which must have been constructed with great care and at great expense, at some remote period, in order to collect the rainwater which falls at rare intervals in torrents. These tanks are so constructed that the overflow of the upper one fills the lower, and in this way when the fall is considerable a great quantity can be gathered. They were all filled with rubbish, and it is very possible that there may be many besides these which have been already discovered, but when they are cleared out they are in perfect preservation. Some of them are of great capacity, and it is difficult to understand how they come to have been filled up so completely. The Governor told me that he had a few months before driven in his gig over the largest, which I went with him to see. At that time he had no idea of its existence. After we had visited the tanks we returned to his residence, which was a sort of one-storeyed cottage surrounded by a verandah, with an out-house adjoining, to which he conducted me. . . . Dinner was laid out in the open air; we were not troubled with mosquitoes, and as there was some lively champagne, and much better food than that supplied in the

Bentinck, this part of the performance was rather pleasant. ...
At about ten I proposed to retire, and found beds in the verandah, besides a grand one in the room. I was persuaded to take one in the verandah as being the cooler. ... I cannot say that I slept much, for the heat was intense. ... The Governor informs me that the thermometer in his house is sometimes 106°; but he removes during the hot season to a cottage on the shore where it does not rise above 90°. At four A.M. I started, after a bath, and by the light of the dawning morning saw the white cantonments, and passed along a road made in the rock through walls of sixty or seventy feet in height, till we opened up the sea and the harbour where the steamer was lying. When we got on board we found that the coaling was not quite completed, and all the passengers miserable, having passed a wretched night in the inn,—the ladies lying in the verandah, and the gentlemen passing the time as they best could by amusing themselves in the vicinity; the chances of sleep for the former being therefore reduced to zero. The ship was dirty, and everybody looking miserable, and the glowing sun was beginning to dart at us those slanting rays against which it is so difficult to protect one's-self; so after watching the antics played by the morning mists, as in all manner of fantastic shapes they curled around the Peak of Aden, before being finally dispersed by the sun, I retired to my cabin to prepare myself for the labours of the day.

May 20*th.*—And such a day! Greatly worse in point of heat than any day in the Red Sea; and Sunday was no better. My cabin is on the wrong side for the breeze, which blows steadily during the north-west monsoon on the other quarter of the ship. The only advantage I enjoy is, that when the wind is high, the opposite cabins are more frequently exposed to have their ports closed. We had service on Sunday on deck as before. On Monday began our blow, which has continued with only a kind of lull while passing the island of Socotra. What a wearisome life it is! I am beginning to pine to be at the end of my voyage and at work, for the alternation of burning sun and scorching wind is only bearable when one has a great deal to do. It affects one's health a little. ... We are getting on slowly and miserably through the sweltering sea. This old vessel has got her copper all out of order, and ought to be docked, so we are making some eight or nine knots, when in one of the new screws we should be making twelve. Luckily for me, I have sufficiently recovered to be able to read blue-books, and to seek relief in writing this. ...

May 22*d.*—I did not write yesterday. I had a bad night, and was not fit for much, so I got L. to enter into a negotiation, by means of which I moved into a cabin on deck, and as the night was quiet, I profited a great deal by the change. I shall feel the motion, as it is over the stern; but the difference in point of coolness is great. I think I should have been regularly laid up if I had remained below. . . . The sea is calmer; there was a heavy shower in the morning, which somewhat lightened the air. . . . As each of these wearisome days passes, I cannot help being more and more determined that, in so far as it rests with me, this voyage shall not have been made for nothing. However, the issues are in higher hands. Half-past two has now struck, and my watch, which I have not altered since I left London, is at a quarter to ten!

Sunday, 24th.—At about two A.M. yesterday, I was awoke by a most tremendous noise, followed by a hurry-skurry among the passengers sleeping on the deck, among whom were some of the fair sex, and found that a violent storm of wind and rain was passing over us. It did not last long, but it was almost immediately followed by a second, which blew from another quarter, and into the windows of my cabin. These storms have done us some service in cooling the air a little. We had another yesterday, and one already this morning. We may expect a succession of them between this and Ceylon. . . . The heat, want of exercise, indifferent feeding, etc., are enough to make one feel unwell, and I am laid up to-day, and writing to you from my cabin, which I have not yet left. . . . We are now told we shall reach Ceylon in two days. . . . I have got dear B.'s large speaking eyes beside me while I am writing, and mine (ought I to confess it) are very dim, while all these thoughts of home crowd upon me. There is nothing congenial to me in my present life. I have not elasticity of spirits to keep up with the younger people around me. It may be better when the work begins; but I cannot be sanguine even as to that, for the more I read of the blue-books and papers with which I have been furnished, the more embarrassing the questions with which I have to deal appear. . . .

May 26th.—*Galle, Ceylon.*—This is a very charming place; so green that one almost forgets the heat. Ashburnham is here; we go on together to Singapore this evening. Bad news from India. I think that I may find in this news, if confirmed, a justification for pressing matters with vigour in China, and hastening the period at which I may hope to see you again. . . .

Steam-ship Singapore.—*May 27th.*—We landed at Point de Galle yesterday at about nine, and remained on shore till six. I should have enjoyed the respite from the sea a good deal if I had felt well, for the place was snug and green, and for a tropical spot, cool. I took a walk, however, along the ramparts, and a drive along the shore, through a grove of cocoa-nut trees, which run almost into the sea, the great surfy waves beating against their roots. This grove is very thick, and extends all the way to Colombo, seventy-two miles. The cocoa is the all-in-all of the natives of Ceylon. Of the latter, one saw abundance. For a long time I found it impossible to distinguish the sexes; but at last I discovered that the gentlemen wear a comb in their hair, while the ladies dispense with that ornament. I was received with all honours, and conducted to a Government building called the Queen's House, which Sir H. Ward had ordered to be prepared for my reception. He would have come to me, but he was engaged in doing the honours of the Queen's birthday at the seat of Government. General Ashburnham was already lodged at the said Queen's House, having arrived from Bombay four days before. He brought with him a report of a most serious mutiny in the Bengal army. Perhaps he sees it in the worst light, because he has always (I remember his speaking to me on the subject at Balbirnie) predicted that something of the kind would occur; but apart from his anticipations the matter seems grave enough. The mutineers have murdered Europeans, seized the fort and treasure of Delhi, and proclaimed the son of the Great Mogul. There seems to be no adequate European force at hand to put them down, and the season is bad for operations by Europeans. Such is the sum and substance of this report, as conveyed by telegraph to Elphinstone, the evening before Ashburnham left Bombay. I was a good deal tempted to remain at Galle for a few hours, in order to await the arrival of the homeward-bound steamer from Calcutta, and to get further news; but, on reflection, I came to the conclusion that the best course to take was to view this grave intelligence as an inducement to press on to China. I wrote officially to Clarendon to say, that if this intelligence was confirmed, it might have a tendency to lower our prestige in the East, and to increase the influence of the party opposed to reason in China; that this state of affairs might make it more than ever necessary that I should endeavour to bring matters in China to an issue at the earliest moment, so as to anticipate this mischief, and to place the regiments destined for China at the disposal of Government for service elsewhere. This despatch will prepare Clarendon for any measures of vigour which I may find it advisable to adopt. . . . I feel better to-day, and I think that our food is better here than in the other ship. We have very good bread, baked by a Chinaman, who certainly has a chance if he wishes to earn fame as a patriot. We ought to sleep, for the cabins smell of laudanum to an extent you can hardly imagine, there being some 1500 chests of opium on board. I did not, however, sleep much, although pretty cool, as I took up my quarters in the saloon,—the cabins, what with opium and closed ports, being unbearable. We have a stiffish breeze, and are to have no smooth water till we get into the Straits at Sumatra.

May 29th.— . . . We are now near the close of our voyage, and the serious work is about to begin. Up to this point I have heard nothing to throw any light upon my prospects. It is impossible to read the blue-books without feeling that we have often acted towards the Chinese in a manner which it is very difficult to justify; and yet their treachery and cruelty come out so strongly at times as to make almost anything appear justifiable. . . . The smell of opium gets worse and worse. We cannot open the portholes, and the cabins are suffocating. . . . We are going on, with a steady monsoon in our favour, but with less roll. . . . On Sunday night or Monday we expect to be at Penang, and I shall leave letters there in case we should pass a homeward vessel between Penang and Singapore. It is only a sail of forty hours between the two. When we reach the latter point my work will, I apprehend, begin, and I am longing for it in the hope that it may be the more speedily over.

May 30th.—We are now passing some of the Islands of Sumatra. They are hilly and covered with wood, but I see no signs of human habitation. They remind me a good deal of West Indian Islands. It is a comfort to see land again, and it brings with it the additional advantage that the swell of the sea is lessened. But it is very hot. We have our portholes open at last. . . .

Sunday, May 31st.—I am a little less miserable this Sunday than I was last. We have had service, the captain officiating. The sea is very smooth, but there is a pleasant breeze. We expect to be at Penang this evening, but it is doubtful whether or not we shall land. . . . We see lofty hills in the distance occasionally, and yesterday we passed pretty near some islands, and have also had the excitement of seeing a steamer in the distance, at first supposed to be an opium-vessel from Calcutta, but we have now ascertained that she is going the other way. . . .

Penang.—June 1st.—We have just returned to our vessel after a few hours spent on shore; or, rather, I have just emerged from a bath in which I have been reclining for half an hour, endeavouring to cool myself after a hot morning's work. We made this place at about eleven last night, running into the harbour by the assistance of a bright moon. The water was perfectly smooth, and I stood on the paddle-box for some hours, watching the distant hills as they rose into sight and faded from our view, and the bright phosphorescent light of the sea, cut by our prow, and which, despite the clearness of the night, was sometimes almost too brilliant to be gazed at. When we dropped our anchor, the captain still professed to doubt whether or not he would have to proceed immediately, but he gave me to understand that if he could not accomplish this, he would not wish to leave until twelve to-day, so that I should in that case have an opportunity of landing and ascending the mountain summit. On this hint I had a bed prepared on deck (fearing the heat of the cabins), and tried, though rather in vain, to take a few hours' sleep. At five A.M. I was told that the Resident, Mr. Lewis, was on board, that carriages and horses were ready, and that if I wished to mount the hill, the time had arrived for the operation. I immediately made a hasty toilette, and set forth accompanied by the General, some of the others following. We were conveyed in a carriage three miles, to the foot of the hill, and on pony back as much more up it, through a dense tropical vegetation which reminded me of my Jamaica days. At the end of the ride we arrived at the Government bungalow, and found one of the most magnificent views I ever witnessed; on the foreground this tropical luxuriance, and beyond, far below, the glistening sea studded with ships and boats innumerable, over which again the Malay Peninsula with its varied outline. I had hardly begun to admire the scene, when a gentleman in a blue flannel sort of dress, with a roughish beard and a cigar in his mouth, made his appearance, and was presented to me as the Bishop of Labuan! He was there endeavouring to recruit his health, which has suffered a good deal. He complained of the damp of the climate, while admitting its many charms, and seemed to think that he owed to the dampness a very bad cold by which he was afflicted. Soon afterwards his wife joined us. They were both at Sarawak when the last troubles took place, and must have had a bad time of it. The Chinese behaved well to them; indeed they seemed desirous to make the Bishop their leader. His converts (about fifty) were staunch, and he has a school at which about the same number of Chinese boys are educated. These facts pleaded in his favour, and it says something for the Chinese that they were not insensible to these claims. They committed some cruel acts, but they certainly might have committed more. They respected the women except one (Mrs. C., whom they wounded severely), and they stuck by the Bishop until they found that he was trying to bring Brooke back. They then turned upon him, and he had to run for his life. The Bishop gave me an interesting description of his school of Chinese boys. He says they are much more like English boys than other orientals. That when a new boy comes they generally get up a fight, and let him earn his place by his prowess. But there is no managing them without pretty severe punishments. Indeed, he says that if a boy be in fault the others do not at all like his not being well punished; they seem to think that it is an injustice to the rest if this is omitted. I am about to do with a strange people; so much to admire in them, and yet with a perversity of disposition which makes it absolutely necessary, if you are to live with them at all, to treat them severely, sometimes almost cruelly. They have such an overweening esteem for themselves, that they become unbearable unless they are constantly reminded that others are as good as they. . . . The Bishop seemed to think that it would be a very good thing if the Rajah were to go home for a time, and leave the government to his nephew, whom he praises much. . . . When we came down from the mountain we went to the house of the Resident on the shore, and there I found all the world of Penang assembled to meet me. Among them a quantity of Chinese in full mandarin costume. It was not easy, under the circumstances, to make conversation for them, but it was impossible not to be pleased with their good-humoured faces, on which there rests a perpetual grin. We had a grand "spread" in which fresh fish, mangosteen, and a horrible fruit whose name I forget (*dorian*), but whose smell I shall ever remember, played a conspicuous part. After breakfast we returned to our ship to be broiled for about an hour, then to bathe, and now (after that I have inserted these words in my journal to you) to finish dressing. . . .

June 2d.—The captain gave me his cabin (on deck, and near the centre of the ship) last night, so I have had a comparatively good night, and I feel vastly better to-day. . . . We are moving through a sea as calm as an inland lake. We have land sometimes on one side, sometimes on the other, and sometimes on both. We shall soon, I apprehend, pass Malacca, and at an early hour to-morrow may expect to be at Singapore. I hope to meet there the home-bound steamer. . . . My stay at Singapore will entirely depend on the Shannon. I cannot, of course, proceed till she arrives, but I am anxious to reach Hong-kong, and enter upon my work. . . . It is chiefly the difficulty of getting sleep that knocks me up. I suppose in time I shall become accustomed to very uncomfortable quarters. . . . We have passed very suddenly into these warm climates. . . . On the whole, our voyage has been a remarkably prosperous one. The weather more favourable than we had a right to expect, and the heat not great for the latitude and the season. I have been sitting on the front of the paddle-box reading for the last two hours, a most delicious breeze fanning me. . . . Keppel has lost his ship, the Raleigh; run her aground. The Bishop told me that he had received a visit from Prince Victor, and another of Keppel's officers, in great distress at the notion that they were likely not to see any fighting. . . . We got no Indian news at Penang. Nobody there had heard of the Mutiny. . . .

June 3d.—Just arrived at Singapore. Urgent letters from Canning to send him troops. I have not a man. Shannon not arrived. So I was right, in spite of all Sir C. W.'s assurances to the contrary.

Singapore.—June 5th.—I am on land, which is at any rate one thing gained. But I am only about eighty miles from the Equator, and about two hundred feet above the level of the sea. The Java wind, too, is blowing, which is the hot wind in these quarters, so that you may imagine what is the condition of my pores. I sent my last letter immediately after landing, and had little time to add a word from land, as I found a press of business, and a necessity for writing to Clarendon by the mail; the fact being, that I received letters from Canning, imploring me to send troops to him from the number destined for China. As we have no troops yet, and do not well know when we may have any, it was not exactly an easy matter to comply with this request. However, I did what I could, and in concert with the General, have sent instructions far and wide to turn the transports back, and give Canning the benefit of the troops for the moment. . . . It is, of course, difficult to conjecture how this Indian business may affect us in China, and I shall await our next news from India with no little anxiety. Await it, I say, for there is no prospect of my getting on from here at present. There is no word of the Shannon, and till she arrives I am a fixture. . . . I am here at the house of the Governor, Mr. Blundell. . . . I am tolerably well since I landed, but I do not sleep very soundly, and I am a little deaf. I have taken to my old habits of exercise in the Tropics, and have a long walk every morning at a very early hour. This morning I daresay I walked five miles, visiting some Chinese temples or joss-houses in the way. Nothing can be more utterly uninteresting than the Chinese religion; a parcel of hideous idols behind altars, somewhat resembling those of Roman Catholic churches. There is here an enormous Chinese population. I should think that they could eat us all up, if they took a fancy to do so. . . . I was interrupted by a card announcing the visit of two French capitaines de vaisseaux, a steamer and gunboat, *en route* for China. They tell me that three others are following. This reinforcement and the new Admiral will strengthen us materially. . . .

June 6th.—I have just had a full-dress levee, and I bore my heavy coat better than I expected. Indeed the heat is so great here, that when one makes up one's mind to it, a few hundredweight more or less of coat makes no great difference, so long as one stands still. The levee was well attended, and I received an address, to which I delivered a reply, which is, I believe, approved. The society is beginning to be excited about my being here, and all sorts of entertainments are on the *tapis* for next week. To-day I dine with the Recorder. This morning the Governor took me on foot to the convict establishment, at which some 2500 murderers, etc., from India are confined, and some fifty women, who are generally, after about two years of penal servitude, let out on condition that they consent to marry convicts. I cannot say that their appearance made me envy the convicts much, although some of them were perhaps better-looking than the women one meets out of the prison. In truth, one meets very few women at all, and those that one sees are far from attractive. *Au reste*, the convicts go about apparently very little guarded, with a chain round the waist and each leg. The church, which we afterwards visited, is rather an imposing edifice, and is being built by convict labour, at the cost of the Indian Government. The heat was very great, and I was not a little glad when the Governor's carriage arrived, to save us the labour of walking home. It is cooler now, for a thundercloud is wandering about, hesitating where it will fall. . . . There was a goodly turn out of Chinese at the levee, robed in mandarin attire, and looking like so many old women. Yesterday afternoon, F. and I went, a second time, to see M— Grant. We were with her only a short time, and we went on horseback (my first ride), and it came on a pouring rain, so we were obliged to borrow a carriage to bring us home. . . .

Sunday, June 7th.-- . . . . I am going to evening church; we are to dine at five for the purpose. . . . My dinner yesterday went off well, and afterwards two Chinese merchants came and spent the evening. I am to visit them at their houses. They profess to wish me great success, and to consider the Cantonese a very bad set. They are enterprising people, very rich, and engrossing all the best trade going. . . . My life here would be dull enough, were it not that anything is a relief after being pent up in a ship for so long. Shall I describe it to you ? I get up at about half-past five; get a cup of coffee, and rush out for a walk; return about half-past seven; bathe, dress, and then breakfast. After breakfast, remain in the house till five P.M.; go out again for an hour; bathe, dress, and dine; after which to bed. Thus my days have been passed till now; but I am told that there are to be gaieties this week to break the monotony.

June 8th.—I went to church last night at half-past six, and heard rather a dull sermon. Punkahs were going all the while, which produces rather a soporific effect. We drove home under a bright full-moon, and I sat for some time in the verandah with Mr. Blundell. My thoughts turned homewards. . . . This morning I visited, in my walk, some of the horrid opium-shops, which we are supposed to do so much to encourage. They are wretched dark places, with little lamps, in which the smokers light their pipes, glimmering on the shelves made of boards, on which they recline and puff until they fall asleep. The opium looks like treacle, and the smokers are haggard and stupified, except at the moment of inhaling, when an unnatural brightness sparkles from their eyes. After escaping from these horrid dens, I went to visit a Chinese merchant who lives in a very good house, and is a man of considerable wealth. He speaks English, and never was in China, having been born in Malacca. I had tea, and was introduced to his mother, wife, and two boys and two girls. I did not much admire the ladies, but the children were pretty well. He intends to send one of his sons to England for education. He denounces opium and the other vices of his countrymen, and their secret societies. All the well-to-do Chinese agree in this, but they have not moral courage to come out against them. Indeed, I suppose they could hardly do so without great risk. . . . Alas! still no sign of the Shannon.

June 11th.—At half-past four this morning the Shannon arrived. Captain Peel came up to breakfast. He has made a quick passage, as he came almost all the way under canvas. Such were his orders from the Admiralty. He says that his ship is the fastest sailer he has ever been on board of; that he has the best set of officers. In short, all is very cheery with him. I told him I should not start till after the arrival of the steamer from England, and he requires that time to get ready, as it appears that he had only twelve hours' notice that he was to take me when he left England. L. has been on board the Shannon, and reports favourably, and certainly she looks magnificent in the harbour. I must now account for two blank days in this journal. On Tuesday at noon, the Chinese arrived with an address to me. I had a reply prepared, which was translated into Malay, and read by a native. It is a most extraordinary circumstance, that in this place, where there are some 60,000 or 70,000 Chinese, and where the Europeans are always imagining that they are plotting, etc., there is not a single European who can speak their language. No doubt this is a great source of misunderstanding. The last row, which did *not* end in a massacre, but which might have done so, originated in the receipt of certain police regulations from Calcutta. These regulations were ill translated, and published after Christmas Day. The Chinese, believing that they authorized the police to enter their houses at all periods, to interfere with their amusements at the New Year, etc., they shut up their shops, which is their constitutional mode of expressing dissatisfaction. It was immediately inferred in certain quarters that the Chinese intended, out of sympathy with the Cantonese, to murder all the Europeans. Luckily the Governor thought it advisable to explain to them what the obnoxious ordinances really meant before proceeding to exterminate them, and a few hours of explanation had the effect of inducing them to re-open their shops, and go on quietly with their usual avocations. Just the same thing happened at Penang. There too, because the Chinamen showed some disinclination to obey regulations of police which interfered with their amusements and habits, a plot against the Europeans was immediately suspected, and great indignation expressed because it was not put down with *vigour!* However, to go back to my address. The answer gave satisfaction, and although some of my European friends told me that the Chinese would not translate it, that they would give an untrue version of it, etc., I am informed that no less than three versions of a translation are being made by them, in order that a perfectly correct one may be prepared for transmission to Canton! After the ceremony, I rode over to call on M— Grant. . . . In the evening we had a very large dinner party, which is a tiresome affair in these latitudes, and next morning I started early on an expedition into the country. We travelled in carriages, and visited a sugar plantation and   plantation on the way; arriving at length at a bungalow fourteen miles from the town, in the jungle, with a nice view of the water and adjoining islands. There we breakfasted and lunched, and returned from it partly by water, in a boat rowed by Malays, through the Straits, and up a river bordered by jungle, with a little village of Malays here and there. After dinner we went to an amateur theatrical representation which I had been invited to patronize. So much for my two days' history. Nothing but Peel's visit has happened to-day, except a visit from the Tumongong, or sort of sovereign of Johore, who came to see me with his two sons, and a sword of state presented to him by Colonel Butterworth. We bought the island from him, and he is now becoming rich, because the emigrants to this place are settling in his territories. There is a Sultan of the place as well, but he has neither authority nor money. I also went, in my morning's walk, to visit the country-place of a Chinaman, who gave me tea and mangosteens, and introduced me to his family. There was a little grand-daughter very finely dressed, of whom the old gentleman seemed very

fond, but I cannot say much for the beauty of the ladies. . . .
I intended to drive, but it is pouring: this is the first regular
rain. This is very, very dull work. . . . I have just finished
reading Kaye's *History of the Affghanistan War*, as an episode
among my Chinese books. It is very well written, and certainly,
if faithful, discloses a series of follies and injustice perfectly
appalling.

June 13*th*.—I returned from a ball this morning at two, and
at six I was on my way to visit a school of Malay boys kept by
an American. . . . The ball went off very well. There were
some 300 people, of whom about seventy ladies. A sitting
down supper, speeches, etc. I always contend that the coolest
place in the Tropics is a ball-room, for as everything is wide
open, it is not pestiferous, which is generally the case in
England, and is not hotter than a ball-room generally is at
home. The beauty was Mrs. C., who was nearly murdered in
Borneo. . . . I have just been interrupted to go and see the
Sultan of Johore, who came to pay his respects. He is a man
of about thirty, very like a prize pig in shape, and perfectly
stupified by sloth and sensuality. The Tumongong does not
seem to be much better. These princes in this country, and
indeed all over the East, are spoilt from their childhood, all
their passions indulged and fostered by their parents, who say,
"What is the use of being a prince, if he may not have more
ghee, etc. etc. than his neighbours?" I do not see what can be
done for them. At the school I visited this morning are two
sultan's sons (of Queddah), but they were at home for some
holidays, when they will probably be ruined. Yesterday it
rained again, and the temperature has been in consequence
much more bearable. During my morning's walk I heard
something like the sound of a school in a house adjoining, and
I proposed to enter and inspect. I found an establishment of
Frères Chrétiens, and one of them (an Irishman) claimed
acquaintance, as having been with Bishop Phelan when he visited
me in Canada. We struck up a friendship accordingly, and I
told him that if there were any *Sœurs* I should like to see them.
He introduced me to the Vicar Apostolic, a Frenchman, and we
went to the establishment of the *Sœurs*. I found the *Supérieure*
a very superior person, evidently with her heart in the work,
and ready for any fate to which it might expose her, but quiet
and cheerful. I told her that a devout lady in Paris had expressed a fear that my mission to China would put an end to
martyrdom in that country. She smiled, and said that she
thought there would always be on this earth martyrdom in
abundance. The sisters educate a number of orphan girls as
well as others. All the missionary zeal in these quarters seems to

be among the French priests. Some one once said that it was not wonderful that young men took away so much learning from Oxford as they left so little behind them. The same may I think be said of French religion. It seems all intended for exportation. . . .

Sunday, June 14*th.*—I am not at church this morning, being on the sick list. . . . Yesterday evening I took a drive with M. G., and at its close sat a short time with her and her hostess. . . . All the Europeans seem afraid of the Chinese, which is not perhaps wonderful, but fear is a bad counsellor, and very apt to be the parent of cruelty. . . .

June 15*th.*—I went on board the Shannon at three P.M. yesterday. She is a magnificent vessel, and I shall be as well lodged as one can be in a ship. . . . To-night is the military ball, which winds up our Singapore gaieties. There is no word yet of the mail-steamer from home. It seems to me to be an age since I landed here. I see from my window that a French steamer has just come into the harbour and dropped her anchor. This reminds me that I have not yet told you what I see from this window—if I may apply the term window to a row of Venetian blinds running all round the house or bungalow, for this residence is not dignified by the title house. I am on an eminence about 200 feet above the sea. Immediately below me the town; on one side a number of houses with dark red roofs, surrounded with trees, looking very like a flower-garden, and confirming me in my opinion of the beauty of such roofs when so situated; on the other, the same red-roofed houses *without trees*, which makes all the difference. Beyond, the harbour, or rather anchorage, filled with ships, the mighty Shannon in the centre—a triton among the minnows. Beyond again, a wide opening to the sea, with lowish shores, rocky, and covered with wood, running out on either side. Such is the prospect ever before me, a very fine one during the day, still more interesting at night when it all sparkles with lights, and the great tropical moon looks calmly down on the whole. . . .

June 17*th.*—No appearance of the steamers either from England or China, both are now due. The French Admiral arrived on Monday, and dined here last night. He seems a gentleman-like man, bedizened with orders innumerable. We have now three French men-of-war in the harbour. The military ball on Monday was successful. The rooms very prettily decorated. E. and K. and "Fuimus," etc., done in a very beautiful description of fern. We had a standing supper and no speeches, which was a relief. . . . On Monday morning I visited the new harbour and the establishment of the Peninsular and Oriental Steam Company, and to-day the residence of the oldest inhabitant, a man of seventy-eight, where I saw nutmeg-trees, coffee, tea, mangosteen, and a great variety of other fruits. The Chinese steamer just signalled. She will convey this letter to England. . . . Peel has been here and proposed most comfortable arrangements for his ship. He suggests that I should be on the footing of admiral, and he of my flag-captain. In short, that I should be master of the house. . . .

June 19*th*.—The steamer from England not yet come, so that I must send this without having heard from you. It is a great disappointment. There has been it appears a considerable battle in China against the junks. The Chinese fought well. Our people here and at Hong-kong are very bloody, and dreadfully afraid lest I should settle matters without carnage. I think of leaving this on Tuesday. . . .

Singapore. — *June* 22*d*. — I little thought that I should have to begin another letter without having received one line from you. But so it is. Just at the time when the packet with my last letter was getting under way, a steamer was telegraphed from the west. We made certain it was the English mail, but it was found to be the Simoom (our old friend, do you not remember her at Quebec), with the 5th Regiment from the Mauritius. I sent her off as soon as she could get coal to Calcutta. . . . I propose to sail to-morrow. If the mail does not arrive before then, it is clear that something must have happened. . . . We had a great field-day on Saturday. Two Sepoy regiments besides volunteers and artillery. We attacked an imaginary enemy with great success. I had a very quiet horse, and as I thought it desirable to show that I was of a pugnacious temperament, rode all the time in the middle of the fire. It was a cool evening, and the ride was really pleasant. Yesterday I had to prepare my letters for Calcutta, as the Simoom sailed at two, but I went to the chapel for afternoon service. . . . Another disappointment; two steamers telegraphed, but they turn out to be a couple more Frenchmen.

June 23*d*.—The French visit went off well. All the French ships manned yards as I passed in my boat, and the admiral received me with a salute, etc. We had dinner, and theatricals after—the performers being sailors. When I left, men were stationed on the yards with blue lights, which had a very good effect. . . . Unless the steamer is telegraphed within two hours we shall be on our way to Hong-kong without having heard a word from you. . . .

H. M. S. Shannon.—*June* 24*th*.—I daresay you will consider me an object of envy when I describe to you where I am,—on board of a magnificent ship-of-war, carrying sixty 68-pounders, our foremast and mainmast sails set, and gliding through the

c

water with just motion enough to tell us that the pulse of the great sea is beating. The temperature of the air is high, but the day is somewhat cloudy, and the sails throw a shadow on the deck. The only thing I regret is, that having no poop, the high bulwarks close us in and shut out both the air and prospect. One can only get these by climbing up on sort of standing-places on the side. We steamed all night, and the motion of the screw was not so bad as I expected it would be. We are now, however, trusting to our sails, which is much more pleasant. We are steering towards the north, but not, alas! to cooler regions. I dread the heat which we are to find at Hong-kong. At present the crew of this ship, as indeed of all the ships which have come to Singapore, is most healthy. Our departure from Singapore was very striking. . . . Not only were all the troops and volunteers under arms, with Chinamen and merchants in crowds, but (may I mention it) the fair ladies of Singapore were drawn up in a row to give us a parting salute. We moved off in our boats, under a salute from the battery, which was repeated by the Spartan as I passed her, and by the Shannon when I got on board, both these vessels manning yards. The French admiral honoured me also with a salute as I passed him after getting under weigh, although the sun had already set. It is not likely that I shall have much to record for some days to come. We shall, we hope, be at Hong-kong in about eight days. We shall pass one mail on the way, but that mail will not reach you empty-handed, as I left a letter for it at Singapore, and I am now beginning another, and still not a word from you! *Three*, P.M.—The wind became so light that we are compelled again to have recourse to the screw. I do not feel very merry, for it is a weary business plodding through the sea in this sweltering climate, and then I sometimes think with awe of the difficulties before me. If one could only see the end!

June 25th.—We are going under sail but slowly. I am very comfortable in my cabin. . . . The only time I spend on deck is from five or six A.M. to eight, and a short time after dinner. All the rest of the day I remain below. Peel, who insists on treating me as admiral, has just reported to me that it is twelve o'clock. I have slept hitherto on a sofa in the large cabin. We have had each night a squall, which has cooled the air and made it tolerable, when before that it was very hot.

June 26th.—We have just had thunder and lightning, but the storm has not yet come on, and it is very close. I was up very early. . . . We are not doing more than four or five miles an hour on the average. . . . As regards our mode of life, Peel has made me master of the house, . . . and I ask two officers of the ship to dine each day. . . .

June 27th.—We have just passed a little island, or rather rock, the abode of innumerable sea-fowl, and named in the charts Pulo Lapata. The navigation is somewhat hazardous just here, and Peel was on deck keeping a look-out when I joined him. The day is pleasant, a good deal more breeze, and we are making ten or eleven knots. I was up at four, and had a bath on deck, which was very refreshing. . . .

June 28th.—We have just had service on deck. It was tolerably cool under the awning, though one felt the glare a little with one's hat off. There was a pretty large congregation, and the sailor-boys sing. The clergyman is much praised by Peel. . . . It was a striking sight—our church on deck, while we were gliding so smoothly through the water. . . . Two months to-day since our parting! . . .

June 30th.—The wind has turned against us. There is very little of it, and I told Peel, who consulted me, that I thought we had better use our screw and get on a little. It is as well that we should reach Hong-kong on Thursday; and we have not four hundred miles to run. We passed the Paracels during the night. . . . I wish to get to work, in the hope, alas! perhaps a vain one, of getting the sooner done with it. An address is to be presented to me, on my arrival at Hong-kong, by the merchants, who are very bloody. This part of our voyage has been very monotonous. We have hardly seen a single sail, but it has been most charmingly smooth.

July 1st.—Another month begun. Last night, at dinner, we were startled by hearing that we seemed to be running on a rock or shoal, where no rock or shoal was known to exist. We backed our screw, and finally went over the alarming spot, and on sounding found no bottom. The sea was discoloured, but whether it was by the spawn of fish or sea-weed we could not discover. Peel took up water in a bucket, but could discover nothing. If we had not been a screw, and had had nothing but sails to rely on, we should have kept clear of this apparent danger, and the result would have been that a shoal would have been marked on the charts, where, in point of fact, no shoal exists. Captain Keppel's adventure makes captains cautious. . . . In all probability we shall arrive at Hong-kong in good time to-morrow afternoon. I trust soon to be able to move on to the north. . . .

Hong-kong.—*July 3d.*— I am headachy and fagged, for I have had some hours of the most fatiguing of all things—a succession of interviews, beginning with the Admiral, General, etc. Sir J. Bowring sent a note to say that he is ill, but that he has rooms for me. I answered, as I always intended to do, that I meant to pay him a visit later, but that for some days I shall be unable to leave the ship. . . . Meanwhile, it is rather cooler than I expected. Yesterday we rolled a great deal, and prepared for a typhoon—the wind and swell menacing one. It seems to be generally supposed that we felt the tail of one, but we got well out of it, and at about half-past six we steamed into the harbour of Hong-kong. The Admiral saluted and came on board. I found him strong on the point that Canton is the only place where we ought to fight. . . . However, I hope we may get off to the north in about ten days,—as soon as we have sent off these letters, and got (as we ought) two mails from home. . . . I have sent off letters to the French and American ministers at Macao, to inform them of my intentions and invite them to co-operate.

July 4th.—Sir J. Bowring has paid me a visit. He was very profuse in his assurances that he wished for my success, and would give me all the assistance in his power. I thanked him, and told him that if the matter ended well, all who had been concerned would get credit, and *vice versâ*. . . . It is clear that there is here an *idée fixe*, that nothing ought to be done till there has been a general massacre at Canton. To-day I am to dine with the Admiral. It is hotter than yesterday, but nothing to complain of. Last night at about ten P.M., it was really cool. They say that the weather is unusual, and that there is generally more sickness when the weather is so cool at this season. . . .

July 9th.—An interval . . . during which I have been doing a good many things, my greatest enjoyment and pleasure being the receipt at last of two sets of letters from home. . . . I have a great heap of despatches, some of which seem rather likely to perplex me. I daresay, however, that I shall see my way through the mist in a day or two. . . . I had a levee last evening, which was largely attended. The course which I am about to follow does not square with the views of the merchants, but I gave an answer to their address, which gave them for the moment wonderful satisfaction. I shall begin my next letter with the history of the last few days. . . . I see in the papers that owing to the accident to the Erin, there will be no second mail from here this month. . . . A document, taken in one of the Chinese junks lately captured, states that " Devils' heads are fallen in price,"—an announcement not strictly complimentary, but reassuring to you as regards our safety. I must now stop my pen. When I send off my letter to you, I seem to have arrived at the end of a stage in my journey. . . .

Hong-kong.—July 12*th*.—I ended my last letter by telling you that you might not hear again for a month, but since then I have seen the proprietor of one of the opium-ships that ply between this and Calcutta; and he says he hopes to be able to despatch her in time to meet the home-bound steamer at Calcutta, but it is uncertain. I felt a little out of sorts yesterday, . . . but was able to go to church, which was fortunate, as the sermon was a good deal to my address. "We are ambassadors," etc., was the text, and sundry references were made to the mission. . . . I have some arrears of history to fill up. . . . On Thursday the 2d, we dropped anchor, steaming into the harbour through the fringe of a typhoon. Friday, Saturday, and Sunday, I remained on board, seeing a good many people, and hearing a good deal. On Saturday we dined with the Admiral on board the Calcutta. . . . On Monday I landed. Each ship of war, as I passed, manned yards and fired a salute. All the military were out. Sir J. Bowring met me on the shore, and conveyed me to the Government House in a pony-carriage. The house is rather a fine one, built of granite, with a magnificent view of the harbour, etc., and in a cool situation. . . . On Tuesday there was a full-dress dinner, with a great many speeches. On Wednesday the levee preceded by the arrival of the mail. Till Friday I was pretty well occupied with letter-writing and reading, and yesterday (Saturday) a few of the leading merchants were asked to dinner. . . .

July 13*th*.— . . . This is the strangest climate. While I am writing, down comes a gust of wind, which blew about the room all my letters and papers. It was hot for a few days, but since then quite cool, with a good deal of rain. I hardly ever leave the house. . . .

H. M. S. Shannon.—July 19*th*.—I wonder what you will think when you receive this letter; that is, if I succeed in despatching it from the point where I wish to post it. Will you think me mad, or what will your view of my proceedings be ? . . . Here I am actually on my way to Calcutta ! To Calcutta ! you will exclaim in surprise. The reasons for this step are so numerous, that I can hardly attempt to enumerate them. I found myself at Hong-kong, without troops and without competent representatives of our allies (America and France) to concert with. Doomed either to *aborder* the Court of Pekin alone, without the power of acting vigorously if I met a repulse, or to spend three months at Hong-kong doing nothing, and proclaiming to the whole world that I am waiting for the Frenchman; *i.e.*, that England can do nothing without France, I considered the great objections which existed to either of these courses. *Sur ces entrefaites*, came further letters from Canning, begging for more help from me, and showing that things are even worse with him than they were when I first heard from him. It occurred to me that I might occupy the three months well in running up to Calcutta, taking with me what assistance I can collect for him, and obtaining thereby an opportunity of conferring with him, and learning from him what chance I have of getting before the winter the troops which I have detached to his support. Sir M. Seymour approved the plan warmly. It occurred to me on Tuesday evening, and on Thursday I was under weigh. Alas! *L'homme propose, mais Dieu dispose!* The monsoon is against us, and as this ship is practically useless as a steamer, as she can only carry coals for five days, we are beating against the wind, and making little progress. Perhaps my whole plans may fail, because I have the misfortune to be in one of H. M.'s ships, instead of in a good merchant steamer, which would be going at ten miles an hour in a direct line, while we are going at six in an oblique one. However, we must hope for the best. I think that my proceeding, though a bold one, is one most wise as regards the public interest. My position at Hong-kong for three months would also have been intolerable. . . . The other alternative was going up to the Peiho; but I believe that it would have been madness to provoke a quarrel with the Emperor of China single-handed, before I know when I can get the force with which I am to act against him.

Whether we are to have peace or war with China, either object will be much more effectually accomplished, when the European forces are acting together, than when we are alone; the Russians meanwhile, no doubt, hinting to the Emperor that we are in a bad way in India. The plan, then, if we can accomplish it, is this: To run up as fast as I can to Calcutta, and to return so as to meet Baron Gros, who is not expected till the middle of September. There will just be time to communicate with the Court of Pekin before winter. I have mentioned the reasons for these proceedings, derived from my own position; but, of course, I am mainly influenced by a consideration for Canning. In both his letters he has expressed a desire to see me, and I am told that my appearance there with what the Indian public will consider the first of a large force, will produce a powerful moral effect. I ought to be there at least two months before he can receive a man from England. . . . On the 17th and 18th it blew so hard that I could hardly attempt to write; it is now calmer, and I hope that Peel will soon begin to use his screw. . . . In three days we have made about 250 miles; so much for Sir C. Wood's crack steam-frigate!

July 20th.—Would that I were at home to-day. You say that I do not appreciate anniversaries, but it is chiefly because it is so sad when the days come when they cannot be celebrated as of yore. "*Nal maggior dolore.*" Do not anniversaries stir this great fountain of sadness? I feel sad when I look at this inhospitable sea, and think of the smiling countenances with which I should have been surrounded at home, and the joyous laugh when papa, with affected surprise, detected the present wrapped up carefully in the paper parcel on the breakfast table. Is it not lawful to be sad? And although perhaps it may turn out for good after all, have not all the anticipations we formed of the premature period of my departure from home been more than justified by the result? This Indian affair could not have been foreseen, but if it had not happened I should still have been unable to act with the small force which I should have had at Hong-kong, and unable to negotiate because I have no colleagues. But a truce to all complaints which do no good. We did steam last night, and have been doing better. Better, however, is not much, for all we had made was *nearly five knots*. The wind remains dead against us, and we are again under sail. . . .

July 23*d*.—Things look much more promising; we are gliding along in a perfectly smooth sea at the rate of nearly nine knots. We are in our seventh day, and have not yet accomplished half the distance to Singapore; but distance is nothing if we are favoured by the weather. We have had no wind to help us, but it is not doing us any harm at present. On the whole, too, there is little to complain of on the score of heat. . . . If we fail in sending our letters home from Singapore, it is not improbable the first news you may receive of my being in India may be a telegraphic message *via* Bombay, which will create some astonishment.

July 25*th*.—Still moving on almost insensibly. The calm is now quite dead, and but for the tremulous motion produced by the screw, it would be impossible to discover that we are not standing still. We have had no favour from wind, and we are obliged to economize our coal, so that we cannot go at great speed. . . . It is very hot to-day. . . . I am getting fidgetty to reach Singapore, because it is of course possible that I might find news there which would affect my movements. . . . The consequences of being at so great a distance from head-quarters are very singular, *e.g.*, in this case I shall not hear whether the Government approve or not of this move of mine until it has become matter of history, until, in all probability, I have carried out my plan of visiting the Peiho with the French Ambassador. It certainly contrasts very strongly with the position of a diplomatic functionary in Europe, now, when reference is made by telegraph to head-quarters in every case of difficulty. . . . This seems a very solitary sea. We have passed in all, I think, two ships. This morning once or twice we have met a log floating with one or two birds standing upon it. Yesterday great excitement was created by the discovery of a cask floating on the surface of the sea. Telescopes were *braqués* from every part of the ship upon this unhappy cask, which went bobbing up and down, very unconscious of the sensation it was creating. This incident will convey to you an idea of how monotonous our life is. . . .

July 27*th.*—At about four yesterday another excitement greater than that created by the floating cask. Peel informed me that there was a steamer in sight, coming towards us. Many were the speculations as to what she could be. It was generally agreed that she was the Transit, as she was due about this time. As we neared her, however, she dwindled in size, and proved a rather dirty-looking merchant craft with an auxiliary screw. On asking whence she came, she informed us that she was from Calcutta, and that she had a letter for me. It proved to be from Canning, in no respect more encouraging than his former letters, and therefore, in so far, confirmatory of the propriety of my present move. We heard, moreover, of the end of the ill-fated Transit, which has been completely lost in the Straits of Sunda. I hope to find her troops at Singapore, and to bring them on to Calcutta. As to the Himalaya, nothing has yet been heard of her, so that my own arrival will be about the first good help which Canning will receive. This vessel met the Simoom in the Hoogly, but I fear that no other portion of the Chinese expeditionary force has yet reached this point from England. So much for the promise of the Government that *at the end of May or beginning of June* I should find 700 men at Hong-kong and 1500 at Singapore! I feel rather better to-day. I had a better night. The wind is more favourable too, and we hope to be at Singapore to-morrow.

July 31*st.*—*En route* for Calcutta, with good hope of catching the mail, which we are assured does not leave Calcutta till the 9th. We reached Singapore on the 28th, at about two P.M. I landed and went to my old quarters at the Governor's. I found it deliciously cool, much more so than it was during my former visit. . . . I saw M— Grant; looking vastly better. . . . My friends at Singapore were very cordial in their welcome of me, and the merchants immediately drew up an address expressive of their satisfaction at my move on Calcutta. We have taken on board 100 men of the detachment of the 90th which was on board the Transit, and put the remainder into the Pearl, so that we are crammed to the hilt. Please God we may reach Calcutta in about a week or less, and then a new chapter begins. Just as we were starting yesterday, an opium-ship from Calcutta arrived, and brought me a letter and despatch from Canning, more urgent and gloomy than any of the preceding ones. The Simoom and Himalaya had both arrived, but he was clamorous for more help, and broadly tells me that I must not expect to get any of my men back. So here I am deprived of the force on which I was to rely in China! . . . Canning's letter is dated the 21st, and therefore contains the latest intelligence. Nothing can be worse. I am happy to say that I have already sent to him even more than he has asked. . . . I trust that I may do some good, but of course things are so bad that one fears that it may be too late to hope that any great moral effect can be produced by one's arrival. However, I have with me about 1700 fighting men, and perhaps we may have more, if we find a transport in the Straits, and take it in tow.

Sunday, August 2d.—We had service on the upper deck to day. . . . What a strange life this is! It seems an age since we parted, and yet only about three months have elapsed. I have been able to do nothing towards the accomplishment of the object of my mission. What we said in London when we protested against the hurried way in which I was sent out, has been completely realized. I found myself in China with nothing to do for three months, except to lose my prestige, by becoming the subject of Hong-kong gossip. I see an article in the *Times* of one of the first days of June, which assumes that nothing can be done by the troops in China till the winter, and that I am to act with the French and American Commissioners, who will not be there till that time. It follows, of course, that I was intended to be for months doing nothing. . . . I hope, at least, I shall not be blamed for having tried to be useful during the period when I was doomed to inaction. . . . But in what condition shall we find Calcutta? . . . A few days will answer these questions. . . . We have at the utmost some 100 miles to make. What wind there is, is in our favour. . . . I really do not know what I should have done if I had remained in China at present, getting despatches perhaps from the Home Government saying that Canning had orders to send on the Chinese troops from India, and letters from him telling me that he could not do so. My position would have been one of great perplexity. My only escape from the difficulty was to seek a personal conference with him. I hope the result will justify this measure.

August 5th.—We have a strong wind in our favour, and are going so fast that we have given up the screw, and are under sail, making about eleven knots. . . . We may hope to arrive at the mouth of the Hoogly to-morrow, exactly three weeks from Hong-kong. There are great mountains of sea rolling behind us, as I look out of my stern window. . . . This is a long letter; but although it will, I trust, reach you within a fortnight of my last, I have had it nearly a month in hand. . . .

August 8th.—We are running up to Calcutta, having at length surmounted all the perils of navigation. On Thursday we had a strong gale, and could get no pilot till late, off the "Sandheads" at the entrance of the Hoogly. This is, I believe, the largest ship that ever went up the river, so we were obliged to stay all night steaming round and round a light-vessel with a heavy sea. When morning came, the pilot still doubted whether he could safely carry us through, but at length he made the attempt, and we ran up yesterday to Diamond Harbour, and anchored for the night. It is only thirty miles from Calcutta, yet I could not, for love or money, get any conveyance for L., whom I wished to send up to Canning! We heard many sinister rumours, but nothing reliable. . . .

Calcutta.—August 9th.—The mail has been delayed for a day, so I can write a line from this place. Our arrival was very timely. Exceedingly well received by the inhabitants, etc. . . . Canning and Lady C. are looking well, all things considered. . . . I am going to give up the Shannon, and take a frigate of the Indian navy, leaving Peel and his fighting men with Canning. I think that this will suit all parties best. . . . I have just been to church at the Cathedral. . . .

Calcutta.—August 11th.—Here I am, writing to you from the Governor-General's Palace at Calcutta! Altogether it is one of the strangest of the *péripéties* of my life. I succeeded, however, in posting a letter, or rather two letters, for you by the last mail, which I should not have been able to do if I had remained at Hong-kong. That is one point gained. Then, again, I think my visit has entirely answered as regards the interests of India. I have every reason to believe that it has had an excellent effect here. I have agreed to give up the Shannon, in order that Peel and his men may be formed into a naval brigade, and march with some of their great guns on Delhi. Peel, for this work, is, I believe, the right man in the right place, and I expect great things from him. He is delighted, and Canning and Sir P. Grant have signified in strong terms their appreciation of the sacrifice I am making, and the service I am rendering. They are in great want of artillery, and no such guns as those of the Shannon are in their possession. The vessel itself, with a small crew, will remain in the river opposite Calcutta, able, if need were, to knock all the city to bits. I shall get a steamer for myself, probably one of the Peninsular and Oriental Company's, to convey me to Hong-kong, and to remain with me till I am better suited. Canning is very amiable, but I do not see much of him. He is at work from five or six in the morning till dinner-time. No human being can in a climate like this, and in a situation which has so few *délassements* as that of Governor-General, work so constantly without impairing the energy both of mind and body, after a time. . . . Neither he nor Lady C. are so much oppressed by the difficulties in which they find themselves, as might have been expected. . . . I shall most likely remain here for about a fortnight. I do not think my ship will be ready before the end of that period. . . .

August 14th.—I have received a mail from Hong-kong with your letters up to the 10th of June, and letters to people here up to the 10th of July have arrived since I began this letter. I find from Canning's letters that my force is to be sacrificed without any reserve or scruple to his necessities. Orders have been sent to Singapore to turn back all troops for China, and to send them to Calcutta. If I had acted on my instructions, I should probably by this time have established a *casus belli* with the Emperor of China. . . . And what am I to expect for the future ? . . . If I had met with a rebuff at the Peiho, without being able to answer it by measures of coercion at Canton, it is clear that not our national honour only but the whole interests of our trade with China might have been seriously compromised. . . . Meanwhile Sir Colin Campbell has arrived to take the command in India. I think I must remain here till the next mail comes from England. The Government will then know that my acts, followed by their recent orders, have deprived me of my *whole force*. . . . In case you hear my proceedings criticised, it may be agreeable to you to know how they are viewed by a man who has seen a good deal of public service, and who bears himself a pretty high reputation. I am hardly acquainted with Sir H. Ward (the Governor of Ceylon), but he writes to me as follows :—" You may think me impertinent in volunteering an opinion upon what in the first instance only concerns you and the Queen and Lord Canning. But having seen something of public life during a great part of my own, which is now fast verging into the ' sere and yellow leaf,' I may venture to say that I never knew a nobler thing than that which you have done in preferring the safety of India to the success of your Chinese negotiations. If I know anything of English public opinion, this single act will place you higher in general estimation as a statesman than your whole past career, honourable and fortunate as it has been. For it is not every man who would venture to alter the destination of a force upon the despatch of which a Parliament has been dissolved, and a Government might have been superseded. It is not every man who would consign himself for many months to political inaction in order simply to serve the interests of his country. You have set a bright example at a moment of darkness and calamity, and if India can be saved it is to you that we shall owe its redemption, for nothing short of the Chinese expedition would have supplied the means of holding our ground until further reinforcements are received." . . .

August 15*th.*—. . . My letters from Hong-kong show that it has not been healthy since I left. Sir J. Bowring has been ill, and Lady B. is, I fear, in a very bad way. It does not appear that my departure has led to any sort of inconvenience. . . . I am taking care of my health, and a proof is that I have kept the doctor of the Shannon who has been attending me, and whom I like both as a medical man and a quiet gentlemanlike person. I am better than when I left Hong-kong. . . . I expect a whole flood of letters at Singapore. I have already given orders for two mails to be brought there from Hong-kong, and shall have a third (yours of the 26th July) stopped *en passant*. . . .

August 17*th.*—The doctor advises me to take a glass of sherry with quinine in it daily, . . . though I feel at present pretty well. It is the fashion here to have punkahs going all night, which is certainly a great comfort, and makes one sleep better, although it makes it rather public, for there are black fellows looking through the keyhole at all moments both of the day and night, in order that they may see when they may take a little rest, and cease pulling the string of the punkah. I asked a lady who dined here whether she did not find this rather inconvenient, and she said that in most houses the punkahs are pulled from down stairs by strings through the floor. In the rooms I occupy in this house the pullers stand outside the door, and are perpetually peeping in. The house is of immense size, but with little accommodation in proportion. . . . At about six we generally go out riding or driving, that is Lady C. and some of us; Canning seldom goes out himself, and is rarely visible till dinner-time. . . .

August 19*th.*—It is very dull work staying here, and I wish I could get away. . . . Yet I think I must wait for the next mail. . . . From Canning's letters by it, or at any rate from the debates in Parliament, I think I am sure to be able to form some idea of the policy which Her Majesty's Government intend to adopt in China. And it is important for me to know the truth on this point as soon as possible. I went on board the Shannon yesterday, saw the Naval Brigade drawn up, and made a speech to the officers and men, which was, I believe, acceptable. Peel did not get off till to-day. . . .

August 21*st.*—. . . It is a terrible business, however, this living among inferior races. I have seldom from man or woman since I came to the East heard a sentence which was reconcilable with the hypothesis that Christianity had ever come into the world. Detestation, contempt, ferocity, vengeance, whether Chinamen or Indians be the object. There are some three or four hundred servants in this house. When one first passes by their *salaaming* one feels a little awkward. But the feeling soon wears off, and one moves among them with perfect indifference, treating them, not as dogs, because in that case one would whistle to them and pat them, but as machines with which one can have no communion or sympathy. Of course those who can speak the language are somewhat more *en rapport* with the natives, but very slightly so, I take it. When the passions of fear and hatred are engrafted on this indifference, the result is frightful, an absolute callousness as to the sufferings of the objects of those passions, which must be witnessed to be understood and believed.

August 22d.—L. tells me he met —— yesterday at dinner. The fact that Government had removed some commissioners who, not content with hanging all the rebels they could lay their hands on, had been insulting them by destroying their caste, telling them that after death they should be cast to the dogs to be devoured, etc., was mentioned. The rev. gentleman could not understand the conduct of Government; could not see that there was any impropriety in torturing men's souls; seemed to think that a good deal might be said in favour of bodily torture as well! These are your teachers, O Israel! Imagine what the pupils become under such leading!

August 23d.—This is a day of an absolute pour of rain. I got up at six to go to church, and after having dressed found we were not to go because of the rain. . . .

August 26th.—This letter will be left here, to be sent by the next mail from this place. . . . I have been living here a most monotonous life, hardly seeing anybody, and in a position perhaps a little false. However, I still think that I am better here than I could have been anywhere else. . . . We are now in the middle of a Mohammedan festival—the Mohurrum—a festival which the Sheiks hold in commemoration of the death of Ali. They have processions, and Dr. Duff told me yesterday very exciting addresses are made in the mosques, picturing the death of this martyr, and they generally contrive to work themselves up into a state of frenzy. Great fears have been expressed here by the British population, who think that something serious may happen; but the authorities are on their guard, and hitherto, at least, the festival has been kept very tranquilly. Yesterday Dr. Duff, the great Free Church missionary, dined here. He is an interesting person. Has a large educational establishment, which is always full, and holds about a thousand. The Scriptures are read. Up to about thirteen or fourteen the lads are quick, more so, perhaps, than Europeans; but after that age they degenerate, which he attributes chiefly to the dissipation into which they then fall. A very small proportion of the students become Christians. Dr. Duff visited Canada early in 1854, before my return. He was very emphatic in his admiration of what he had seen there. He was astonished to find the people so prosperous, so contented, so proud of their position, *vis à vis* the Yankees. He expected something quite different, knowing Canada only from books. This morning I got up very early, and sallied out to visit the Fort, where I found some of the marines I brought here with me in the Shannon. It is a magnificent place, covering about three miles of ground. The great subject of anxiety here now is Lucknow, where a small party of soldiers, with some two hundred women and an equal number of children, are beleaguered by a rebel force of 15,000. The attempts hitherto made to relieve them have failed, and General Havelock, who commands, says he can do nothing unless he gets the 5th and 90th Regiments (the two I sent from Singapore on my own responsibility). The men of the Pearl and Shannon and the marines are guarding Calcutta, or on their way up to Allahabad, so that it is impossible to say what would have become of Bengal if these reinforcements had not come.

August 28*th*.— . . . I was to have gone to-day to visit a country-place of the Governor-General's—Barrackpore—about fifteen miles off, but on consideration I determined not to go during the Mohurrum. There are a good many disarmed sepoys there, and one of the regiments has volunteered to go to China. This has created a good deal of excitement among some of the others, and if I went, they might suppose my visit had reference to this affair. Another vessel with China troops has arrived, the Blevie Castle, with the Military Train. The men are for the most part dragoons, and will be invaluable here. . . .

August 30*th*.—The mail from England has arrived. No letters, of course, for me. I gather from the newspapers and Canning's letters that some troops, though only to a small extent, I fear, are to be sent to Hong-kong, to replace those which have been diverted to India. From Palmerston's speeches I gather that he adheres to the policy of my first visiting the North, and making amicable overtures; and secondly, taking Canton, if these overtures fail. I believe I have adopted the only mode of carrying out that policy. It is rather perplexing, however, and sometimes a little amusing, to be working at such a distance from head-quarters, as one never knows what is thought of one's proceedings until it is so much too late to turn to account the criticisms passed upon them. . . . I have nothing now to keep me here longer, so I shall be off probably on the 2d September. I dined yesterday with Sir J. and Lady Colvile. Great fears are felt for Lucknow. There was a report yesterday that the garrison had made overtures to the rebels to allow them to surrender, on condition of the women, etc. being taken safely to Cawnpore, but that these overtures were rejected. . . .

August 31*st*.— . . . I am to go with Lady C. to-morrow to Barrackpore. It is pretty they say, and one ought to see it. The Mohurrum ended to-day. There was a great deal of drumming last night, but it has been very quietly kept. I am glad there has been no riot, for it is sad to have quarrels with these wretched natives about their religious observances. I am to end this letter at Barrackpore, as there are several hours of the day during which we can do nothing out of doors. We go at six A.M., and return to dinner. I propose to embark next morning at half-past five. I am told my ship is comfortable, and her captain experienced. . . . I visited Lady C. in her own apartments to-day.

September 2*d*.—I put off my departure for a day, as a steamer from Hong-kong was telegraphed, and I wished to get her news. . . . I have been informed that an address would have been presented to me here, but that something disagreeable about the Government would probably have been said, and the idea was therefore abandoned. I think that it was quite right to abandon it for such a reason. . . . We had, on the whole, a pleasant trip to Barrackpore. . . . I embark to-morrow at 6.30 A.M. We shall reach Singapore probably in about seven days. . . . Eight days more should bring me to Hong-kong. I may get four sets of home-letters within a short space of time. . . .

Steamer Ava.—September 3*d*.--Here I am reduced to a merchant steamer, and moving down the Hoogly. . . . There are no bulwarks here to intercept the air and prospect. We carry a good supply of ice, and we have power to beat against the wind, but the cabins are hotter than on board the Shannon, and closer, etc. I am taking with me General Van Straubenzie and two A.D.C.'s.

Two p.m.—Kedgeree.—We must remain at anchor here till the morning, *stewing*. . . .

Steamer Ava.—September 10*th*.—I have had a very bad time of it since I finished my last letter on my way down the Hoogly. Probably it may have been something of the Calcutta fever brought with me. . . . But on the second night after our departure, it came on to blow hard towards morning. I was in my cot on the windward side. First, I got rather a chill, and then the ports were shut, leaving me very hot. I remained all day in a state of feverish lethargy, unable to rise, and constantly falling off into dreamy dozes; kaleidoscopes, with the ugliest sides of everything perpetually twirling before my eyes. I panted so for air that they opened my ports towards evening, as an experiment. It turned out better than might have been expected. A sea washed in, and filled my cot half full of water, which decided me on rising. No gentler hint would have mastered my lethargy. After I got on deck, as you may imagine, it was about as difficult, or rather more so, to overcome the *vis inertiæ* which fixed me there. So a bed was made for me under the awning. I remained on deck for four nights; the fourth, in a cot slung up to the boom, and though I slept little, was cool. - Last night I came down to the cabin again. I have taken the turn, and am on the mend, though I do not yet feel the least inclination for food, and my nerves are so shaky that I can hardly write. That little pretty book of Guizot's which you sent me, I have been trying to read, but I find that it is too touching for me, and I have been obliged to lay it aside.

September 11*th.*—I am now at Singapore again, which is my kind of oasis in this desert of the East; the only place where I have felt well or comfortable, and where there has been a sort of cordiality in the people, which makes one feel somewhat at home. I shall stay here two days, to gain a little strength before plunging again into the sea. Baron Gros is not yet come. I am before him, after all. Commodore Keppel is in this house (the Government) on his way home. He is going to Borneo, on a visit to the Rajah, to-morrow. M. Grant and her child went to Sarawak a few days ago. The Recorder, who used to walk with me in the mornings, is gone to Malacca for the sessions, so that I have lost even here many of my old avocations. . . . I have been indulging in the perusal of your letters of the 26th June and 10th July. . . .

September 12*th.*—I have had a much better night. To the astonishment of everybody, a steamer has made her appearance in the harbour, and proves to be the mail from England, some days before her time. I have hardly any hope of getting my letters out of the Hong-kong boxes. It is most tantalizing. . . . I am much better. Singapore has proved as usual a restorer. . . . I am glad to say that arrangements have been made about the feeding of the native sailors in the Ava, to diminish, at least to some extent, the smells which have so distressed me. They employ a horrid material, made of butter, called *ghee*, and the smell produced by heating and frying this is frightful. . . . I have just returned from church, where it was very hot, and where I thought of you all. This will not reach you until the end of October! How long! how long!

Hong-kong.—September 20*th.*—I did not attempt to write on my way from Singapore to this place, because, though we were much favoured by the weather (as this is the worst month in the China seas and the most subject to typhoons), the motion of the screw in the Ava is so bad, that it is almost impossible to write when she is going at full speed. However, I may now tell you that we made out our voyage in six days of beautiful weather, and that I have gone on gradually recovering my health, which I lost between Calcutta and Singapore. I believe I do not look quite as blooming as usual; but it is of no use my claiming 'sympathy on this score, for, as the Bishop of Labuan appears to have said, I always have a more florid appearance than most people, and never therefore get credit for being ill, however ill I may feel. I found two mails from home. . . . The Government approves of my having sent my troops to India, and Clarendon's letter seems to imply that they are not quite insensible to the difficulties of my position. . . . As it is, I now find myself in a very puzzling position. If I go to the north I shall lose prestige, and perhaps also time; it is even possible that I may force the Emperor to declare himself against us, and to direct hostilities against us at the northern ports, where hitherto we have been trading in peace. On the other hand, if I do not go to the north, and make pacific overtures to the Emperor, I shall go dead against my instructions, and against the policy which Palmerston has over and over again told Parliament I am to pursue. . . . I must think over the matter for a day or two. . . . I regret my man-of-war; though, as I have said, there are some compensations, and among them speed. I do not think I shall live on land here. . . . My great desire is to get all this business over, so as to be able to return home. . . . I do not know that what has happened as yet is likely to protract affairs here. It never was intended, as it now appears, that I should do anything serious before the winter; and if we have force enough sent to take Canton, we shall be as far advanced before the winter is over as we should have been if nothing had happened in India.

September 22*d.*—I have discovered the source of another smell, by finding that my steward had ingeniously contrived to store his onions immediately below my cabin! Only conceive the abomination of such an arrangement! . . . The doctor has pronounced me convalescent, and put me off his list. I intend, however, to continue to be careful, at least until the heat is

D

over. I have taken to dining at three, in order that I may land and get a walk at nightfall. I always go on deck soon after five A.M., and walk for about two hours before dressing. We have had floods of rain, and it has been blowing in this harbour in such a way as to make us suppose that there must be great storms outside. . . . I have almost determined to remain here myself, and send Frederick with a letter to the mouth of the Peiho. . . . The Admiral and others are delighted with this plan, as they are very averse to my going in person. . . . I have not yet quite made up my mind. . . .

September 23d.—It is going on raining, with short intervals, not of sunshine, but of dryness, both night and day, and I have remained for these last two days a prisoner on board. I ask you to imagine the dulness of my life. If I do not move to the north, I do not suppose that I shall have anything to interrupt this dulness for months to come. . . .

September 25th.—I have charged Captain Rolland with a little box with some *misères* which I have picked up at Hong-kong for you. He is going home. . . . I cannot find any slippers bigger than those I have enclosed, and which are really made to be worn here! There is a Chinese compass and two sunpans (boats) carved in peach-stones, etc. . . .

Hong-kong.—September 25th.—I sent a letter off to you this day. . . . I used to dislike to begin writing a letter, when I thought I should receive one from my correspondent before it was finished; but I have got over all these scruples now. Our correspondence is kept up in a kind of constant flow, and our letters so cross each other, that we hardly know where one is begun or ended. Therefore, although I sent off one this forenoon, and although I may calculate on hearing from you again before this is despatched, I feel that it is quite natural to take up my pen, and to have some talk with you this evening before I retire to my cot. I have been dining with the Admiral, quietly, at three P.M., and I went on shore with him afterwards to take a walk. We strolled through the Chinese part of the town—crowded with Chinese all returning from their work—and looking good-humoured as usual. The town is more extensive than I had supposed it to be; but it was close and hot, and I was rather glad when we got into our boat again to pull off to our ship, which is lying about two-and-a-half miles from the shore. It was calm and cool on the water; and after reaching my ship, and taking a bottle of soda-water to quench my thirst, I have sat down to my writing desk, having placed one of the ship's attendants (a disbanded sepoy I believe) at the punkah which has lately been fitted up in my cabin. It is wonderful what a comfort these punkahs are! I was suffocated with heat before my sepoy began to pull, and every now and then I have to hallo to him when he seems disposed to take a nap. . . . When you wrote your letter of July the 10th you were very unhappy, because you had just heard of my troops being ordered, not by me, but by the Government, to India. I was on that day sending you and Lord Clarendon my first despatches from Hong-kong, in which I argued triumphantly in favour of going to the Peiho in accordance with my instructions, against what seemed to me then the only alternative, doing nothing, or making a fruitless attempt at a bad season against Canton; and I begin to answer this letter on the very day on which I have been writing to Lord Clarendon, to prove to him that I had better not go to the Peiho until Canton is settled! This seems inconsistent, but I believe it is not so. The voyage to Calcutta got me out of my difficulty of remaining during the summer inactive at Hong-kong; and the season, the absence of my French and American colleagues, and the loss of prestige occasioned by Indian difficulties, have added greatly to the objections to going to the Peiho. Besides which, the plan of sending F. is a *mezzo termine*, which did not occur to me before, and gets me out of a good deal of embarrassment. . . . When you were writing to Clarendon on the 16th July to ask for news of me, and Clarendon was telling A. that there was to be a good understanding between me and Canning (that is to say, that I was going to sacrifice everything to him), I was actually weighing anchor in Hong-kong harbour, *en route* for Calcutta! How strange are these *rapprochements!* . . .

September 29*th.*— . . . The whole of my party are gone to dine with Sir J. Bowring. I excused myself on the plea of being in delicate health. It is lucky, for the day has been an absolute pour of rain. Since we came here we have had I should think as much rain as falls in England in six months. I keep to my habit of early rising, and two hours' walk on deck before seven A.M. This preserves my health pretty well, and moreover qualifies me for the hulks, if I ever should be sentenced to recreation in that quarter. I have only been on shore four or five times here. You may judge of the liveliness of my life. . . . Poor boys! You must tell them that I hope to be back with them soon. . . . Nothing could be more inconsistent than the tone in which the Ministers write about Canton, and the language which they use in Parliament about our being at peace with China, and my having a chance of settling matters amicably. I shall act as I think for the best, and if they don't like what I am doing, they must send another. . . . The thing which bores me most is the absence of the French and American

Plenipotentiaries. They will not, I fear, be half so anxious to finish matters as I am, who have been left in this horrid region all summer. . . .

October 1st.—What a climate! after raining cats and dogs for forty-eight hours incessantly, it took to blowing at about twelve last night, rain still as heavy as ever. Our captain, who is a man of energy, apprehending that he might run ashore or foul of some ship, got up steam immediately, and set to work to perform the goose step at anchor in the harbour. You may imagine the row,—wind blowing, rain splashing, ropes hauled, spars cracking, everybody halloing:—"A stroke a-head! ease her! faster! stop her!" and other variations of the same tune. All this immediately over my head! After expending the conventional number of hours in my cot, in the operation of what is facetiously called sleeping, I mounted on deck at about five A.M. . . . I wish I could send you a sketch of that gloomy hill at the foot of which "Victoria" lies, as it loomed sullenly in the dusky morning, its crest wreathed with clouds and its cheeks wrinkled by white lines that marked the track of the descending torrents. It was still blowing and raining as hard as ever, but I took my two hours' exercise notwithstanding, clad in Mackintosh. F. and O. who went on shore the day before yesterday to dine with Sir J. Bowring, have not yet returned. *Seven P.M.*—The weather cleared about noon. I remained in my cabin as usual till after five, when I ordered my boat and went on shore. There were signs of the night's work here and there. Masts of junks sticking out of the water, and on land verandahs mutilated, etc. etc. L. accompanied me, and we walked up the hill to a road which runs above the town. The prospect was magnificent—Victoria below us, running down the steep bank to the water's edge; beyond, the bay, crowded with ships and junks, and closed on the opposite side by a semicircle of hills, bold, rugged, and bare, and glowing in the bright sunset. . . . When we got beyond the town, the hill along which we were walking began to remind me of some of the scenery in the Highlands—steep and treeless, the water gushing out at every step among the huge granite boulders, and dashing with a merry noise across our path. After somewhat more than an hour's walk we turned back, and began to descend a long and precipitous path, or rather street, for there were houses on either side, in search of our boat. By the time we had embarked the tints of the sunset had vanished, a moon nearly full rode undisputed mistress in the cloudless sky, and we cut our way to our ship through the ripple that was dancing and sparkling in her beams.

Sunday, October 4th.—I attended church on board the

Admiral's ship to-day. It was very hot on deck under the awning. After dinner, I paid Sir J. B. a visit. . . . It was raining when I left his house, so I performed my first trip in a Hong-kong chair, protected from the rain by a Japan waterproof cloak, which, strange to say, is made of paper.

October 5th.—I am to get a guard of marines and a boat's crew to-day. The Admiral's captain, who is rather a wag, made a speech to them, and said they were going to guard Lord Elgin, and that they had better take good care of him, because he had come to get cheap tea for their wives and children. I am likely therefore to be well protected.

Hong-kong.—October 8th.—I am in daily expectation of the mail, so that I ought perhaps not to begin this letter now, but I may as well tell you how I have passed my time since I despatched my last on the 5th. On the 6th, I went to the anchorage of the French fleet, about twelve miles off. It was rather a nice sail—calm weather, smooth water, narrow passages through hills which have all the same character as that of Hong-kong—green, treeless, and steep. When I reached the anchorage, the French Admiral saluted, and I went on board his ship. He asked me to dinner, and promised me a play afterwards, as I had appreciated the one he gave me at Singapore. The play was really very fairly acted, and the ladies' dresses were supplied from the wardrobe of Madame Bourboulon, wife of the French Minister. The Admiral was very amiable, and called on me the next morning before I started to return. On our way back we made the tour of the island. Every spot at the foot of the hills on which anything will grow is cultivated by the industrious Chinese, whose chief occupation in these parts seems, however to be fishing. Where the French fleet is anchored it is very healthy, but in an entire solitude, and my belief is that they are so dreadfully dull that they would willingly fight anybody in any cause, for the sake of distraction. Last evening I dined with our own Admiral. Sir J. B. and a good many men were there. An opium-ship from India had just arrived, so we had a plentiful crop of topics of conversation. The news from India is rather better. The whole of Bengal was dependent not only on the China force, but on that portion of it which I took or sent them on my own responsibility. The 5th and 90th regiments are marching to the relief of Lucknow. The crews of the Shannon and Pearl are protecting other disturbed districts, and the marines garrisoning Calcutta. . . . It cannot therefore be said that I have not done Canning a good turn. I think, however, that there is a disposition, both in Calcutta and in England, to underrate our needs in China, and I am disposed to write to Canning a despatch which will bring this point out.

... The Government having sent me out with the intention that I should make war, and a war which would require a military force, are quietly giving the public to understand that I came here to make peace, and that if I have any fighting to do, it is fighting for which a naval force only is necessary. ... I think I must tell a little of the truth, however disagreeable. ... If we take Canton by naval means alone, we shall probably not be able to hold the city, in which case we shall probably occasion a great deal of massacre and bloodshed, without influencing in the slightest degree the Court of Pekin. Meanwhile I have a letter to-day from Baron Gros, who has at length reached Singapore. ... He tells me that his "machine" is out of order, and that he must stay at Singapore to re-fit.

October 9th.—Mail not yet arrived. The monsoon is now unfavourable for coming here, and the departure of the mails from here is also delayed, to the 15th instead of the 10th as in the other monsoon. ... I do not think that the naval actions here have really done anything towards solving our questions, and perhaps they may have been injurious, in so far as they have enabled the Government and the Press to take up the tone that we could settle our affairs without troops. All these partial measures increase the confidence of the Chinese in themselves, and confirm them in the opinion that we cannot meet them on land. They have never denied our superiority by sea. ...

October 13th.—No steamer from England yet. I have just despatched letters to Canning, in the sense I have already explained to you. ... General Ashburnham's position is a very cruel one,—at the head of a whole lot of doctors and staff-officers of all kinds, without any troops. The enormous amount of supplies sent out passes belief. Oceans of porter, soda-water, wine of all sorts, and delicacies that I never even heard of, for the hospitals. *I am told*, even tea and sugar, but that may be a calumny. This is the reaction, after the economies practised in the Crimea, and will be persevered in, I suppose, till Parliament gets tired of paying, and then we shall have counteraction the other way. By dint of grumbling about the heat, I have got my captain to put a spring on the cable, so that we may turn our side instead of our prow to the breeze. I dined yesterday on board the Nankin, Captain Stewart, Lord Galloway's brother. The Admiral was there. It was very hot. I am to have my first dinner on Thursday, and I think of having it on deck if the weather is fine.

October 16th.—I have your letters to August 24th. Those from the Government are more satisfactory in *tone* than their earlier ones. I had intended to write more, but a salute is now firing, which informs me that Baron Gros is entering the harbour, so I must close.

Hong-kong.—October 18*th*.— . . . I wound up my last letter to you while salutes were honouring the advent of Baron Gros. Never were there such salutes. I believe the Audacieuse, his frigate, had to fire 180 *coups* in return. Before the noise had well ceased, he came on board my vessel. He is civil, cautious, diplomatic; does not commit himself. I was rather surprised at his declining to dine with me, but I have since been led to suspect that he is the *guest* of his captain, and that he finds some difficulty in returning civilities of that sort. . . . Meanwhile Sir J. Bowring has asked him to dinner, . . . and made him consent to go, if I would agree to meet him. Of course, I agreed at once. My business is to take Canton, to settle Chinese treaties, and to get away from the country, in order that I may find myself at home again, and I do not stick at trifles of this kind. Meanwhile the instructions brought by the last mail give me much greater latitude of action; in fact, untie my hands altogether. I hope I shall get him to go with me; but if not, I shall go at Canton alone. The Admiral is quite ready for the attempt, as soon as his marines arrive. Gros seems to have been most uncomfortable in his frigate. She rolls sixty five degrees. For three weeks near the Cape they never had their ports open; and as all the men sleep on the main deck—some close up to the doors of the cabins of the suite—you may imagine the odours! We were better off in the Shannon. I am thinking of getting out of this ship when I can find a lodging on shore. The Indian Government is paying a great price for her, on the assumption that I should be constantly consuming coal. As there seems to be now little chance of moving to the north till January or February, there is no use in my keeping this expensive ship, and I may probably get the Shannon again before I want to put to sea. . . . I am already beginning to hope for the next mail. . . .

October 23*d*.— . . . The dinner at Sir J. Bowring's went off very well. . . . Baron Gros is now gone with his frigate to the French anchorage, and he tells me that when he comes to see me again, he will borrow a *cannonière* from his Admiral. In that case he will get out of his difficulty about dinners. He is a great artist; paints in oils; and is first-rate, I believe, as a photographer. I gave a dinner on Wednesday. It was on deck, and was rather hot, otherwise not marked by any incident. . . .

October 30*th*.—How little was I prepared for the sad intelligence brought to me by your last! How constantly we shall all feel the absence of that good genius!—that Providence always on the watch to soothe the wretched and to console the afflicted. I had never thought of her early removal by death, and yet one ought to have done so, for she complained much of suffering last year, and all who knew her well must have felt that to make her complain her sufferings must have been great. She is gone; and she will leave behind her a blank in many existences. . . . Many years ago we were much together. She was then in the full vigour of her faculties. . . . I had ample opportunity then of appreciating the remarkable union of heart and head and soul which her character presented. Many of her letters written in those days were of rare excellence. . . . I feel for you. . . .

October 31*st.*—I shall hardly recognise Scotland without her, so much did she, in her unobtrusive and quiet way, make herself the point to which, in all difficulties and joys, one looked. . . . Poor M. has the satisfaction of knowing that all that was great and loveable in her, flourished under his protection and with his sympathy. Perhaps that is the best consolation which a person bereaved as he is can enjoy. It is not a consolation which will arrest his progress along the path which she has trodden before, but it is one which will strew it with flowers. . . . Already, when this letter reaches you, the green weeds will have begun to creep over the new-made grave, and the crust of habit to cover wounds which at first bled most freely. It is also a soothing reflection that hers was a life of which death is rather the crown than the close. So that it will not be in gloom, but in the soft sunset light of memory that they who have been wont to walk with her, and are now deprived of her companionship, will have henceforward to tread their weary way. I see in that sunset light the days when we were much together—when she used to call herself my wife. In those days her nervous system was stronger than it was when you became acquainted with her. Her soul spoke through more obedient organs. Nothing could exceed the eloquence and beauty of her letters in those days, when written under the influence of strong feeling. She is gone. I do not expect ever to see her like again.

November 1*st.*—Poor Balgonie, too. It is another loss; very sad, though different in its character. When I saw him at Malta I had not a conception that he would last so long. . . . On *November* 1*st* I am reading your thoughts of *September* 1*st.* How far apart this proves us to be! . . . I sympathize deeply in all those feelings. . . . To whatever side one looks there is the sad blank effected by her removal, even in my public interests. I cannot say how much since I returned home I owed to her thoughtfulness and affection. . . . Cut off as we are here at present from all immediate contact with home interests, it is difficult to realize her removal and its consequences to the full. It is a stunning blow from which one recovers gradually to a consciousness of a great and undefined loss. God bless you! . . . and grant that you may share her inexpressible comfort. . . .

November 8th.—I have been absent for four days on a tour. We started on Wednesday, and went up as far as the Bogue Forts, where we anchored for the night. On the following morning we took Commodore Elliot and some others on board, and after proceeding some twenty miles further up the river, got into a gunboat and went on to the Macao Fort, about two miles from Canton, and now occupied by us. This day was one of the hottest I have felt since I have been in these parts, but the temperature fell suddenly on Thursday, and we have had cool weather since. Our trip was most pleasant. When the river narrowed we saw villages composed of houses well built; brick walls and pottery roofs, surrounded by sugar and rice fields, and every appearance of ease and comfort. The people took hardly any notice of us, and it was difficult to realize the fact that we were in an enemy's country. Macao Fort is a tolerably strong place; thick granite walls. From the top I got a view of Canton, and although it was considerably shielded by the island of Honan, by dint of a spyglass and a good deal of cross examination, I was able to make out pretty well the character of the place. On our return we took a channel of the river, which has not been travelled since the war began. We took a second gunboat and an armed boat with us in case of mishap, and charged our own big gun, but we had not the satisfaction of even creating a sensation. The poor labourers looked very listlessly at us as we glided by. We returned to the Ava soon after nightfall, and started next morning from our anchorage to Macao (not fort, but town). We had a gunboat to meet us there as the Ava could not approach within four miles of the shore. We landed at about three P.M., without accident, except that the Secretary to the French embassy, M. Duchene de Bellecourt, whom I had taken with me, tumbled into the water in getting from my row-boat into the gunboat, and was nearly made a sandwich of between the two. On landing I called first on the Governor, and then on M. Bourboulon, the French minister, with whom I dined; and as it was blowing very hard I yielded to his hospitable invitation to take a bed on shore. I liked Macao, because there is some appearance about it of a history,—convents and churches, the Garden of Camoëns, etc. The Portuguese have been in China about three hundred years. Hong-kong was a barren rock fifteen years ago. Macao is Catholic, Hong-kong Protestant; so these causes combined give the former a wonderful superiority in all that is antique and monumental. We returned to this place yesterday, calling on Baron Gros on the way. On my arrival I found that the American Envoy, Mr. Reed, is in the harbour in his monster ship, the Minnesota. Notes have passed between us, and he is to visit me to-morrow. I went to church this morning on shore. We had a sermon by the chief military chaplain, on behalf of the Institution for the Daughters of Soldiers. . . . After church I went up to the Government House with Sir J. B. and remained there an hour. . . .

November 10*th.*—I have just returned from the Minnesota, where I returned the visit which Mr. Reed paid me yesterday. She is a magnificent ship, thirty-five feet longer and five feet wider than the Shannon. I never saw such a deck. The accommodation for the envoy is splendid. The captain is removed to a sort of house on deck. . . . We had enough firing this morning again, to take Canton. The American Commodore arrived during the night, and a regular volley of salutes took place. We are told to expect the Russian Plenipotentiary in a day or two, and the whole affair will be repeated. . . .

November 14*th.*—I have received your letters to September 24th. . . . The Government approve entirely of my move to Calcutta, and Lord C. writes very cordially on the subject. . . .

November 15*th.*—I have seen the Russian Plenipotentiary. . . . He has been at Kiatcha and the mouth of the Peiho, asking for admission to Pekin, and got considerably snubbed at both places, as I should have been if I had gone there. It will devolve on me, I apprehend, to administer the return, which is not, I think, a bad arrangement for British prestige in the east. . . .

Steamer Ava.—*Hong-kong, November* 17*th.*—I am about to *déménager* to-day, and to take up my abode on shore. . . . When General Ashburnham informed me that he was under orders for India, and that he was to take several officers with him, I thought it a good plan to offer them a good ship, save their passage-money, and get a good house for myself on shore. He accepted the offer at first, but since then there has been an interval of hesitation and delay. I did not much care personally; but I still think it was right that I should endeavour to relieve the Indian Government of the expense of this ship. . . . However, the upshot is, that General A. comes on board, and I go on shore to-day. I am to dine at the Government House, to meet the American and Russian Plenipotentiaries. I have given B. a hint to avoid speeches, which I hope he will take. The Russian is miserably lodged in a very small steamer, with a poorly furnished cabin. He presents a great contrast to his republican neighbour, who is lying beside him in his magnificent ship, with accommodation to match. He carries only six guns, and as he has had about 120 *coups* to fire in salutes, it must have been hot work. I went to church on board the Admiral on Sunday, and I found the American Plenipotentiary there. He went yesterday to call on the Frenchman at his anchorage, and we heard the booming of cannon over the waters as they interchanged salutes.

My serious work is about to begin. I must draw up a challenge for Yeh, which is a delicate matter. Gros showed me a *projet de note* when I called on him some days ago. It is very long, and very well written. The fact is, that he has a much better case of quarrel than we. At least one that lends itself much better to rhetoric. An opium-ship came in from Calcutta yesterday. It brought me nothing from Canning. It is clear, however, that things are getting better with him. I think it probable that my despatch anticipating a favourable turn of affairs there, and founding on that anticipation a demand for reinforcements, will reach England at the very time when the news from India justifying that anticipation will be received. . . . The Government and public in England would not believe there was any danger in India for a long time, and consequently allowed the season for precautionary measures to pass by, and then made up for their apathy by the most exaggerated apprehensions. My mind has been more tranquil, for it has not presented these phases. As soon as I heard of Canning's difficulties, I determined to do what I could for him; but it never occurred to me that we were to act as if the game was up with us in the East. . . .

My crew are doing me a kindness. They have taken to their *ghee* again, by way of reconciling me to my departure from the ship. . . . We are so far separated, that now, when I hear of the impression produced on your mind by the news of my arrival at Calcutta, I am looking for troops from thence to repay my advances made at their time of need. Shall I get any ? . . . The secret of governing a democracy is understood by men in power at present. Never interfere to check an evil until it has attained such proportions that all the world see plainly the necessities of the case. You will then get any amount of moral and material support that you require; but if you interfere at an earlier period, you will get neither thanks nor assistance ! I am not at all sure but that the time is approaching when foresight will be a positive disqualification in a statesman. But to return to our own matters. The Government and public are thinking of nothing but India at present. It does not however follow that quite as strong a feeling might not be got up for

China in a few months. If we meet with anything like disaster here, that would certainly be the case. . . .

Head-Quarters House, Hong-kong.—November 18*th.*—I dined yesterday with the Governor, and returned to sleep here, though the house is in sad confusion. It is a good house, roomy and airy, with hardly any furniture; there is certainly some comfort in being in a house for a change. B. avoided speeches, and the dinner went off well enough. He came to me in a fuss about the precedency of his three ambassadors. So I proposed to represent Lady B. (the dinner being a man's dinner), which relieved him from his difficulty. . . . General Ashburnham has been with me to take leave. . . . I am to dine with General Straubenzie, his successor, as I have no means of dining at home to-day. The Admiral sailed this morning to take up a station in the river, preparatory to operations against Canton.

Sunday, November 22*d.*—I had a visit from Gros on Thursday. He remained till yesterday morning. Nothing would induce him to accept a room here, so he lived at the Club. Notwithstanding his unsociability, I like him. We have drawn up plans of united operation, which will, I hope, do well. I shall have some difficulty, however, on my own side. . . . The Admiral has a plan of his own for capturing Canton, which may be a right one, but which is certainly open to great criticism. Its principal recommendation, I suspect, in the eyes of the Navy is, that it promises to make this exploit a naval operation. Its chief condemnation in mine is, that it will probably lead to much destruction of life and property. . . . About three weeks ago, Sir J. B. stated officially that the black troops here might be sent back to Singapore, "as he knew of no danger to the colony from any quarter." I protested against this, and they were not sent back. The General came to me on Friday with a letter he had written to B., proposing to take a considerable part of the garrison to assist at Canton, as the Governor had stated "he knew of no danger to the colony." He told me also that he had spoken to B. on the subject, and that he had expressed his perfect readiness that the troops should go. Yesterday morning Sir J. B. came to me with the General's letter, and the draft of a reply, protesting against the General's proposal. I told him that I must decline to offer any opinion on the subject unless he submitted the papers, and gave me an opportunity of stating it in writing (experience has taught me the necessity of this precaution); but that, as he had mentioned the matter, I could not help expressing my regret that he should have written as he had done three weeks before to Singapore. . . .

The climate now is, I am bound to say, delicious. The thermometer, I should think, between 60° and 70°, a bright sun, and fresh breeze. I was a little laid up by a chill, I suppose, on Friday, but I am quite well again. I wish you could take wings and join me here, if it were even for a few hours. We should first wander through these spacious apartments. We should then stroll out on the verandah, or along the path of the little terrace garden which General A. has surrounded with a defensive wall, and from thence I should point out to you the harbour, bright as a flower-bed with the flags of many nations, the jutting promontory of Kowloon, and the barrier of bleak and jagged hills that bounds the prospect. A little later, when the sun began to sink, and the long shadows to fall from the mountain's side, we should set forth for a walk along a level pathway of about a quarter of a mile long, which is cut in its flank, and connects with this garden, and from thence we should watch this same circle of hills, now turned into a garland, and glowing in the sunset lights, crimson and purple, and blue and green, and colours for which a name has not yet been found, as they successively lit upon them. Perhaps we should be tempted to wait (and it would not be long to wait, for the night follows in these regions very closely on the heels of day), until, on these self-same hills, then gloomy and dark and sullen, tens of thousands of bright and silent stars were looking down calmly from heaven. . . .

November 25th.—I have your letters to October 8th. . . .

November 28th.—I am going to Macao to-day to see Baron Gros, so I must put up this letter before the day of the packet's departure. . . .

Macao.—December 2d.—. . . Baron Gros and I have been settling our plans of proceeding, which we are conducting with a most cordial *entente*. . . . As he is well versed in all the forms and usages of diplomacy he is very useful to me in such points. . . . I have been living here in the house of Mr. Dent, one of the merchant princes of China. He is very obliging, and I have remained at his request a day longer than I intended. I return, however, to-day. I like Macao with its air of antiquity; in some respects almost of *décadence*. It is more interesting than Hong-kong, which has only existed fifteen years, and is as go-a-head and upstart and staring as "one of our cities," as my Yankee friend informed me a few days ago. We have been a regular constellation of Ambassadors here. Besides myself and the Frenchman, we have had the American and Russian both living in the same house, and both I must say looking very foolish.

Hong-kong.—December 4th.—I was interrupted by Baron Gros, who came to have a last word with me, and then I went on board my gunboat and came back to Hong-kong, a very pleasant and smooth voyage. I found that one of the steamers with marines had arrived, and that the Colonel of Engineers, a very superior man, had died suddenly. Both these occurrences are favourable to the pretensions of the navy, who wish to oust the army from the affair. . . . However, I trust I shall get things right in time. . . . Sir J. B. admitted to me to-day that while I was at Calcutta he had intimated that he was ready to receive communications from Yeh. This was directly in the teeth of the instructions of the Government and of my directions. . . . The American Plenipotentiary told me to-day that he had received a letter from Yeh. He is to come to me to-morrow to speak about it. For some days past it has been much warmer again, but generally speaking the weather is at present very perfect. . . . My present difficulty arises from my fear that to gratify certain feelings of professional vanity we shall be led to attack Canton before we have all our force, and led therefore to destroy (if there is any resistance) both life and property to a greater extent than would otherwise be necessary. . . . How long I shall remain in this house (which is a good one) I cannot tell, for when operations commence I must go up the river. . . .

December 5th.—The General has returned from visiting the Admiral, whom he went to see in consequence of my official demand that they should give me their joint opinion as to the sufficiency of the means at their disposal for taking Canton. The interview appears to have gone off very well. I think, therefore, that I have succeeded in getting things into their right places, and I hope they may go on smoothly. I had also a visit of two hours from the American Plenipotentiary. He is new to the trade, and in a false position, but I trust that we may keep him tolerably straight. The Russian also called on me. . . . When I went out to walk with O., I was informed by a person I met in a very public walk just out of the town, that a man had been robbed very near where we were. I met the person immediately afterwards. He was rather a *mesquin-* looking Portuguese, and he said that three Chinamen had rushed upon him, knocked him down, thrown a quantity of sand into his eyes, and carried off his watch. This sort of affair is not uncommon. I have bought a revolver, and am beginning to practice pistol shooting. . . .

December 9th.—Baron Gros came here on Monday. We have been busy, and all our plans are settled. I sent up this evening to the Admiral my letter to Yeh, which is to be delivered on Saturday the 12th. He is to have ten days to think over it, and if at the end of that time he does not give in, the city will be taken. We are in for it now. I have hardly alluded in my ultimatum to that wretched question of the Arrow, which is a scandal to us, and is so considered, I have reason to know, by all except the few who are personally compromised. I have made as strong a case as I can on general grounds against Yeh, and my demands are most moderate. If he refuses to accede to them, which he probably will, this will I hope put us in the right when we proceed to extreme measures. The diplomatic position is excellent. The Russian has had a rebuff at the mouth of the Peiho. The American at the hands of Yeh. The Frenchman gives us a most valuable moral support by saying that *he* too has a sufficient ground of quarrel with Yeh. We stand towering above all, using calm and dignified language, moderate in our demands, but resolute in enforcing them. If such had been our attitude from the beginning of this controversy it would have been well. However, we cannot look back. We must do for the best, and trust in Providence to carry us through our difficulties. Count Putiatine (the Russian Plenipotentiary) dined with me on Monday. I had a good deal of talk with him, but not much that stuck to the memory.

December 13*th*.—The home mail only arrived to-day. It has been a humiliation day here for the Indian difficulties. The Bishop preached a sermon which was in some parts eloquent, and as good perhaps as a semi-political sermon can be. I had letters from India yesterday. It appears that Lucknow has been relieved after a severe fight. Canning writes as if he had still serious work to do, but then he is writing partly to persuade me that he can spare me no troops. . . . Few people have ever been in a position which required greater tact—four ambassadors, two admirals, a general, and Sir J. B.! and notwithstanding this luxuriancy in the shape of colleagues, no sufficient force. I am anxiously awaiting the return of Mr. Wade, my Chinese secretary, who went up the river to deliver my letter to Yeh at Canton. The Admiral moves on Friday to Honan Island, opposite the city. I dined yesterday with Mr. Reed, the American. I had written to him in the morning a despatch replying to one that he had addressed to me, and I was not sure how he would like my answer, but he was very amiable and seemed in very good humour. I have been invited to dine by Count Putiatine on Thursday, but I have declined, as I expect by that time to be up the river. . . .

December 15*th*.—The mail was to have gone to-day, but is detained till to-morrow. I suppose that Clarendon will receive about forty letters of my writing, either addressed to himself, or copies of what I have written to others, by this mail, so you may suppose I have been rather busy. Reed has given me a good deal of trouble by writing to very little purpose. I have also had all the affair of the movement on Canton to arrange. The delivery of the letter to Yeh was accomplished successfully, but the move to Honan was to take place to-day, and I shall be anxious to hear how it went off. It is my intention to embark on Thursday to go up the river. Yeh has till the 22d to make up his mind. If he does not give in, the army and navy will take him in hand. My difficulties are, of course, much enhanced by the wretchedness of the lorcha case in which our quarrel began. . . . The American is here to look on, and take note of what is rotten in our case, and I have got to fight everybody's battles, and make myself sponsor for everybody's follies. . . .

December 16*th.*—I have just heard that Honan was occupied without conflict or difficulty. I have also got an answer from Yeh, which is, though civil in terms, no concession to my demands.

H. M. S. Furious, Canton River.—December 17*th.*—You see from my date that I am again in a new lodging. It promises to be, I think, more agreeable than any of our previous marine residences. We have paddles instead of a screw. Then the captain has not only given up to me all the stern accommodation, but he has also done everything in his power to make the place comfortable. . . . He is the Sherard Osborne of Arctic regions notoriety. I am on my way to join Gros, in order to decide on our future course of action. I mentioned yesterday that Honan was occupied, and that I had received a letter from Yeh which must, I suppose, be considered a refusal. This was the fair side of the medal. The reverse was an ugly quarrel up the river, which ended in the loss of the lives of some sailors, and the destruction of a village,—a quarrel for which our people were, I suspect, to some extent responsible. I fear that under cover of the blockade instituted by the Admiral, great abuses have taken place. . . . It makes one very indignant, but unfortunately it is very difficult to bring the matter home to the culprits. All this, however, makes it most important to bring the situation to a close as soon as possible. It is clear that there will be no peace till the two parties fight it out. The Chinese do not want to fight, but they will not accept the position relatively to the strangers under which alone strangers will consent to live with them, till the strength of the two parties has been tested by fighting. The English do want to fight; and although I made the most moderate proposals to Yeh, with a most *bonâ fide* intention that he should have the option of accepting them, and thus avoiding a conflict, I am sure that if the result had been pacific I should have been famously abused. . . . Referring to your last letter, . . . I am quite aware that the Government could not well help sending the China force to India, and since they have begun to acknowledge the difficulties which this has created in my situation, I am satisfied. Of course, if the interest about the Chinese quarrel had been originally real, and not *created* for political purposes, they would have been obliged to find a force for both purposes; but as that interest was wholly factitious, it burst as an airbubble in presence of a real interest such as that of the Indian quarrel. . . . There is no cold here as yet, though it is cooler to-day. They say that the winter till now has been unusually hot.

December 18*th.*—This does not promise to be a lively sojourn. We are anchored at present at a point where the river forks into the Whampoa and Blenheim reaches. We have the Blenheim reach, and my suite wish me to go up it to the Macao Fort, from which they think they would have a good view of what goes on when the city is attacked. I wish, however, to be with Gros, and he will go up the Whampoa reach as far as his great lumbering ship will go. Meanwhile we are here confined to our ships, as it would not of course do for me to go on shore to be caught. Poor Yeh would think me worth having at present. What will he do? His answer is very weak, and reads as if the writer was at his wits' end; but with that sort of stupid Chinese policy which consists in never yielding anything, he exposes himself to the worst consequences without making any preparations (so far as we can see) for resistance. Among other things in his letter he quotes a long extract from a Hongkong paper describing Sir G. Bonham's investiture as K.C.B., and advises me to imitate him for my own interest, rather than Sir J. Davis, who was recalled. Davis, says Yeh, insisted on getting into the city, and Bonham gave up this demand. Hence his advice to me. All through the letter is sheer twaddle. His letter to Reed, who wrote him a toadying note, was much sharper, and had in it a spark of the old fire, which seems extinct in this.

December 22*d.*—On the afternoon of the 20th, I got into a gunboat with Commodore Elliot, and went a short way up towards the barrier forts, which were last winter destroyed by the Americans. When we reached this point, all was so quiet that we determined to go on, and we actually steamed past the city of Canton, along the whole front, within pistol-shot of the town. A line of English men-of-war are now anchored there in front of the town. I never felt so ashamed of myself in my life, and Elliot remarked that the trip seemed to have made me sad. There we were, accumulating the means of destruction under the very eyes, and within the reach of a population of about 1,000,000 of people, against whom these means of destruction were to be employed! "Yes," I said to Elliot, "I am sad, because when I look at that town, I feel that I am earning for myself a place in the Litany, immediately after 'plague, pestilence, and famine.'" I believe, however, that as far as I am concerned, it was impossible for me to do otherwise than as I have done. I could not have abandoned the demand to enter the city after what happened last winter, without compromising our position in China altogether, and opening the way to calamities even greater than those now before us. I made my demands on Yeh as moderate as I could, so as to give him a chance of accepting, although, if he had accepted, I knew that I should have brought on my head the imprecations both of the navy and army and of the civilians, the time being given by the missionaries and the women. And now Yeh having refused, I shall do whatever I can possibly do to secure the adoption of plans of attack, etc., which will lead to the least destruction of life and property. Yesterday we had a conference of the Commanders-in-chief and Plenipotentiaries on board the Audacieuse, which I suggested. It went off pretty well. I hope that the Admiral will abandon the greater part, if not all, of the most objectionable parts of his original plan. We dined with the French Admiral, and had a theatrical performance as usual. The weather is charming; the thermometer about 60° in the shade in the morning; the sun powerful, and the atmosphere beautifully clear. When we steamed up to Canton, and saw the rich alluvial banks covered with the luxuriant evidences of unrivalled industry and natural fertility combined; beyond them, barren uplands, sprinkled with a soil of a reddish tint, which gave them the appearance of heather slopes in the Highlands; and beyond these again, the white cloud mountain range, standing out bold and blue in the clear sunshine,—I thought bitterly of those who, for the most selfish objects, are trampling under foot this ancient civilisation.

December 24*th*.—I am somewhat better satisfied to-day, because I hear that the Admiral's plan is altogether abandoned, and that the one fixed upon is likely to be attended with less sacrifice of life and property. My letter telling Yeh that I had handed the affair over to the naval and military commanders, and Gros to the same effect, were sent to him to-day; also a joint letter from the commanders, giving him forty-eight hours to deliver over the city, at the expiry of which time, if he does not do so, it will be attacked. I postponed the delivery of these letters till to-day, that the expiry of the forty-eight hours might not fall on Christmas day. Now I hear that the commanders will not be ready till Monday, which the Calendar tells me is "the Massacre of the Innocents!" If we can take the city without much massacre, I shall think the job a good one, because no doubt the relations of the Cantonese with the foreign population were very unsatisfactory, and a settlement was sooner or later inevitable. But nothing could be more contemptible than the origin of our existing quarrel. . . . We moved this evening to the Barrier Forts, a spot within about two miles of Canton, and very near the place where the troops are to land for the attack on the city. I have been taking walks on shore the last two or three days on a little island called Dane's Island, formed of barren hills, with little patches of soil between them and on their flanks, cultivated in terraces by the industrious Chinese. The people seemed very poor and miserable, suffering, I fear, from this horrid war. The French Admiral sent on shore to Whampoa some casks of damaged biscuit the other day, and there was such a rush for it, that some people were, I believe, drowned. The head man came afterwards to the officer, expressed much gratitude for the gift, but said that if it was repeated, he begged notice might be given to him, that he might make arrangements to prevent such disorder. The ships are surrounded by boats filled chiefly by women, who pick up orange-peel and offal, and everything that is thrown overboard. One of the gunboats got ashore yesterday, within a stone's-throw of the town of Canton, and the officer had the coolness to call on a crowd of Chinese, who were on the quays, to pull her off, which they at once did! Fancy having to fight such people! I hope that Christmas day may bring me a gift, in the shape of a letter from you.

Christmas Day.— . . . Who would have thought, when we were spending that cold snowy Christmas day last year at Howick, that *this* day would find us separated by almost as great a distance as is possible on the surface of our globe! and that I should be anchored, as I now am, within two miles of a great city, doomed, I fear, to destruction, from the folly of its own rulers, and the vanity and levity of ours. We have moved a little further up the river this morning, and as we are, like St. Paul, dropping an anchor from the stern, I have had over my head for several hours the incessant dancing about and clanking of a ponderous chain-cable, till my brains are nearly all shaken out of their place.

December 26*th.*—Still no letters. Our post should leave this on Monday the 28th, on which day the attack on Canton is to begin. I understand that the two Admirals and Generals are to land together at a spot near that at which we are anchored. They will advance to a fort called Lin's Fort, and establish themselves there on the Monday, and assault the town on Tuesday. This is a much more rational plan. It is probable that the mail-steamer may be delayed, and take home the result of

Tuesday's operations. I have a second letter from Yeh, which is even more twaddling than the first. They say that he is all day engaged in sacrificing to an idol, which represents the God of Physic, and which is so constructed that a stick in its hand traces figures on sand. In the figures so traced he is supposed to read his fate.

December 28*th, Noon.* —We have been throwing shells, etc., into Canton since six A.M., without almost any reply from the town. I hate the whole thing so much, that I cannot trust myself to write about it. . . .

December 29*th.*—The mail was put off, and I add a line to say that I hope the Canton affair is over, and well over. . . . The English mail is just arrived with your letters to the 8th November. . . . When I say this affair is over, perhaps I say too much. But the horrid bombardment has ceased, and we are in occupation of Magazine Hill, at the upper part of the city, within the walls. . . .

H. M. S. Furious, Canton River.—*January* 2*d*, 1858.— . . . The last week has been a very eventful one. Not one of unmixed satisfaction to me, because of course there is a great deal that is painful about this war, but on the whole the results have been successful. On Monday last I was awakened at six P.M. by a cannon-shot, which was the commencement of a bombardment of the city, which lasted for twenty-seven hours. As the fire of the shipping was either not returned at all, or returned only by a very few shots, I confess that this proceeding gave me great pain at the time. But I find that much less damage has been done to the town than I expected, as the fire was confined to certain spots. I am on the whole, therefore, disposed to think that the measure proved to be a good one, as the terror which it has excited in the minds of the Cantonese is more than in proportion to the injury inflicted, and therefore it will have the effect, I trust, of preventing any attempts on their part to dislodge or attack us, which would entail very great calamities on themselves. At ten A.M. on Monday the troops landed at a point about two miles east of the city, and marched up with very trifling resistance to Lin Fort; which they took, the French entering first, to the great disgust of our people. Next morning at nine A.M. they advanced to the escalade of the city walls, and proceeded, with again very slight opposition, to the Magazine Hill, on which they hoisted the British and French flags. They then took Gough Fort with little trouble, and there they were by three P.M. established in Canton. The poor stupid Chinese had placed some guns in position to resist an attack from the opposite quarter—the quarter, viz., from which Gough attacked the city; and some people suppose that if we had advanced from that side we should have met with some resistance. My own opinion is, that the resistance would have been no great matter in any case, although, no doubt, if we had made the attempt in summer, and with sailors only, as some proposed when I came here in July, we should probably have met with disaster. As it is, my difficulty has been to enforce the adoption of measures to keep our own people in order, and to prevent the wretched Cantonese from being plundered and bullied. This task is the more difficult from the very motley force with which we have to work, composed, firstly, of French and English; secondly, of sailors to a great extent—they being very imperfectly manageable on shore. All, moreover, having, I fear, a very low standard of morality in regard to stealing from the Chinese. There is a word called "loot," which gives, unfortunately, a venial character to what would, in common English, be styled robbery. . . . Add to this, that there is no flogging in the French army, so that it is impossible to punish men committing this class of offences. . . . On the other hand, these incomprehensible Chinese, although they make no defence, do not come forward to capitulate, and I am in mortal terror lest the French Admiral, who is in the way of looking at these matters in a purely professional light, should succeed in inducing our chiefs to engage again in offensive operations, which would lead to an unnecessary destruction of life and property. It may seem presumptuous, but I feel confident that I could settle the whole matter in a very few days without shedding a drop more of blood. All that is required now is some talent for administration. Meanwhile, by way of getting up to the front, and putting myself into communication with the chiefs, I proposed to Gros that we should land on the first of the year, and march up to the Magazine Hill. He consented, and the chiefs agreed, so we landed at about one P.M. at a point on the river bank immediately below the south-east angle of the city wall, which is now our line of communication between the river and Magazine Hill. As we landed, all the vessels in the river hoisted English and French flags, and fired salutes. We walked up to the hill along the top of the wall, which is a good wide road, and which was all lined with troops and sailors, who presented arms and cheered as we passed. We reached the summit at about three. The British quarter, which is a sort of temple, stands on the highest point, the hill falling pretty precipitously from it on all sides. The view is one of the most extensive I ever saw. Towards the east and north barren hills of considerable height, and much of the character of those we see from Hong-kong. On the west, level lands cultivated in rice and otherwise. Towards the south, the town lying still as a city of the dead. The silence was quite painful, especially when we returned about nightfall. But it is partly owing to the narrowness of the streets, which prevents one from seeing the circulation of population which may be going on within. We remained at the top of the hill till about half-past five, during which time we blew up the Blue-Jacket Fort and Gough Fort, and got back to our ships about eight P.M., having spent a very memorable 1st of January, and made a very interesting expedition; although I could not help feeling melancholy when I thought that we were so ruthlessly destroying the prestige of a place which had been for so many centuries intact and undefiled by the stranger, and exercising our valour against so contemptible a foe.

January 4th.—I have not given you as full a description as I ought to have done of the views and ceremony of Friday, because I saw "Our own Correspondent" there, and I think I can count on that being well done in the *Times*. . . . This day is a pour of rain, rather unusual for the season. . . . Some of the Chinese authorities are beginning to show a desire to treat, and some of the inhabitants are presenting petitions to us to protect them against robbers, native and foreign. . . .

January 6th.—Yesterday was a great day. The chiefs made a move which was very judicious, I think, and which answered remarkably well. They sent bodies of men at an early hour into the city from different points, and succeeded in capturing Yeh, the Lieutenant-Governor of the city and the Tartar General, etc. This was done without a shot being fired, and I believe the troops behaved very well, abstaining from *loot*, etc. Altogether the thing was a complete success, and I give them great credit for it. Yeh has been carried on board the Inflexible steamer as a prisoner of war. He is an enormous man. I can hardly speak to his appearance, as I only saw him for a moment as he passed me in a chair on his way to his vessel. M., who has taken a sketch of him to-day speaks favourably of him; but it is the fashion to abuse even his looks. The Lieutenant-General has been allowed to depart, but the Lieutenant-Governor and Tartar General are still in custody at head-quarters. At my suggestion a proposal was made to the Lieutenant-Governor to-day to continue to govern the city under us; but the stolidity of the Chinese is so great that there is no saying what he may do. We have given him till to-morrow to determine whether he will accept. My whole efforts have been directed to preserve the Cantonese from the evils of a military occupation; but their stupid apathetic arrogance makes it almost impossible to effect this object. Yeh's tone when he was taken was to be rather bumptious. The Admiral asked him about an old man of the name of Cooper, who was kidnapped. At first he pretended that he knew nothing about him. When pressed he said, "Oh! he was a prisoner of war. I took him when I drove you away from the city last winter. I took a great deal of trouble with him and the other European prisoners, but I could not keep them alive. They all died, and if you like I'll show you where I had them buried." M. says that to-day when he saw him on board the Inflexible, he was very civil and *piano*. He takes it easy, eats and drinks well, etc. He said to his captain, that if it was not an indiscreet question, he would be glad to know whether it was likely that we should kill him. The captain had no difficulty in re assuring him on that point.

January 8th.—We had rather an important day's work yesterday. The Lieutenant-Governor showed some symptoms of a willingness to govern on our conditions. This gives some chance of our getting out of the difficulties of our situation. You may imagine what it is to undertake to govern some millions of people (the province contains upwards of 20,000,000), when we have *in all* two or three people who understand the language! I never had so difficult a matter to arrange. . . . Each man has his own way of seeing things, and the real difficulties of the question being enormous, and the mysteries of the Chinese character almost unfathomable, . . . the problem is well nigh insoluble. However yesterday we seemed to make some progress towards an understanding. We walked up to the front along the wall as usual, and very hot it was; but we returned through the town itself with the General and Admiral and a large escort. I rode on a pony. It was a strange and sad sight. The wretched-looking single-storeyed houses on either side of the narrow streets almost all shut up, only a few people making their appearance, and these for the most part wan and haggard, and here and there places which the fire from our ships had destroyed, all presented a very melancholy spectacle; and one could hardly help asking one's-self, with some disgust, whether it was worth while to make all the row which we have been making, for the sake of getting into this miserable place. However, I presume that the better part of the population have either fled or hid themselves. I daresay if they had returned, and the shops had been opened, the aspect of the town would have been different.

January 9th.—Yesterday I went up again to the front without Gros, and pressed matters forward towards a solution. The result was, that my plan of getting the Governor of the province to consent to return to his Yamun and resume his functions, a board of our officers, supported by a large body of troops, being appointed to inhabit his Yamun with him, and to aid him in the maintenance of order, prevailed. . . . To-day we went, Gros and I, in great procession to the Governor's Yamun, to reinstate him in his office on the above conditions. We were carried in chairs through the town, attended by a large escort. The city seemed fuller of people than on the occasion of my former visit, and they looked more cheerful.

January 10*th.*—By a ludicrous mistake, no orders had been given to release the Governor and Tartar General, so that, after waiting for them for an hour, we heard that the sentry would not let them leave the room in which they were confined. The consequence was that it was getting late, and as I wished to get my escort out of the streets before it was dark, we were obliged to hurry through the ceremony a little. We began with a kind of squabble about seats; but after that was over, I addressed the Governor in a pretty arrogant tone. I did so out of kindness, as I now know what fools they are, and what calamities they bring upon themselves, or rather on the wretched people, by their pride and trickery. Gros followed; in a few words endorsing what I had said. The Governor answered very satisfactorily. I then rose, saying that we must depart, and that we wished him and the Tartar General all sorts of felicity. They were good-natured looking men, the General being of great size. They conducted us to the front door, where we ought to have found our chairs, but they had disappeared, to the infinite wrath of Mr. Parkes. . . . I say the front door; but in fact the house consisted of a series of one-storeyed pavilions, placed one behind the other, and connected by a covered way with trellis-work panels running through a sort of garden. We got at last into the chairs, and hastened off to the city wall, which we reached just as it was getting dark, having thus terminated about the strangest day which has yet occurred in Chinese history,—the Governor of this arrogant city of Canton accepting office at the hand of two barbarian chiefs!

January 13*th.*—No mail from England yet. To-morrow at twelve this letter goes. You get the least agreeable picture of the concerns in which I am engaged; because as I write this record from day to day, all my anxieties and their causes are narrated. . . . On the whole, I think the last fortnight has been a very successful one. I walked through the city to-day with the Admiral and an escort, and saw evident signs of improvement in the streets. The people seemed to be resuming their avocations, and the shops to be re-opening. My "Tribunal" is working well. In short, I hope that the evils incident to the capture of a city, and especially of a Chinese city, have been in this instance very much mitigated. The season is very changing. Three nights ago the thermometer did not fall below 72°, and last night it fell to 40°. There is a cold wind; and it was necessary to walk briskly to-day to keep one's-self warm.

January 14*th.*—Last night the thermometer fell to 38°. I send you rather a good sketch of Yeh by Morrison. . . .

January 16*th.*--Though I was able to send off the last despatches with something of a satisfactory report; we are by no means I fear yet out of the wood. I took a long walk in the city of Canton yesterday. I visited the West Gate, where I found a stream of people moving outwards, and was told by the officer that this goes on from morning to night. They say, when asked, that they are going out of town to celebrate the New Year, but my belief is that they are flying from us. The streets were full, and the people civil. Quantities of eating stalls, but a large proportion of the shops still shut. As we got near the wall in our own occupation, some people ran up to us complaining that they had been robbed. We went into the houses and saw clearly enough the signs of devastation. I have no doubt, from the description, that the culprits were French sailors. If this goes on one fortnight after we have captured the town, when is it to stop ? . . . It is very difficult to remedy. . . . Nothing could, I believe, be worse than our own sailors, but they are now nearly all on board ship, and we have the resource of the *Cat.* . . . All this is very sad, but I am not yet quite at the end of my tether. If things do not mend within a few days I shall startle my colleagues by proposing to abandon the town altogether, giving reasons for it which will enable me to state on paper all these points. No human power shall induce me to accept the office of oppressor of the feeble.

Sunday, January 17*th.* — Your letters to November 24th arrived yesterday. . . . The calling together of Parliament so suddenly I was not prepared for. I am glad however to think that probably the Government will know before the 3d of December the course which I finally determined to follow. As you know by this time, the mission of F. to the Peiho was ultimately abandoned. It could not have done any good, and it might have compromised us in other parts of China. . . . I took another walk all about Canton yesterday. In fact I act the part of chief-constable. . . .

January 20*th.*—I hinted at my ideas as to the evacuation of the city, and it has had an excellent effect. . . . There is a notable progress towards quiet in the city. Still, I fear the tide of emigration is going on. Parkes is exerting himself with considerable effect, and he is really very clever. There were a great many more shops open in the streets yesterday than I had seen before. . . . What a thing it is to have to deal with a sober population ! I have wandered about the streets of Canton for some seven or eight days since the capture, and I have not seen one drunken man. In any Christian town we should have had numbers of rows by this time arising out of drunkenness, however cowed the population might have been. The Tribunal convicted a Chinaman the other day for selling "Samshoo" to the soldiers. I requested Parkes to hand him over to the Governor Pehkwei for punishment. This was done, and the arrangement answered admirably. The Governor was pleased, he presented himself before the Chinese as the executor of our judgments, and at the same time we to a certain extent seemed to be conceding to the Chinese the principle of ex-territoriality which we assert as against them. The weather continues cool though the sun is hot during the day. This morning the thermometer stood at 49°. . . . I am rather anxious for the next mail. . . . C. is generally very complimentary about my despatches, which I suppose tell their story, and leave nothing to the imagination except what I intend they should. The fact is, that I never before was in a position where I could write, because I have always hitherto been obliged to give others the credit both of thinking and acting for me. I have no responsible ministers here, though the presence of a colleague, and since military operations began the position of the naval and military commanders-in-chief, has required me to act with some caution, in order to make the wheels of the machine work smoothly and keep on the rails. For this reason it was that I suggested a few days ago the plan of evacuation. The maintenance of order in a city under martial law was, I felt, an affair rather for the Commander-in-Chief than for me, therefore I was in a false position when I meddled with it directly. But the question of remaining in the city or not was a political one. By letting it be known that I had there my lines of Torres Vedras, upon which I should fall back if necessary, I obtained the influence I required for insuring as far as possible the adoption of satisfactory arrangements within the city. I must add that this evacuation plan was not intended by me to be a mere threat. I have it clearly matured in my mind as a thing feasible, and which would be under certain circumstances an advisable plan to adopt. In taking Canton we had, as I understand it, two objects in view: the one to prove that we could take it; the other to have in our hands something to give up when we come to terms with the Emperor,—" a material guarantee." I believe that the capture of the city, followed by the capture of Yeh, has settled the former point. Indeed from all that I hear I infer that the capture of Yeh has had more effect on the Chinese mind than the capture of the city. I believe, therefore, that we might abandon the city without losing much if anything on this head. No doubt we should lose on the second head. We should not have Canton to give up when a treaty was concluded if we had given it up already; even then however we might, by retaining the Island of Honan, the forts, etc., do a good deal towards providing a substitute, so that you see my threat was made *bonâ fide*. I certainly should have preferred the loss to which I have referred, to the continuance of a state of things in which the Allied troops were plundering the inhabitants. . . .

January 21st.—I have a letter from Mr. Reed, the United States Plenipotentiary, to-day, in which the following passage occurs :—"I cannot omit this opportunity of most sincerely congratulating you on the success at Canton—the great success of a bloodless victory, the merit of which, I am sure, is mainly due to your Lordship's gentle and discreet counsels. My countrymen will, I am sure, appreciate it." This from the representative of the United States is gratifying both personally and politically.

January 24th.—Baron Gros and I were conversing together yesterday on affairs in this quarter, and among other things he told me that we were both much reproached for our laxity, and that I was more blamed on that account than he. I said to him: "I can praise you on many accounts, my dear Baron, but I cannot compliment you on being a greater brute than I am."

. . . I hear from L., who has just returned from Hong-kong, that the thirst for blood is not yet slaked among the meek Christians of that locality.

January 28th.— . . . I am glad to say that this mail conveys, on the whole, a satisfactory report of the progress of affairs, though this letter puts you in possession of all the ebbs and flows which have taken place during the fortnight. I send a leaf of geranium, which I culled in the garden of the Tartar General. . . .

H. M. S. Furious, Canton River.—*January 29th.*—No letters yet from England. The mail is after its time, and it is reported that the Alma steamer has met with an accident, in which case we may still have to wait. . . . Yesterday, after sending off my letters, I went to Canton, where I found that a sensation had been created by the arrival of a tall, fair, and slender youth, who turned out to be Madame de B., who took this method of visiting the town, which has been hitherto closed. I have not yet met her, but I hear that she was walking about to-day in her male attire, under the escort of her friend, the French Admiral.

January 31st.—Still no letters. I visited yesterday two of the Canton prisons, and witnessed there some sights of horror beyond what I could have pictured to myself. Many of the inmates were so reduced by disease and starvation, that their limbs were not as thick as my wrist. One man who was in this condition was in the receptacle for untried prisoners, and said he had been there seven years. In one of the courts which we entered, there was a cell closed in by a double row of upright posts, which is the common style of gate at Canton, and I was attracted to it by the groans of its inmates. I desired it to be opened, and such a spectacle as it presented! The prisoners were covered with sores, produced by severe beatings; one was already dead, and the rats,—but I cannot go further in description. The others could hardly crawl, they were so emaciated, and my conviction is that they were shut in there to die. The prison authorities stated that they had escaped at the time of the bombardment, for which they had been punished as we saw. If the statement was true, they must have been systematically starved since their recapture. Our pretext for visiting the prisons was to discover whether any Europeans, or persons who had been in the service of, or had had relations with Europeans, were confined in them. We took out some who professed to belong to the latter classes. I went a step further, by taking out a poor boy of fifteen, whom we found in chains, but so weak that when we took them off he was unable to stand. I told Mr. Parkes to take him to Pehkwei, from me, as a sample of the manner in which his prisons are managed. And if Gros consents, I shall send him a letter which will astonish him. I suppose I was on foot for at least seven hours, but these incidents of the latter part of my walk almost put out of my head those of the earlier part. I made, however, a long tour in the western suburb. Among other things of interest, I saw a temple which contains statues of the 500 disciples of Buddha; about as ugly a set of customers as I ever clapped my eyes on. This temple is contained in a monastery, and several priests attended us when we went round it. They have shaven heads and no tails, and seem particularly stupid.

February 2d.—This is a desperately cold day, although the thermometer is, I believe, 54°. There is a stiff breeze from the north, which makes one feel like below zero in Canada. I am trying to get rid of a cold by staying on board to-day. . . . Pehkwei was very indignant at our visit to his prisons, and hinted that he would make away with himself, in a letter which he wrote to me on the subject. However, he was obliged to admit that some of the things we found were very bad, and quite against the Chinese law. On reviewing the whole, I must admit that, except in the case of the one cell that I have described, it was rather neglect, want of food, medical care, cleanliness, etc., than positive cruelty, of which one found evidence in the prisons.

February 4*th.*—Still no letters. To-morrow, F. is to go to Macao, to take to Messrs. Reed and Putiatine copies of all my diplomatic correspondence with Yeh, etc., and an invitation to each that he will join us in an attempt to settle matters by negotiation at Shanghae. It is the commencement of the third act in this Chinese affair. Yesterday, Baron Gros and I paid a visit to the Magazine Hill, where we had a meeting to settle the arrangements under which foreigners are to be admitted to Canton when the blockade is raised. . . . I hear that wonderful stories against me pass current at Hong-kong, but on the whole they are useful, for I am represented as determined to have my own way, etc. I confess that I am pretty determined to have it, but I achieve that object under great difficulties, as the responsibility for all that goes wrong will certainly fall on me.

February 6*th.*—I have a letter from Mr. Reed, saying that he is going to the North this day, so that perhaps F. will not find him. This would be a great disappointment. I am beginning to feel low about my prospects here, so great are the difficulties. . . . I feel in conscience bound to mitigate as far as possible the evils which we are inflicting on these unhappy Chinese; besides which, I believe that the Government intended that my voice should be heard in all that takes place. As yet, I believe that the system which we have established at Canton has been a great success. I do not think that above 200 or 300 Chinese were killed during the whole attack of the city, and that we should be established with so small a sacrifice of life in actual mastery of the city is a great achievement. But I am quite aware that we have some danger, and much difficulty before us, and I know that I shall be held responsible for everything that goes wrong. I should not care about the responsibility if I had all the power in my hands; but in fact I have very little, though I own I assert a good deal. The Commanders-in-Chief are the ostensible governors of the town, and everything I do is an intrusion. . . .

Sunday, February 7*th.*—A month without news is very long to wait. Perhaps time passes a little more quickly than when one was dawdling and doing nothing at Hong-kong; but still this life is tiresome enough. I do not suppose that there ever was a town of the same extent, or a population of the same number, more utterly uninteresting than the town and population of Canton. Low houses, narrow streets, temples containing some hideous idols, which are not apparently in the least venerated by their own worshippers. The only other resource is the curiosity-shops, and as you know, I have not the genius for making collections. . . .

February 9*th*.—Things have taken a better turn. F. by steaming at night from Macao to Hong-kong, caught Reed about an hour before that fixed for his departure for the North. He was delighted with my communication, and has written undertaking to co-operate cordially with us. This is, I think, a very great diplomatic triumph, because it not only smoothes the way for future proceedings, but it greatly relieves our anxiety about Canton, as the Americans are the only people who would be likely to give us trouble during the military occupation. We have not got an answer from Putiatine, but it is of little comparative importance what he does. . . . Seymour showed me yesterday a letter which he had received from Peel from Cawnpore, 16th December. It concludes in these words: "Please give my kind respects to Lord Elgin. Should he have felt any inconvenience in the change from the Shannon to the Ava, I am sure he will be still heartily glad that he made the change, and that he will have followed our course with pride. It was the Chinese expedition that relieved Lucknow, relieved Cawnpore, and fought the battle of the 6th."

February 10*th*.—We have got Putiatine's letter for Pekin. It is very good; perhaps better than any of the lot. . . . However, the *entente* is now established. My mind, too, is a good deal relieved to-day by seeing the wretched junks which have been shut up so long by the blockade, with their sails set, gliding down the river. I sent Mr. Wade to visit Yeh yesterday, to see how he took the notion of being sent out of the country to Calcutta or elsewhere. He adhered to his policy of indifference, real or affected, I cannot tell which. I suppose it is a point of pride with him never to complain.

February 12*th*.—At last! Two mails from England arrived this morning. I have your letters to the 26th December. . . . Reed has been with me for the last two hours. The new alliance is established. . . . I wonder how the Government and Opposition will like this phase of the affair. . . . —— ought to know that there is now only one policy to follow here. . . . It is my firm belief that I have done more than most men would have even attempted, to avert great calamities from the Chinese. I should like to see him try to fight his own battle against enemies who will never either yield or resist effectually. . . . If I can only conclude a treaty at Shanghae, and hasten home afterwards! . . .

H.M.S. Furious.—*February* 20*th*.—I am now off from Canton, never I hope to see it again. Two months I have been there—engaged in this painful service—checking, as I have best been able to do, the disposition to maltreat this unfortunate people. ... On the whole I think I have been successful. There never was a Chinese town which suffered so little by the occupation of a hostile force; and considering the difficulties which our alliance with the French (though I have had all support from Gros, in so far as he can give it) has occasioned, it is a very signal success. The good people at Hong-kong, etc., do not know whether to be incredulous or disgusted at this policy. ... I am told a parcel of ridiculous stories about arming of braves, etc. I heard that in the western suburb the people "looked ill-natured," so I have been the greater part of my two last days in that suburb, looking in vain into faces to discover these menacing indications. Yesterday I walked through very out-of-the-way streets and crowded thoroughfares with Wade and two sailors, through thousands and thousands, without a symptom of disrespect. ... I know that our people for a long time used to insist on every Chinaman they met taking his hat off. Of course it rather astonished a respectable Chinese shopkeeper to be poked in the ribs by a sturdy sailor or soldier, and told, in bad Chinese or in pantomime, to take off his hat, which is a thing they never do, and which is not with them even a mark of respect. I only mention this as an instance of the follies which people commit when they know nothing of the manners of those with whom they have to deal. ... We are steaming down to Hong-kong on a beautiful fresh morning. I feel as if I was a step on my way home.

Sunday, February 21*st.*—*Hong-kong.*—I am on shore for a few days, till my ship is fitted to go north. I have been taking my morning walk. The climate here at this season is really delicious, brighter and clearer than up the river, and with a touch of sea-air which makes it more bracing. I arrived yesterday, at about two P.M. My gentlemen went off to see the races. I walked to the Government House. ... I have been reading over your last letters. ... I think that the Government can hardly fail to perceive, when the results of my policy here are known, that I have done them, even in a party sense, immense service. I have carried out their original Canton policy, but in such a way that I very much doubt whether much of a case can be made against it. I have extorted even from the representatives of the Powers who would not join us in that policy an approval of it. It is something that both the Russian and United States Plenipotentiaries should compliment us on the moderation of our proceedings at Canton. And finally, I have united all the Great Powers in an appeal to the Chinese Court. ... Moreover, the distance at which I am acting is so great that it is clear I must be acting for myself.

On the whole, I am disposed to take the silence of my friends and the press very easy. . . .

February 22*d.*—Yeh is off this morning. I have just sent my despatch to Canning to be written out. "Our Own" is to accompany Yeh to Calcutta. Perhaps he may get something out of him, but I fear not. He seems an uninteresting monster.

February 24*th.*— . . . Nothing is going on here of any moment. . . . The newspapers go on writing the most absurd nonsense. But the weather is charming, so that the evils of exile are not for the moment aggravated by discomfort on that head. . . .

February 26*th.*—To-morrow this letter goes, and still no mail from England. I think of starting in a few days, and calling at the other ports—Foochow, Amoy, and Ningpo. I have a line from O., who took up my letter to Shanghae, and made a quick though rough passage. We shall be a good deal longer on the way, and my captain advises me to be off, to anticipate the equinox. I have just written a despatch to Lord Clarendon, to tell him that perhaps I may go direct from Shanghae to Japan, and so home. It is almost too good a prospect to be realized.

February 27*th.*—I had Reed to dine with me yesterday. He is in very good humour, and is off this morning to Manila, *en route* for Shanghae. The Russian returns on Monday, and we are going to Shanghae by the same route most fraternally. Your accounts of the boys . . . make me feel as if I had been an age away from home. God grant that I may get through this business soon, and return to find you all flourishing ! . . .

March 1*st.*—I received your letters yesterday. . . . This will probably be a short letter, as I intend to leave it here when I sail for the north to-morrow. . . . How I wish that I had joined that merry dance on Christmas day at Dunmore, and seen B. and R. performing their reel steps, and F. snapping his fingers ! You know now how differently my New Year was passed. Traversing that vast city of the dead—meditating over that 28th December which Herod had already hallowed. . . . These letters are my conscience and memory, the only record I keep of passing emotions and events. . . . Depend upon it the true doctrine is one I have before propounded to you : Do nothing with which your own conscience can reproach you ; *nothing* in its largest sense ; *nothing*, including *omission* as well as *commission;* not nothing only in the meaning of having done no ill, but nothing also in the meaning of having omitted no opportunity of doing good. You are then *well with yourself.* If it is worth while to be well *with others*—SUCCEED. . . .

March 2*d*.—I am a little afraid of the weather. It has been desperately hot for two or three days, and a storm is likely to follow. I had some of the leading people here to breakfast yesterday morning, in order to talk to them a little on Canton affairs. . . .

H. M. S. Furious, Swatow.—*March* 5*th*.—I am again on the wide ocean, though for the moment at anchor. We started at four A.M. on the 3d. When I got up I found a calm sea, hot day, and thick mist. This I considered a very good compromise, as we were going against the north-east monsoon. But it was too good to last. The wind gradually rose, it got colder, and by midnight waxed into pretty much of a gale, and we only reached this place at two P.M. on the 4th, instead of nine A.M., as we had expected. It has been too thick to see much of the coast, but what we have seen is barren and bleak, with ranges of hills at a short distance from the shore. We could not observe much indication of human dwellings, but the shoals of fishing-boats prove the existence of a dense population. The settlement here is against treaty. It consists mainly of agents of the two great opium-houses, Dent and Jardine, with their hangers-on. This, with a considerable business in the coolie trade—which consists in kidnapping wretched coolies, putting them on board ships where all the horrors of the slave-trade are reproduced, and sending them on specious promises to such places as Cuba—is the chief business of the "foreign" merchants at Swatow. Swatow itself is a small town some miles up the river. I can only distinguish it by the great fleet of junks lying off it. The place where the foreigners live is a little island, barren, but nicely situated at the mouth of the river. A number of Chinese are resorting to it, and putting up rather good houses for Chinese. The population has a better appearance than the Cantonese. The men powerful and frank-looking, and some of the women not quite hideous. Our people get on very well with the natives here. They have no consuls or special protection; so they act, I presume, with moderation, and matters go on quite smoothly. I went into the house of one of the "Shroffs" (bankers or money-dealers) connected with Jardine's house. And I found the gentleman indulging in his opium-pipe. He gave us some delicious tea. . . . The Shroffs here are three brothers. They come from Canton, their father remained behind. The mandarins wanting money to carry on the war with us, called upon him to pay 12,000 taels, about £4000. They used him as the screw to get this sum from his sons who were in foreign employ. Though the old man had resolved to leave his home and his patch of ground rather than pay, his sons provided the money and sent him back. Such cases are constantly occurring here, and they show how strong the family affections are in China. Another case was mentioned to me yesterday which illustrates the very roundabout way in which justice is arrived at among us all here. The coolies in a French coolie ship rose. The master and mate jumped overboard, and the coolies ran the ship on shore, where the crew had their clothes, etc., taken from them, but were otherwise well treated. On this a French man-of-war comes, proceeds to Swatow, which is fifty miles from the scene of the occurrence, and informs the people that they will bombard the place immediately unless 6000 dollars are paid. They got the money, but the mandarins at once squeezed it out of these same Shroffs, saying that as they brought the barbarians to the spot, they must pay for the damages they inflicted. Meanwhile, the "foreigners" have it, I apprehend, much their own way. They are masters of the situation, pay no duties except tonnage dues, which are paid by them at about one-third of the amount paid by native vessels of the same burthen! Hearing that a Mr. Burns, a missionary, whose case is narrated in the series of "insults by the Chinese authorities" submitted to Parliament (he having been in fact very kindly treated, as he himself acknowledges) was at the island, I invited him to breakfast. I found him a very interesting person, really an enthusiastic missionary, and kindly in his feelings towards the Chinese. He wears the Chinese attire, not as a disguise, but to prevent crowds being attracted by his appearance. He does not boast of much success in converting, but the Chinese are very willing to listen to him and to take books. They approve of all books that inculcate virtue, morality, etc. But they have no taste for the distinctive doctrines of Christianity. As Yeh said, when a Bible was presented to him from the Bishop:—" I know that book quite well, a very good book. It teaches men to be virtuous, like the Buddhistic books;" and then turning very politely to his captain, " Will you be good enough to take care of this book till I want it." The country in this neighbourhood is very lawless. Burns, a few days before he was arrested, slept with his two companions, two native Christians, in a large village. During the night the house he was in was broken into, and all they had stolen. Nothing remained but a few of their books, which they carried tied to sticks over their shoulders. A peasant came up to him and said, " I see you are not accustomed to carry loads," and took his burden and carried it for him six miles, asking for nothing in return. Other natives bought the books (they had previously given them gratuitously), and thus they got money enough to go on with. When they got into this principal town, and were arrested by the police, the authorities seemed rather to regret it. They underwent some interrogatories which Burns seems to have turned into a sort of sermon, for he went at length into Christian teaching, and the judges listened most complacently. They confined them in prison, but did everything they could to make Burns himself comfortable. His companions were not so well treated. He joined them at one time at his own request, under circumstances curiously illustrative of Chinese manners. A subordinate of the gaoler with whom he was lodged died from swallowing opium. The gaoler was at once held responsible, and his house was mobbed. On which Dr. Burns, not knowing the cause of the disturbance, asked to rejoin his companions. He found them shut up in a very loathsome cell, with several other prisoners. A place something like my Canton prisons, but he said they did very well while there, for they were able to preach to the other prisoners. At one of the interrogatories, one of his companions, the more zealous of the two, on being asked why he had brought a foreigner to the place, answered that it was because he was a Christian, and that their books said, "It is better to die with the wise than to live with fools." This sentiment was not considered complimentary by the mandarins, who immediately ordered him to be beaten, upon which he got ten blows on each side of his face with an instrument like a sole of a shoe. Mr. B. told this story, but added that he believed the beating had been determined on before, for his other companion who was the more worldly of the two, and who had probably found his way to the heart of the gaoler, was told that he too would be beaten that day, but that the blows would be laid on by a friendly hand, and that if he kept his cheek loose, he would not feel them much.

March 6th.—Amoy.—I can hardly go through all Dr. Burns' stories. He was very fluent, delighted to have listeners, and went on for some two' hours without intermission. We left Swatow at about noon, kept well in shore, and had not much sea. But the weather was misty, and at last it began to blow pretty hard. Captain Osborne, however, took us into a bay, and anchored for the night, thus saving us a very disagreeable one. We started early this morning. When I got on deck, I found a bright sun. Thermometer about 60°, and a fanning breeze.

March 7th.—I leave this letter here. The weather is so fine that we proceed this evening. . . .

March 8th.—We are entering Foochow; a most beautiful day; the sea smooth as glass. We left Amoy last night. I went to church in the forenoon at the Consulate. An American missionary preached. There are several missionaries at Amoy.

They have, as they say, about 300 converts. The foreigners and natives get on very well there. The town is a poor enough place, and the island seems rocky and barren. How it can sustain the great population which inhabits the villages that cover it, is a mystery. . . . We have just reached the anchorage at Pagoda Island. I find the mail for England has not left yet, so I may probably send this line. . . . The run up the *Min* river to this point is very pretty; bold hills on either side, cultivated in terrace-patches up to their very summits by the industrious Chinese. The weather became gloomy as we entered the mouth of the river, and the north-east wind began to presage a blow; but we were safe, and had only to be thankful that it had been so calm while we were in the open sea. . . . They say it is apt to be fine and to blow for three days at a time alternately. In that case I think we may remain where we are for three days. . . .

March 14*th*.—On this day last year I accepted the mission in which I am now engaged! and here I am now at anchor under the shelter of Fuh Yan cliff, after a day of tossing from Foochow Foo. I do trust that there may be some hope of a termination before very long of this wearisome separation. A vessel from Shanghae brought me this morning a letter from O., which shows that he has got well through the business which I entrusted to him. He went with my letter for the Prime Minister of the Emperor, to a city named Soochow, which is not open to foreigners, and which is moreover the seat of beauty and fashion in the empire, and he seems to have been well received. This is a good sign. An edict has moreover been issued by the Emperor degrading Yeh, and moderate in its tone as regards foreigners. All this looks as if there would be at Pekin a disposition to settle matters. God grant that it may be so, that I may get home, and not be required to do farther violence to these poor people. . . . On the 10th, I went up the river to the Consulate, which is situated on Nantai Island, a suburb of the city. The scenery of Foochow Foo and the neighbourhood is far more beautiful than any which I have before seen in China; but unfortunately the weather during the whole period of my stay was thick and rainy. I spent a good deal of time in the shops, though I took advantage of some glimpses of sunshine to visit the views in the city, and to take a walk in the country. Besides the Consulate at Nantai, there is another residence for the Consul within the town, in a most beautiful site on a hill, looking all over the town and adjoining country. My walk in the country was very interesting, through a rich district, studded with horse-shoe tombs and monuments to faithful widows, all surrounded with little patches of wheat and vegetables. The whole country is a sort of *Père la Chaise* in a kitchen garden. The people whom we met in our peregrinations were perfectly civil. The Consul, too, and Europeans were civil likewise. They were willing to give me information. I do not know that I carried much away with me, except the general impression, that our trade is carried on on principles which are dishonest as regards the Chinese, and demoralizing to our own people. It is, unfortunately, easier to see these evils than to devise a remedy for them. We started at six this morning. It has been blowing pretty hard all day, so that we have not been able to enjoy ourselves much, or to have service. Captain Osborne has, however, anchored for the night, under shelter of a lofty cliff. . . .

It seems a very long time since I last heard from you, though in truth only the usual fortnight has as yet elapsed, and though the fortnight has been more pleasantly passed than my fortnights have usually been since we parted, as there has been more variety of interest and fewer *désagrémens*. There has been, however, a succession of incidents which have filled up the time and made it appear to pass slowly. . . . I met the Bishop of Victoria at Foochow. He is travelling in about the best steamer on the station, which the Admiral has placed at his disposal, and he is engaged in getting up chaplaincies at the ports. He gets a subscription from the residents, which is doubled by the Government. As the missionaries at Amoy, Foochow, and Ningpo very nearly equal the laity in number, it may be a question whether it be necessary to throw this additional charge on the British public. At Foochow, I saw one of the American missionaries, a very worthy man I should think, but not of the stamp of Mr. Burns. He had been about eight years at Foochow, and he computed the converts made by himself and his brother missionaries at fifteen. He said that they were particular as to the conduct of their converts; but I cannot affirm that he satisfied me that they accepted in any very earnest way the peculiar doctrines of Christianity. However, I daresay, that these missionaries do good, for the Chinese are not fanatics, and it must do them a benefit to see among them some foreigners who are not engaged exclusively in money-making.

March 16*th*.—We are at anchor off Chinhae at the mouth of the river which leads to Ningpo. We have just returned from a walk on shore. We passed through a small walled town, and climbed up a hill to a temple on the summit, from which we had a magnificent prospect. On the east and north, the sea studded with the islands of the Chusan group; on the west, a rich plain, through which the river meanders on its way from Ningpo; on the north, a succession of mountain ranges. We were accompanied by some curious but good natured Chinamen, who seemed anxious to give us information. A very dirty lad, without a tail, proved to be the priest. After looking about us for some time, we entered the building, which contained a sort of central shrine, in which were some gilt figures of large size, besides rows of smaller gilt figures round the walls. I observed a number of slips of paper with Chinese characters upon them; and being told that they were used for divination purposes, I asked how it was done; upon which one of the Chinamen took from before the shrine a thing like a match-holder, full of bits of stick like matches, and kneeling down on a hassock, began to shake this case till one of the bits of stick fell out. He picked it up, and finding a single notch upon it, selected from the slips of paper which I had noticed the one which had a corresponding mark. We carried it away, and I intend to get Mr. Wade to translate it that I may send it to you. The other Chinamen present seemed very much amused at what was going on. They do not appear to have a particle of reverence for their religion, and yet they spend a good deal of money on their temples. We have had gloomy weather lately; in fact, it has really been cold, but on the whole we have been most fortunate. Wade's teacher (so the Chinaman who aids him in the work of interpretation is styled) has told him that the lot which fell to me at the Buddhist temple is the No. 1 lot, the most fortunate of all. Their system of divination is rather complicated, but, as I understand it, it appears to be that Noah, or some one who lived about his time, discovered eight symbols on the back of a tortoise. These, multiplied into themselves, make sixty-four, which constituted the Book of Fate. It appears that my lot is the first of the eight, and therefore the best that can be got!

TRANSLATION.

" The Chán Pau Shán, or mountain that invites or calls the jewel."

This may be the name of the hill itself, or simply of the immediate position of the temple. The words have reference to a part of Buddhistic mythology. Below this (which is the meaning of the three characters at the top of the slip of paper), and inside the marginal line, are—

" Lot No. 1," or " Lot the first."

Then follow four verses of seven words each, of which the first, second, and fourth verses are in rhyme:

1. " When the heaven was opened and the earth rent, there was knit with yours a goodly destiny;" that is, at the creation of the world, fate predestined you to be happily associated

with some other person in one of the relations of life, such as father to son, husband to wife, minister to prince, etc. The concluding verse of the four shows that here the last is meant.

2. "The day auspicious, the hour good, everything complete," or "in perfection."

3. "If you obtain this lot (or slip), it is no little that is in your power."

4. "In your ways unerring and true (or honest), the monarch will summon you;" that is, you will be officially employed.

Following this, on the left, is a column of small characters, stating: "The most eager haste is not too great haste. The word that comes (to you) is in the nick of time. Kwanyin (a deity whom we call the Goddess of Mercy) signifies this to you, sir. This symbol is typical of the heaven open and the earth rent;" that is, is typical of the influences in combination dominant at the time of creation.

This last sentence may be that of which Kwanyin desires you to take notice, but the other is the better version.

In the last column are, above, two characters, signifying "The uppermost uppermost;" that is, the very first or best, or the uppermost line of that symbol in the Classical Book of Changes, which has reference to the phenomenon of the Creation, and has in Chinese philosophy a value which it would take too much time to explain.

Below is written, "Printed with reverence by the Buddhist Fuh Yuen and his wife at the Pillar of Buddha."

Ningpo.—March 18th.—We arrived here yesterday, and I have been walking both days about the town with Mr. Meadows, the author, who is vice-consul here. I am disappointed with the city, of which I had heard a great deal. But the people are even more amiable than at any other place I have visited. . . . O. has rejoined us in high spirits, after his visit to Foochow. I cross-examined a Church of England clergyman about his converts. When pressed, he could only name one who seemed to be conscious of the want which we believe to be supplied by the Atonement. About 100, however, including children, attend churches in Ningpo, of whom thirty have been baptized. . . .

H. M. S. Furious.—March 20th.—We are off from Ningpo. It has been cold and gloomy. I have taken, for the first time since we parted, to fires in my cabin. Yesterday, I called on a clergyman to see Miss Aldersey,—a remarkable lady, who came out here immediately after the last war, and has been devoting herself and her fortune to the education and Christianization of the Chinese at Ningpo. She seems a nice person, but

I could not get as much conversation with her as I wished, because the Bishop, etc., were present all the time. She has to pay the girls a trifle, as an equivalent for what their labour is worth, for coming to her school, or to board them and keep them, as it is not at all in the ideas of the Chinese that women should be educated. She does not seem to have got the *entrée* into Chinese houses of the richer class. Mrs. Russell (wife of the English clergyman), who speaks the language, has obtained it a little. I cannot make out that when she visits them, they ever talk of anything except where she got her dress, etc.; but on great occasions, when they assemble for ceremonies in the temples, they seem very devout. In private, they treat these matters with great indifference. I had some of the missionaries to dinner. They put the converts at a larger number than I understood Mr. Russell to do, but otherwise their report did not differ materially from his.

Chusan.—March 21st.—We arrived here last night. To-day, after church, we went on shore. It was the first sunny day for some time, but quite cold enough for walking. I forgot to mention that yesterday all the tops of the high hills round Ningpo were covered with snow. This is a most charming island. How any people, in their senses, could have preferred Hong kong to it, seems incredible. The people, too, that is to say, the lower orders, seem really to like us. We walked through the town of Tinghae, and asked at the shop of a seller of perfumed sticks for the "Mosquito Tobacco," but in vain. We then passed through the further gate of the city into the country beyond, and seeing something like a chapel, made towards it. A man, dressed as a Chinaman, came out to meet us. He addressed us in French, and proved to be a Roman Catholic priest. He was very civil, and asked us into his house, where he gave us some tea, grown on his own farm. He has been here two years quite alone, and he was ten years before in the province of Kiangsù. He says that he has some 200 converts. Some twenty boys, deserted children, he brings up, and works on his farm. I saw them, and I must say I never beheld a more happy and well-conditioned set of boys. In the town was an establishment for younger children, chiefly girls, under the charge of a Chinese female convert. After he had given us tea, the missionary accompanied us in our walk. He first took us to a sort of cottage-villa, belonging to one of the rich inhabitants, consisting of about a couple of acres of ground, covered by kiosques and grottos and dwarf-trees, and ups and downs and zigzags,—all in the most approved Chinese fashion. From thence we clambered up a mountain of, I should think, some 1200 feet in height, from which we had a very extensive view, and beheld ranges of hills, separated by cosy valleys, on one side; on the other, the walled city of Tinghae, surrounded by rice-fields; beyond, the sea studded with islands of the Chusan group. It was a beautiful view, and we returned to the ship, very much pleased with our scramble.

March 22*d*.—I have just returned from a walk to the top of a hill, on the opposite side of the flat on which the town is situated from that which we mounted yesterday. The day is charming, clear, with a fanning, bracing air. We had a finer view almost than yesterday. The same character of scenery all round the island. Spacious flats on the sea-board under irrigation; about one-half of the fields covered (now) with water, and the other half in crop, chiefly beans, wheat, and rape, which, with its yellow flower, gives warmth to the colouring of the landscape. These flats, fringed by hills of a goodly height,—say from 600 to 1200 feet,—which cluster together as they recede from the sea-board, compressing the flats into narrow valleys, and finally extinguishing them altogether. The hills themselves barren, with patches here and there of Chinese cultivation, and fir plantations, the first I have seen in China. Turn your eyes to the sea, and you have before you innumerable islands dotting its surface, the same in character, though smaller in size, than that on which you are standing. I have seldom seen a more delightful spot. In going on our walk, we passed by the burying-ground of the British who died while we occupied the island, and we did something to put order among their neglected graves. On our return, we passed by a cottage where an old lady was seated at her spinning-wheel. I entered. She received us most courteously, placed chairs for us, and immediately set to work to prepare tea. When she found that one of the party was a doctor, a son (grown up) was produced who was suffering from ague. We brought him on board, and gave him some quinine. He showed us the medicine he was taking. It appeared to be a sort of mash of bits of bamboo and all sorts of vegetable ingredients. The doctor who tried it said it had no taste. I should mention that at the landing-place we met some of the French missionary's boys, who brought me a present of eggs and fowls and salad from the farm, in return for a dollar which I gave them yesterday to buy cakes withal. We have been steaming since half-past one, and now at six P.M. we are at anchor again, in "the sea of water-lilies" between Chusan and the sacred island of Potou. We have had to make a detour, however, to reach this point, threading first through the islands of the group, on a sea smooth as a lake, then passing between two bold and lofty bluffs into the heaving sea, and then gliding along the rugged coast until we reached our present anchorage, immediately behind Chusan. We have been steaming about thirty miles, but we might have crossed on foot to where we now are in about fifteen (as the crow flies). Potou is a sacred island covered with temples.

March 23*d*.—We set off this morning to visit Potou. After landing on the beach, we proceeded along a spacious paved path to a monastery, in a very picturesque spot under the grey granite hills. We entered the buildings, which were like all other Buddhistic temples—the same images, etc.—and were soon surrounded by crowds of the most filthy and miserable-looking bouzes, some clad in grey and some in yellow. All were very civil, however, and on the invitation of the superior—who had a much more intelligent look than the rest—we went into an apartment at the side of the temple and had some tea. After a short rest we proceeded on our way, and mounted a hill about 1500 feet in height, passing by some more temples on the way. I never saw human beings apparently in a lower condition than these bouzes, though some of the temples were under repair, and on the whole tolerably cared for. The view from the top of the hill was magnificent, and there was glorious music here and there, from the sea rolling in upon the sandy beach. We met some women (not young ones) going up the hill in chairs to worship at the temples, and found, in some, individuals at their devotions. In one, there was a monk hidden behind a great drum, repeating in a plaintive tone, over and over again, the name of Buddha "ameta fo," or something like that sound. I observed some with lumps on the forehead, evidently produced by knocking it against the ground. The utter want of respect of these people for their temples, coupled with this asceticism and apparent self-sacrifice in their religion, is a combination which I cannot at present understand. It has one bad effect, that in the plundering expeditions which we Christians dignify with the name of war in these countries, idols are ripped up in the hope of finding treasure in them, temple ornaments seized, and in short no sort of consideration is shown for the religious feelings of the natives.

March 24*th*.—We are gliding through a perfectly smooth sea, with islands on both sides of us, in a beautifully calm and clear day, warmer than of late, but still tart enough to feel healthy. We passed a fleet of some hundreds of junks, proceeding northward under convoy of some lorchas, of the "Arrow" class, carrying flags which they probably have no right to. These lorchas exact a sort of black mail from the junks, and plunder them whenever it is more profitable to do so than to protect them. They often have Europeans on board. Poor Yeh has suffered severely for our sins in respect to this description of craft. We are on our way to Chapoo now, a port not opened to trade, but one which I am ordered by the Government to induce the Chinese to open. As it is very little out of the way to Shanghae, I wish to look at it in passing.

March 25th.—We reached Chapoo at about five P.M. I did not land, but some of the party did, and mounted a hill from whence they looked down upon a walled town of no great size, and a plain, perfectly flat, stretching for any number of miles beyond it. The people, as usual, were civil, and made no difficulties, although we have no right to land there. The bay in which we anchored is open, and not in any particular way interesting. At about three this morning we started, and have been favoured with as good a day as yesterday. We have had nothing of the bold coasts of previous days, and passed occasionally islands flatter than those seen before. We are now in the mouth of the Yang-tze-kiang, with a perfectly flat and low shore on one side, and an equally flat one just discoverable with the aid of the telescope on the other. A good many junks are sailing about us, their dark sails filled with a lively breeze. Before us is a large man-of-war, which I am just told is the American Minnesota. So our cruise is coming to an end, which I regret, as it has been a very pleasant break, and at least for the time has kept me out of reach of the bothers of my mission. We have reason too to be most thankful for the weather with which we have been favoured, and if Mr. Reed is before me he cannot complain, as I am here on the very day on which I said I should reach Shanghae. This is a very strange coast. The sea seems to be filling up with the deposits of the rivers. We have an island (inhabited) beside us, which did not exist a few years ago. We have not during all yesterday and to-day had ever more than eight fathoms of water.

March 29th.—Shanghae.—Here I am in the Consul's house a very spacious mansion. The climate, character of the rooms, etc. etc., all make me feel in Europe again. I reached this harbour on the 26th, but only landed to-day. Mr. Reed and Count Putiatine arrived before me, but Baron Gros has not yet made his appearance. The Prime Minister of the Emperor says that he cannot write to me himself, but sends me a message through the Governor-General of the province to say that a Commissioner has been sent to Canton by the Emperor to replace Yeh, and that I must go there and settle matters with him. This will never do, so I must move on to the mouth of the Peiho. I am only waiting for Gros and the Admiral before I start. The Shanghae merchants presented an address to me to-day, and as I was obliged to say something in reply, I thought that I might as well take advantage of the opportunity to let the Chinese (who are sure to get a translation of my answer) know, that there is no chance of my going back to Canton. I also endeavoured to give the British manufacturers a hint that they must exert themselves and not trust to cannon if they intend to get a market in China. I was compelled to fly a little high in my language, in order to make the disagreeable truths I had to tell palatable. I found here your letters to the end of January. . . . I shall be a little curious to see my next letters. . . . The truth is that the whole world just now are raving mad with a passion for killing and slaying, and it is difficult for a person in his sober senses like myself to keep his own among them. However I shall be glad to see what Parliament says about Canton. . . .

March 30*th*.—Baron Gros arrived to-day. I forgot to mention that I visited the town of Shanghae yesterday, and among other things went into a bathing establishment, where coolies were getting steamed rather than bathed at rather less than a penny a head, which penny includes, moreover, a cup of tea. So that these despised Chinamen have bathing-houses for the million. With us they are a recent invention : they have had them, I believe, for centuries. I am told that they are much used by the labouring class. I was struck by an instance of the malevolence towards the Chinese, which I met with to-day. Baron Gros told me that a boat with some unarmed French officers and seamen got adrift at a place called the Cape of Good Hope, as he was coming up from Hong kong. They found themselves off an island, on the shore of which a crowd of armed Chinese collected. Their situation was disagreeable enough. Next day, however, the body of the Chinese dispersed, and a few who remained came forward in the kindest manner offering them food, etc. They stated that they came down in arms to defend themselves, fearing that they were pirates, but that as they were peaceful people they were glad to serve them. I have heard the first part of this story from two other quarters, but the latter part was in both cases omitted.

April 3*d*.---I took another walk yesterday into the country, and saw a kind of tower where dead children whom the parents are too poor to bury are deposited. It is a kind of pigeon-house about twenty feet high, and the babies are dropped through the pigeon-holes. After that I walked into a spacious building where coffins containing dead bodies are stored, awaiting a lucky day for the burial, or for some other reason. The coffins are so substantial and the place so well ventilated that there was nothing at all disagreeable in it. There is something touching in the familiarity with which the Chinese treat the dead. . . . The Admiral is not yet come, and has, notwithstanding my earnest entreaties, sent no gunboats. This may compromise my whole policy. . . .

Shanghae.—Easter Sunday.—I have been at church. . . . In the afternoon I walked to the Roman Catholic cathedral, which is about three miles from the Consulate. I found a really handsome, or at any rate, spacious building, well decorated. The priests were very civil. They count 80,000 converts (a considerable portion, I take it, descendants of the Christian converts made by the missionaries ages ago) in this province. It is impossible to help contrasting their proceedings with those of the Protestants. They come out here to pass the whole of their lives in evangelizing the heathen, never think of home, live on the same fare and dress in the same attire as the natives. The Protestants (generally) hardly leave the ports, where they have excellent houses, wives, families, go home whenever self or wife is unwell, etc. etc. I passed an American missionary's house yesterday. It was a great square building, situated in a garden, and at the entrance gate there was a modest barn-like edifice large enough to hold about twenty sitters, which on inquiry I found to be the church. These people have excellent situations, good salaries, so much for every child, allowances for sickness, etc. etc. They make hardly any converts, but then they console themselves by saying that the Roman Catholics who make all these sacrifices do it from a bad motive, teach idolatry, etc. I cannot say, but I must admit that the priests whom I met to-day talked like very sensible men, and that the appearance of the young Chinamen (*séminaristes*) whom I saw was most satisfactory. They had an intelligent, cheerful look, greatly superior to that of the Roman Catholic seminarists generally in Europe. The priests bear testimony to their aptitude in learning, their docility and good conduct. They have an organ in the cathedral, the pipes of which are all made of bamboo. It seems to have an excellent tone.

April 7th.—I went on Monday to visit a college which the priests have about six miles off, with about seventy scholars. It appeared to be in good order. I walked back with a priest who had been in Canada in our time. He was talkative, and gave me a good deal of information about the Jesuits. It came on to rain very hard as we returned, but we found our letters from home to reward us on our arrival. . . . No doubt, as you say, one cannot help sometimes regretting that one is mixed up with so bad a business as this in China, but then in some respects it is a great opportunity for doing good, or at least for mitigating evil. I had a visit to-day from a Dr. Bridgeman, who is I believe the most eminent of the American missionaries in China. He began by expressing his gratitude to me for the merciful way in which matters had been conducted at Canton, adding that they were *bad* people, that they insulted foreigners. He had lived among them fifteen years, and had never been insulted when alone. He always went about without even a stick, and they knew that he did not wish to injure them, etc. etc. I then asked him whether there was not some inconsistency in what he had said about their treatment of himself and the epithet "bad" which he had applied to them. He said that perhaps the word was too strong, that he was much attached to the Chinese, but that certain classes at Canton were no doubt very hostile to foreigners, and that the chastisement they had received was quite necessary. I really believe that what Dr. B. said is pretty nearly the truth of the case, and it is satisfactory to me that the fact that I laboured to spare the people should be known, known not only by those who approve, but by those who abhor clemency. . . . Meanwhile I wish we could finish this matter. . . . I have taken it on myself to send off to the Gulf of Pecheli all the ships that can be spared from hence, and I propose to sail myself on Saturday, with Gros, Reed, and Putiatine. . . . You must not be surprised if you do not hear by the next mail. I am going beyond the region of regular posts, and I must depend on chance opportunities. . . .

H. M. S. Furious, at sea.—April 11*th.*—Here we are, gliding through the smoothest possible sea, with a gentle wind, and this time favourable, which relieves us of all the smoke and ashes of the funnel,—an advantage for our eyes as well as conducive to our comfort. We are in the midst of the Yellow Sea, going about eight knots, dragging a gunboat astern to save her coal. This is the only gunboat I have got out of about twenty which the Admiral has on the station. This will throw much greater difficulties in my way. . . . I requested *officially*, and he promised *officially*, to send up here all the gunboats *drawing little water* which he could spare. He sends only one or two; and instead of sailing on the 16th from Hong-kong, as he also promised to do, puts off his departure, without giving me any reason for it, to the 25th. . . . Meanwhile, the French Admiral has also remained longer at Hong-kong, and left Gros in the lurch. I trust, both on private and public grounds, that we may succeed, notwithstanding this want of support, because otherwise the consummation might be put off for a year, or at least till the autumn, and God knows what might happen in the interval. The Russian Plenipotentiary, with his own small vessel—dragging behind him, however, a junk well laden with coals and provisions—sailed the day before me. I followed on the 10th (yesterday). The French and American are to follow. It is amusing to see how we play our parts. Putiatine and I are always together, visiting every port, looking into everything with our own eyes. Our colleagues, with their big ships, arrive sooner or later at the great places of rendezvous. However, a change has come over the spirit of the Russian Government. I *suspect* that they hoped that we should not be able to act vigorously because of India. They affected at one time to regret that this difficulty should have arisen, as, said they, it would add to the arrogance of the Chinese Government, etc.; but since they have found that we *do* act they have entirely changed their tone. . . .

April 12*th*.—The wind changed as I was writing yesterday, and it begins to blow from the north; no great amount of sea got up, however, and this morning I found the wind round again to the south. At this moment it is impossible to imagine anything more perfect than the temperature of the air and the smoothness of the sea. We are about fifty miles (at two P.M.) from the Shantung Promontory, on the other side of which we find the Gulf of Pecheli.

April 13*th*.—We have rounded the Shantung promontory and are opposite the harbour of Chefoo. It is a little misty over the shore, but we can see rocky islets forming a sort of advance-post into the sea, and around them we are going. Our object is to get up to the Meautau Strait (the entrance to the Gulf of Pecheli) to-night, so that by good time to-morrow we may reach the rendezvous off the river Peiho. The most serious work for me will then commence. . . . *Nine* P.M.—We had an adventure this afternoon. I was on the paddle-box bridge, watching, as we passed between the town of Tung-Chow Foo (a long wall, as it seemed, stretching for about four miles, with a temple at the nearest end) and the island of Meantau, when I felt a shock,—and, behold! we were aground. Our gunboat, which we towed, not being able to check its speed at a moment's notice, ran foul of us, and we both suffered a little in the scuffle. We got off in about two hours. On the whole, I am rather glad that we have a gunboat with us, for if anything serious did happen, it would be rather awkward, under existing circumstances, to be cast on the coast of China. It is as well to have two strings to one's bow. The coast to-day seems rather bleak—hilly, though not quite so bold as the coasts of the south of China.

April 14*th*.—This morning it was thick and pretty rough. It is now (four P.M.) very bright and comparatively smooth. We have seen no land to-day, nor, indeed, anything but sea and a few junks. Shall we meet any vessels at the rendezvous? A few hours will tell.

April 15*th*.—We saw, at about five P.M. yesterday, the

Russian at anchor, and went towards her, but were afterwards obliged to remove to some distance, as we had not water enough where she is. While we were going to our berth, the Pique came in sight. So here we are—Pique, Furious, and Slaney (gunboat), in an open sea; land not even visible. Captain O. started off this morning, in the gunboat, to sound and find out what chance we have of getting over the bar at the mouth of the Peiho. Putiatine came on board this morning. He has sent to the shore a note announcing his arrival. I am not disposed to do anything of the kind. The best plan, as it appears to me, is to move steadily up the river as soon as we can get over the bar, and let the Chinese stop us if they dare. Putiatine says that he will follow me, if I pass without any resistance being offered, but that he must not go first, as his Government forbids him to provoke hostilities. This division of labour suits me very well. . . . I have been reading an article in the *Quarterly* on the Peerage, which names Lord Elgin as descended in the direct male line from a baron by tenure, at the time of the Conquest, and the Lambtons from a knightly family of the same date. So B. ought to do for old blood. The De Braose of those days must have been an amiable party, for it is said of him that he would salute any children that he met, " to the end that he might have a return of the benediction of the Innocents."

April 19*th*.—I have nothing to write about. You may imagine what it is to be at anchor in this gulf with nothing to do. . . . If I had had my gunboats, I might have been up the Peiho ere this. I might perhaps have brought the Emperor to his senses. . . . Meanwhile Reed is arrived. Gros is last, but he is bringing his Admiral and force with him. . . . I went to call on the Russian to-day. I went under sail, but had to row back against a sea—very rough and slow work. . . . When shall I be able to send this ? . . . At last, I fear, you will have a blank mail. . . . Perhaps a chance may present itself. I shall always have a letter ready.

April 21*st*.—Gros arrived last evening. He is very well disposed, and ready to act with me. The French Admiral may be expected any day. We are going to make a communication to Pekin to invite a plenipotentiary to meet us here, as we cannot go up to Tientsin. . . .

April 22*d*.—An American vessel is come up with the news that there is no mail from England this time, in consequence of the loss of the Ava. There is, however, some news from England *via* Bombay. . . . I learn that Ministers are beat, and likely to go out. . . . All this complicates my difficulties. I am here without any definite instructions for my guidance, not properly supported by the Admiral, and ignorant of whether there may not be in power at home a Government opposed on principle to all this Chinese policy. Add to this, I am in this open roadstead, which appears to be agitated by a perpetual breeze or gale; the only change being that it sometimes blows from the north-east and sometimes from the south-west.

April 24th.—The Admiral arrived this forenoon. He has actually left all his gunboats behind him! It is very hard, that after having made so good a combination, which would have enabled me to carry everything here hand-over-hand, I should be thus thwarted. . . . The French Admiral has just come, with *four gunboats.* He will actually have in the Peiho a greater force than we have! . . . Not even economy is gained, for the gunboats which I ought to have are running up and down the Canton river. . . .

April 28th.—I have written to the Admiral to suggest that he should send to Hong-kong for gunboats; in which case, this letter will be despatched. I have no answer yet; he is at the bar trying to push over it his *despatch* boats—a larger class of vessels—as, out of his *eighteen* gunboats, he has only *one* here. As far as we can judge at this distance, his vessels have stuck on the bar. The French are over. . . . I am at my wits' end! . . .

Nine P.M.—The Admiral has consented to send a steamer down to the South, so you will receive this, I fear, only after the interval of a blank mail. I hope I may send better news in my next.

April 29th.— . . . This letter goes to-day, and leaves me in the most humiliating position. The flag of France is at this moment represented by two gunboats *within the bar of the Peiho river;* that of England by two despatch-boats *on the top of it,* *aground!* . . .

H. M. S. Furious.—*Pecheli, May 6th.*—I continue the not very creditable history which was interrupted by the despatch of the mail on the 29th ult. . . . In the afternoon of the same day, the despatch-boats, by the help of an unusually high tide, by getting everything possible taken out of them, and by the exertions of the officers, were dragged over and anchored *within range* of the fire of the forts. On the morning of the 1st of May, Baron Gros and I, for diplomatic reasons with which I need not trouble you, came to the conclusion that the time had arrived when we should call on the Admirals to take the forts, and stop the junks going up the river, to show the Chinese Government that we are in earnest. We called a meeting of the Admirals and Plenipotentiaries on board of the Furious, with this view. You may imagine our surprise when we were informed by the Admirals that as they had made *no reconnoissance,* they did not know when they would be able to take the forts, if at all; and that, therefore, if we suspended diplomatic action, we must do so without any assurance as to the steps by which this suspension of action would be followed. The speaker on behalf of the Admirals was Rigault. ... It is enough for me to point out the professional position which they had created for themselves. On the 28th and 29th of April, four or five days after their arrival, they had pushed their vessels over the bar into a position where the English ones, at least, were under the fire of the forts, and from whence they *could not retire* until the next spring tides. On the 1st of May they inform us that they cannot undertake to take the forts because they have made no *reconnoissance;* therefore it follows that the Admirals had placed these vessels in a position where they were exposed to the fire of the enemy, and from whence they could not retreat, without ascertaining whether or not they would be able to advance from it. In a word, they had recklessly exposed them to the most imminent risk of destruction. Either they consider the Chinese so contemptible a foe, that the most ordinary precautions may be dispensed with in dealing with them; in which case, the whole fuss they are making about taking the forts is a pretence, or they have by the step they have already taken rendered themselves liable to the severest censure. Of course, the former branch of this alternative is the true one. It is almost impossible to convey to any one who has not seen them, an idea of the utterly contemptible character of these so-called forts. Putiatine, who is here with one little vessel, has, I believe, said that he would take them. ... But Rigault is sharp enough to put his hesitation on the absence of Seymour's gunboats. ...

Sunday, May 9th.—Two English mails arrived to-day. ...

May 15th.—I cannot write, I am like a person in a bad dream. ... I foresaw before I came out that difficulties might arise from my want of authority over the naval and military forces who were to carry out my policy; but I little dreamt that my anticipations were to be so cruelly realized. ...

May 21st.—I have spent during the last three weeks the worst time I have passed since 1849, and really I have not been capable of writing. Things are a little better to-day, and I have given up an intention of sending F. to England. I drove the Admirals into such a corner, that they were obliged to say yes or no to my request, that I might be escorted in person by the gunboats up the river towards Tientsin. They said they would not allow me to be so escorted unless the forts at the mouth were previously in their hands. I said, I authorize you to take them if you agree to convoy me up afterwards. They could not get out of this, and agreed. I knew that they were *now* anxious to take the forts, although they had refused to do so when I first asked it. Accordingly the forts were taken yesterday. The Chinese had had, thanks to the Admirals, several weeks to prepare, and their *morale* was greatly raised by our hesitations and delays. The poor fellows even stood at their guns and fired away pretty steadily. But as they hardly ever hit, it is of very little consequence how much they fire. As soon as our men landed they abandoned the forts and ran off in all directions. We have hardly had any loss, I believe; but the French, who blundered a good deal with their gunboats, and then contrived to get blown up by setting fire to a powder-magazine, have suffered pretty severely. I fancy that we have got almost all the artillery which the Chinese Empire possesses in this quarter. We have now again some hope of getting our Treaty before we are compelled by the heat to leave this place, but I cannot speak with confidence when I see how my hands are tied. The weather is very beautiful now, but getting much hotter, like delicious summer weather in England, with of course a clearer and brighter atmosphere. Till now it has generally been very uncomfortable. A great deal of wind and tossing, though perhaps I have felt it more from the state of mental disgust in which I have been kept. . . . This affair of yesterday, in a strategical point of view, was a much more creditable affair than the taking of Canton. Our gunboats and men appear to have done well, and though they were opposed to poor troops, still they were troops, and not crowds of women and children, who were the victims of the bombardment at Canton. You will perhaps, however, not have so brilliant an account of it as the romance written by "Our Own" in the Canton case. I know how much of that was the work of imagination, as the writer witnessed not what he describes, but what he really saw was from the deck of the Furious.

May 22*d.*—This letter goes to-day to Shanghae. . . . Would that you had been a true prophet. Yet there is something of inspiration in your writing on the 1st of March: "I was fancying you even now, perhaps, ascending the Peiho with a train of gunboats!" How I wish that you were in command of the fleet! . . . On the whole my health has been good, considering the worry which I have endured of late, and this sedentary life on board ship and never landing. . . .

May 23*d.*—I sent my letter off to you yesterday. . . . These wretched Chinese are for the most part unarmed. When they are armed, they have not a notion of directing their firearms. They are timorous, and without either tactics or discipline. I will venture to say that twenty-four determined men, with revolvers and a sufficient number of cartridges, might walk through China from one end to another. . . . However, after losing the good season, losing the chance of stopping junks, and nearly driving me wild with vexation, the Admirals now find themselves in the famous Tientsin river without any enemy to face them. They are delaying to move up, and therefore doing their best to allow the Chinese to collect for resistance. But it is doubtful whether that wretched people will take advantage of the chance. You know that I induced the Admirals to move by asking them to escort *me*. However, I got a hint that they would prefer my room to my company. . . . All I care for is to get the work done, so I keep back, though I must do so cautiously. . . . I shall, of course, be nervous till I hear that they have reached Tientsin, as I believe they have written to their Governments to say that they *cannot* do so. I trust, however, that the Chinese will not give them even a pretext for turning back.

May 25*th*.—No news since I began this letter, except a vague report that the Admirals are moving up slowly, meeting with no resistance, rather a friendly reception, from the people. I am rather surprised that we have not yet heard anything from Pekin. I hope the Emperor will not fly to Tartary, because that would be a new perplexity. I am not quite in such bad spirits as last week, because at least now there is some chance of our getting this miserable war finished, and thus of my obtaining my liberty again. . . . We ought to have a mail from England any day. . . . Changes of Government have this inconvenience, that of course the new-comers cannot possibly take time to read over previous correspondence, so that they must be but partially informed on many points, . . . but no doubt at this distance it is practically impossible for Government to give instructions, and all the responsibility must rest on the agent on the spot. At this moment, when I am moving up to Pekin, I am receiving the despatches of the Government commenting upon the Canton proceedings, and asking me: What do you intend to do next?

May 26*th*.—I see the steamer Sampson, which we sent off on the 29th ultimo to Hong-kong for reinforcements, coming into the gulf with two gunboats. This is a good sight, ominous, I trust, of a better state of things at Canton, as well as an increase to our strength here. Perhaps, too, it may bring the English mail of the 25th of March. . . .

May 27*th*.—I have been pacing the deck looking at the dancing waves sparkling under a bright full moon. It is the third time, I think, that I have seen it since I have been in this gulf. I had a message last night late from the Admiral, stating that he is within two miles of Tientsin! I sent F. up that he might see what is going on, and let me know when I ought to advance. I had also a communication from the Chinese Plenipotentiaries, but it was not of much importance. I do not think that these poor, timorous people have any notion of resisting. I only trust that they may make up their minds to concede what is requisite at once, and enable us all to have done with it.

May 28*th.*— . . . The Sampson did *not* bring the mail of the 25th March. It had been sent to Shanghae! . . . The last news from Canton shows that the kind of panic which had been, in my opinion most needlessly, got up, is subsiding, and the General has sent up a few men— for which I ought to thank him, as the Admiral only asked him whether he could supply any if wanted. . . .

May 29*th.*—The Cruiser, with your letters to the 23d of March, arrived yesterday. . . . I have a short despatch from the new Government, giving me latitude to do anything I choose if I will only finish the affair. Meanwhile F. writes from Tientsin to recommend me to proceed thither, and I intend to be off this afternoon. There appears to be on the part of the Chinese no attempt at resistance, but on the other hand no movement to treat. This passivity is, of course, our danger, and it is one which slowness on our part tends to increase. However, we must hope for the best. I forgot to mention that Lord C., in his last letter, refers to his *private* letters for proofs of his appreciation of my services! . . .

May 30*th.*—*Yamun, Tientsin.*—Only look at my date, does it not astonish you? I hardly yet realize to myself where I am. I started at about 4.30 P.M. yesterday from the Furious, crossed the bar, at the forts at the entrance of the river picked up Gros and the French mission—whose vessel could not get on—and moved on to this place. The night was lovely—a moon nearly full. The banks, perfectly flat and treeless at first, became fringed with mud villages, silent as the grave, and trees standing like spectres over the stream. There we went ceaselessly on through this silvery silence, panting and breathing flame. Through the night-watches, when no Chinaman moves, when the junks cast anchor, we laboured on, cutting ruthlessly and recklessly through the waters of that glancing and startled river, which, until within the last few weeks, no stranger keel had ever furrowed! Whose work are we engaged in, when we burst thus with hideous violence and brutal energy into these darkest and most mysterious recesses of the traditions of the past? I wish I could answer that question in a manner satisfactory to myself. At the same time, there is certainly not much to regret in the old civilisation which we are thus scattering to the winds. A dense population, timorous and pauperized, such would seem to be its chief product. I passed most of the night on deck, and at about four A.M. we reached a point in the centre of the suburb of Tientsin, at which the Great Canal joins the Tientsin or Peiho river. There I found the Admirals, F., etc. F. had got this yamun for us, half of which I have had to give to my French colleague. It consists of a number of detached rooms, scattered about a garden. I have installed myself in the joss-house, my bedroom being on one side, and my sitting-room on the other, of the idol's altar. We have a letter informing us that the Emperor has named two great Officers of State to come here and treat, and our Admirals are in very good humour, so that matters look well for the present.

June 1st.—It is settled that the Fury is to go down to Hong-kong for troops, and to take this mail. . . . I found that almost the whole of the marines and sailors here were to be sent back to their ships the very day after my arrival! I am not much afraid of the Chinese, but still there are measures of common prudence which it is folly to neglect, . . . and I have had to interpose to prevent this, etc. All this is very awkward, because, of course, these things are not my business, and it is difficult for me to interpose without giving offence. Our present plan is to remain here to treat with the new Commissioners if they have sufficient powers, and if they have not, we shall move on to Pekin when the troops arrive. My belief is, that all this would have been done, and better done, by this time, if I had been supported as I ought at first. With people like the Chinese, promptitude is everything; as, while we remain doing nothing, their innate self-sufficiency regains its sway. But what can I do? . . . I found my joss-house so gloomy and low, that I have returned to my first quarter in the garden, on a mound overlooking the river. It consists of a single room, part of which is screened off by a curtain for a bedroom. It is hot during the day, but nothing much to complain of. I took a walk yesterday. The country is quite flat, cultivated in wheat, millet, etc. Instead of the foot-paths of the southern parts of China, there are roads for carriages, and wheeled carts dragged by mules in tandem going along them. I have not been in the town, but some of the party were there this morning, and one had his pocket picked, which is a proof of civilisation. They say it is a poor place, the people stupid-looking and curious, but not as yet unfriendly.

June 3d.—I was laid up yesterday, . . . but I am right again to-day. Last night the two functionaries of the Chinese Government arrived. I have not yet heard from them. . . .

June 4th.—I am to have an interview with the Chinese Plenipotentiaries to-day. I devoutly hope it may lead to a speedy and satisfactory pacific settlement; but I am sending to Hong-kong for troops, in order to be prepared for all eventualities. In sum, my policy has resulted in this:—I have complete military command of the capital of China, without having broken off relations with the neutral powers, and without having interrupted, for a single day, our trade at the different ports of the empire. . . .

Tientsin.—June 5th.—After sending off your letter yesterday, I went to have my first official interview with the Chinese Plenipotentiaries. I made up my mind, disgusting as the part is to me, to act the *rôle* of the " uncontrollably fierce barbarian," as we are designated in some of the confidential reports to the Chinese Government which have come into our hands. These stupid people, though they cannot resist—and hardly even make a serious attempt to do so—never yield anything except under the influence of fear; and it is necessary therefore to make them feel that one is in earnest, and that they have nothing for it but to give way. Accordingly I got a guard of 150 marines and the band of the Calcutta, and set off with all my suite in chairs, *tambour battant*, for the place of rendezvous. It was about two-and-a-half miles off, and the heat of the sun very great. The road carried us through several narrow streets of the suburb, then across a plain, till we reached a temple at which the Plenipotentiaries were awaiting us. A dense crowd of Chinese men—I saw not one woman—lined the route. Curiosity chiefly was depicted on their countenances; some looked frightened; but I observed no symptoms of ill-will. At the entrance of the temple were two blind musicians, playing something like squeaking bagpipes. This was the Chinese band. We marched in with all our force, which drew up in a sort of court before an open verandah, where refreshments were set out, and the dignitaries awaited us. I was received by the Imperial Commissioner, and conducted to a seat at a small table covered with little plates of sweatmeats, etc. One of the Chinese Plenipotentiaries sat on either side of me. It was a very pretty scene, and the place was decorated in very good taste with flowers, etc. As my neighbours showed no disposition to talk, I began by asking after their health and that of the Emperor. They then said that they had received the Emperor's orders to come down to treat of our affairs. I answered, that although I was much grieved by the neglect of the Prime Minister to answer the letters I had addressed to him, yet as they had on their cards stated that they had " full powers," I had consented to have this interview in order that we might compare our powers, and see whether we could treat together. I told them that I had brought mine, and I at once exhibited them, giving them a translation of the documents. They said they had not powers of the same kind, but a decree of the Emperor appointing them, and they brought out a letter which was wrapped up in a sheet of yellow paper. The chief Plenipotentiary rose and raised the paper reverentially over his head before unfolding it. I thought the terms of this document rather ambiguous, besides which I was desirous to produce a certain effect; so when it had been translated to me, I said that I was not sufficiently satisfied with it to be able to say on the spot whether I could treat with them or not. That I would, if they pleased, take a copy of it and consider the matter, but that I would not enter upon business with them at present. So saying I rose, moved to the front of the stage, and ordered the escort to move and the chairs to be brought. This put the poor people into a terrible fluster. They made great efforts to induce me to sit down again, but I acted the part of the " uncontrollably fierce" to perfection, and set off for my abode. I had hardly reached it when I received two cards from my poor mandarins, thanking me for having gone so far to meet them, etc. . . .

June 9th.—Things are moving here, though slowly. Keying the man who made a treaty with Pottinger, and who is supposed to be friendly to the barbarians, has been restored to his rank, and is come down here. This is a proof that there is at Pekin a sincere desire to settle matters pacifically. . . . I expect to be able to prove that the Americans are doing all they can to thwart us, though they are here only because we have opened the door for them. Russia is better, but not of course to be trusted out of sight. The weather is very tolerable, and I am nearly, though not quite, right. I am confident that no one was ever placed in a situation of more difficulty. . . .

June 12th.—Last night things looked promising. The Russians and Americans had made an attempt to check me, by affecting to believe that my interpreter, Mr. Lay, had spoken too roughly to the Chinese Plenipotentiaries. . . . Of course my great object is to get the Chinese to make the requisite concessions here, so as to prevent its being necessary to resort to further acts of violence; and these gentlemen, while affecting to support the Chinese, act as their worst enemies. However, I made my language stronger instead of weaker in consequence of their remonstrance, and the result was, that at a late hour last night I received from the Chinese Plenipotentiary a most promising communication. God grant that it may enable us to finish this wretched affair! I am reading over your last letter. . . . Your visit to Dunnikier takes me a generation back, when another two sets of cousins, divided much the same as to sexes, used to spend many pleasant days together there. . . . I have gone through a good deal since we parted. Certainly I have seen more to disgust me with my fellow-countrymen than I saw during the whole course of my previous life, since I have found them in the East among populations too timid to resist and too ignorant to complain. I have an instinct in me which loves righteousness and hates iniquity, and all this keeps me in a perpetual boil. I must tell you that I do not think "Our Own's" letters in the *Times* give a really correct view of this country. I saw very well, from his case, what the great evils are of this way of informing the public mind. It was always necessary for him to write a telling letter. Everything was exaggerated for effect. The fighting was a work of the fancy, and the poor Chinese were of use only as *matériel* for caricatures and epigrams. He never entered into or ever approached the heart of Chinese life. He looked at them entirely from without, with the eyes of a man whose whole stock of ideas has been laid in at Temple Bar, and who had not room for any importation from any other quarter. As he said of the Chinese in one of his letters, "they are not only a 'cute, but a cutaneous people;" that was pretty much the sum of his observations. . . .

June 15*th*.—We have got really, I hope, to work with our Treaty. At one time I almost hoped that we might be able to send it home by this mail, but I hardly think that is likely. Indeed, one has so many disappointments that one does not like to anticipate anything. . . .

June 16*th*.—The French Admiral's aide-de-camp told me yesterday that by the last mail they had received letters from Paris telling them that Admirals Guérin and Cécile had told the Emperor that it was impossible to move up the river to this place ! . . .

June 19*th*.—This letter goes off now. . . . The Treaty is going on rapidly to completion. . . . I begin to look forward with hope to seeing you again. . . .

June 19*th*.—I sent off a letter this morning. Will this one reach you by the same mail ? I have some hopes. Good progress was made in the Treaty yesterday. The Chinese seem ready to concede everything.

June 23*d*.—What can be the meaning of it ? I am in despair. My mail is arrived, and with nothing from you at all. . . . I can only suppose that the Government have deprived me of my bag just at the time when it might be of service. . . . Matters here are advancing, though somewhat slowly. . . . I fear this will not reach you as soon as I once hoped. Meanwhile our troops have contrived to sustain a kind of defeat at Canton, which will, of course, be productive of bad effects, and which will naturally be laid to my charge. People will say that if I had murdered all the inhabitants of the city and villages, they would never have given us any trouble afterwards. I am not so sure about that. . . . The proper policy at Canton was the one I prescribed, to act fairly by the natives, set up a firm and just government, and punish signally any attempts on the part of braves or others to dislodge you. . . . But this business may have a bad effect here on the Chinese. I thought it better to anticipate the effect of any rumours from the south, by sending to the Imperial Commissioners here to say that I was very indignant at hearing that some assassinations, etc., had been committed on our people in the South, and that I was strongly inclined to proceed to Pekin and demand satisfaction from the Emperor. On one point I am agreeably disappointed, namely, the climate. There are occasionally two or three hot and heavy days, but then they end in some kind of storm, which clears and cools the air. Generally, too, the nights are very tolerable.

June 29th.—I have not written for some days, but they have been busy ones. . . . I hope to carry this letter in person to Shanghae, and probably F. will convey it from thence to England. We went on fighting and bullying, and getting the poor Commissioners to concede one point after another, till Friday the 25th, when we had reason to believe all was settled, and that the signature was to take place on the following day. . . . On Friday afternoon, however, Baron Gros came to me with a message from the Russian and American Ministers, to induce me to recede from two of my demands—1. A resident minister at Pekin; and, 2. Permission to our people to trade in the interior of China; because, as they said, the Chinese Plenipotentiaries had told them that they had received a decree from the Emperor, stating that they should infallibly lose their heads if they gave way on these points. . . . The resident minister at Pekin I consider far the most important matter gained by the Treaty; the power to trade in the interior hardly less so. . . . I had at stake not only these important points in my treaty, for which I had fought so hard, but I know not what behind. For the Chinese are such fools, that it was impossible to tell, if we gave way on one point, whether they would not raise difficulties on every other. I sent for the Admiral; gave him a hint that there was a great opportunity for England; that all the Powers were deserting me on a point which they had *all*, in their original applications to Pekin, demanded, and which they all intended to claim if I got it; that therefore we had it in our power to claim our place of priority in the East, by obtaining this when others would not insist on it. Would he back me? . . . I felt, however, that all depended on myself. This was the forenoon of Saturday 26th. The Treaty was to be signed in the evening. I may mention, as a proof of the state of people's minds, that Admiral S. told me that the French Admiral had urged him to dine with him, assuring him that no treaty would be signed that day! Well,

I sent F. to the Imperial Commissioners, to tell them that I was indignant beyond all expression at their having attempted to communicate with me through third parties; that I was ready to sign at once the Treaty as it stood; but that, if they delayed or retracted, I should consider negotiations at an end, go to Pekin, and demand a great deal more, etc. . . . F. executed this most difficult task admirably, and at six P.M. I signed the Treaty of Tientsin. . . . I had told the Admiral that any of the officers of the squadron who liked to see the ceremony might attend, and this was made an excuse for the presence of a disorderly crowd, who rushed into the place where we signed the treaty, mobbed the Imperial Commissioners, stole the tea-cups; in short, conducted themselves very ill. . . . I am now anxiously awaiting some communication from Pekin. Till the Emperor accepts the Treaty, I shall hardly feel safe. Please God he may ratify without delay! I am sure that I express the wish just as much in the interest of China as in ours. Though I have been forced to act almost brutally, I am China's friend in all this. . . .

June 30th.—To-day the English mail of the 10th May arrived, with two letters from you. Whether the delay in the first of the two arose from negligence at the Foreign Office, or from any other reason, I cannot tell. . . .

July 2d.—The Chinese are making difficulties about ratification. However, I made a step in advance to-day towards that object, and I have induced the Admiral to consent to bring up the troops from the Gulf, which will increase the pressure. I do not despair of the Treaty's being ready to send by the mail which will take this letter.

July 8th.—At Sea, Gulf of Pecheli.—At last I am actually off—on my way home? May I hope that it is so? I got on Sunday the Emperor's assent to the Treaty, in the form in which I required it. Sent immediately down to stop the troops, and set off myself on Tuesday at noon for the Gulf. We sailed yesterday afternoon, with the intention, if possible, of seeing the great Wall of China on our way to Shanghae, but we have not been very successful, and have now put about, and are moving southwards. It is beautifully calm, though rather hot, and I must also say that it was very hot during the last few days at Tientsin. F. is going home with the Treaty, and I proceed *via* Japan. I trust that nothing will stop me on my way home, but I cannot conceal from myself that much is being tried out here in order to make my mission a failure. A newspaper at Hong-kong never ceases abusing me. I am not properly supported. . . . I feel more at home in my cabin here, and at any rate, I am quiet for a day or two, and one is safe from evil news. . . .

July 9th.—It is less hot, which is more than we were entitled to expect, for at this season the monsoon is supposed to be blowing from the south. . . . I know how miserable my life has been for some time past, by the comparative quiet which I am now enjoying. . . .

Sunday, 11th July.—I have an inflammation in one eye, which has prevented me from leaving my cabin to-day. We are going on as smoothly as ever, never having had a shake since we left our anchorage in the Gulf. It is getting very hot now. . . . We are approaching Shanghae. . . .

Shanghae.—July 12th.—We arrived this afternoon. I am still confined to my cabin; very hot. The first thing that greeted me on my arrival was your letter, finished on the 23d May. . . . I have, as usual now, nothing from the new Government. Bad news from Canton. The community here, having laughed at my audacity when I was last here in announcing what I intended to get, treat my acquisitions, now I have obtained them, as matters of course! . . .

July 14th.—F. embarks to-night, and sails to-morrow morning at four. I shall not know all that I lose, publicly and privately, by his departure, till he is gone. He will tell you what the heat here is. . . .

Shanghae.—Sunday, July 18th.—I have just returned from church. Such an ordeal I never went through. If a benevolent lady, sitting behind me, had not taken compassion of me, and handed me a fan, I think I should have fainted. . . . Every one says that the heat here surpasses that felt anywhere else. They also affirm that this is an exceptional season.

July 19th.—Writing has been an almost impossible task during these few last days. The only thing I have been able to do has been to find a doorway, or some other place, through which a draught was making its way, and to sit there reading. . . . In sending F. away, I have cut off my right arm, but I think, on the whole, it was better that he should take the Treaty home, . . . and of course he is better able than any one else to explain what has been the real state of affairs here. I had no instructions from this Government, except the intimation that they were desirous of finishing the affair, and that they left it to me to determine what the *honour* and the *commercial interests* of England required. I was therefore, of course, open to attack on both flanks, not by the enemy only, but also at the hands of my employers. For if I patched up a peace in order to comply with the desire that I should "finish the affair," I might be accused of not doing enough for the "honour and commercial interests of England;" on the other hand, if I went on fighting for the "honour and commercial interests," I was open to the charge of not "finishing the affair." *Sur ces entrefaites,* I struck out a plan which I firmly believed would enable me to accomplish *both* objects. . . . This plan consisted in a rapid move upon the capital by the route of Tientsin; a diplomatic move, in the first instance, but so supported that it could, if necessary, repel hostility. I was perfectly satisfied that this plan, if carried boldly and rapidly into execution, would not be attended with any serious difficulty. I had therefore, as I believed, difficult as was the feat which I was called to accomplish, the game in my hands. Imagine my position when I found that the whole of my plan, with the important issues involved, was absolutely at the mercy of the naval authorities who had resolved to thwart it. . . . Observe what was at stake: on the one hand, as I believed, and as the result has proved, a complete success; but on the other, if we had left the Gulf of Pecheli, as the Admirals intended, without having brought the Imperial Government to terms, I am not sure that an attack upon the Europeans at all the ports might not have been the consequence. All the blame of this would have been cast on me, and I should have borne the reproach of having, by my rashness and folly, compromised the whole relations of Europe with China. . . . This would have been attended with great mischief to the empire. Indeed, in the present state of India, it is not easy to put a limit to the evils which would have ensued. . . . Such has been my fate during the past few months. . . . However, F. will tell you all. It is impossible to acknowledge too strongly the obligation I am under to him for the way in which he has helped me in my difficulties. *Seven* P.M.—Such a thunder-storm! Lightning flashes in such a hurry, that they nearly ran foul of one another; and no wonder, for the air must be choked with electricity, after these tremendous heats. I trust we may now have a short respite, for it has been wellnigh unbearable. . . .

July 20*th.*—Is it a good omen? There is a slight and almost cool breeze to-day, for the first time since we reached this sweltering place. . . . In old times this anniversary was more noticed at B. than others, because it was my father's birthday as well as my own. . . .

July 21*st.*—We had some rain again yesterday, and the weather is somewhat more bearable. . . . As no orders have yet come from Pekin about the revision of the tariff, I have written a letter to the Imperial Commissioners to-day, to hint that if there is any delay in carrying out the Treaty I may perhaps pay another visit to Tientsin. Baron Gros has arrived, having seen the Great Wall, and made two very nice sketches of it. When he and his party landed several bands of armed and mounted Tartars came galloping down to urge them to return to their ship. They seemed to know nothing of what had been going on at Canton or Tientsin. I think I must wait here for the next letters from home, and also from Canton, and, I hope, from F. . . . I am reading again your last letter. . . . As for Yeh, I cannot say very much for him; but the account given of him by Captain B. of the Inflexible, who took him to Calcutta, differs as widely as possible from that of the *Times'* Correspondent. He was very courteous and considerate, civil to everybody, and giving no trouble. I suppose that there is no doubt of the fact that he executed a vast number of rebels, and I, certainly, who disapprove of all that sort of thing, am not going to defend that proceeding. But it is fair to say that rebels are parricides by Chinese law, and that, in so far as we can judge, nothing could have been more brutal or more objectless than this Chinese rebellion. They systematically murdered all—men, women, and children—of the dominant race, and their supporters, on whom they could lay their hands. Certain Americans and Europeans took them up at first because they introduced a parody of some Christian doctrines into their manifestoes. But these gentlemen are now, I think, heartily ashamed of the sympathy which they gave them. . . .

July 22*d*.—Another comparatively cool day,—almost constant rain and distant thunder. A very severe thunder-storm yesterday, too, brought down the thermometer. I am, therefore, more comfortable in my room, but I am suffering, as I did last year during the heats, from inflammation in the ear. Some news from Canton—not very satisfactory—arrived last night. I cannot make up my mind as to my next step until I hear from F. I have been reading some numbers of the *Indépendance Belge*, and am amused to find from it that there are some *dissentiments* between Gros and me: he being in favour of the go-ahead movements; I holding him back! . . .

July 23*d*.—The last mail brought me just two despatches,—one being about an execution of a barbarous character, which a Hong-kong paper said had taken place at Canton. Somebody in Parliament took the matter up, so the Government, who have passed very jauntily over almost everything I have written to them, thought it necessary to show zeal by addressing me on this newspaper report. Luckily I have been able to send a Report which was drawn up for the Admiral at the time, by the senior naval officer (I had left Canton for the north long before), which states that the cruelties in the Canton prisons ceased after the visit I paid to them in January, and that the story in the paper about the execution was a fabrication. . . .

July 26*th*.—I heard yesterday a good piece of news. The

Emperor has named my friends, the Imperial Commissioners, to come down here to settle the Tariff, etc. This, I think, proves that the Emperor has made up his mind to accept the Treaty and carry it out. I hope also that it will enable me to settle the Canton affair. The Admiral has not yet arrived.

July 30*th.*—On the 28th the mail arrived, bringing good accounts of you all. I am off to-morrow morning for Nagasaki, in order to turn to account the interval which must elapse before the arrival of the Imperial Commissioners. The heat here has completely knocked me up. . . .

August 1*st.*—We left Shanghae yesterday morning, and have had our usual fine weather. We have now disconnected our machinery from the paddle-wheels, and are gliding along over a smooth sea with a light breeze. We have two companions— the Retribution, a paddle steamer, rather larger than this, and a gun-boat. The three look very well, with their sails all set. The fourth vessel, the Cruiser, attached to me, remains at Shanghae, to follow as soon as the Imperial Commissioners arrive. I am already better, though I cannot say that the weather is yet cool. I do not exactly know what I shall do when I get to Nagasaki, but at any rate I shall ascertain what my chances are of making a satisfactory treaty with Japan. The Admiral will join me at Nagasaki. . . . Poor Peel! His death was very sad—though certainly there never was a man who more truly died in his vocation. . . .

Nagasaki.—*August* 3*d.*—We have had beautiful weather, and have reached this point,—a quiet, small-looking town, fringing the bottom of a bay, which is itself the close of a channel passing between ranges of high volcanic hills, rugged and bold, but luxuriant with vegetation and trees, and cultivated in terraces up to their summits. I have seen nothing so beautiful in point of scenery for many a long day. No sort of difficulty has been made to our progress up to the town. The only symptom of objection I observed was an official in a boat, who waved a fan, and when he saw we took no notice, sat down again and went on with a book which he seemed to be reading. On both sides of the channel, however, there is a very formidable display of cannons and works of defence, which I apprehend would not be very formidable in action. I have heard little in the way of news yet, but I am disposed to believe that nothing can be accomplished here, and that if anything is to be done we must go on to Yeddo. It is still hot, but the air, which comes down from these lofty hills, is, I think, fresher than that which passes over the boundless level in the vicinity of Shanghae.

August 4*th.*—I have just had a visit from the Vice-Governor of Nagasaki. One of his own suite did the interpretation. These are the nicest people possible. None of the stiffness and bigotry of the Chinese. I gave them luncheon, and it was wonderful how nicely they managed with knives and forks and all other strange implements. The Admiral arrived this forenoon. He now finds that his instructions direct him to send the Emperor yacht (which is to be a present) to Yeddo. I shall take advantage of this and go to Yeddo myself at once. I may do something, or find out what I can do. I have not yet been on shore, but I intend to land this afternoon, and see some of the marvels of Japan.

August 5th.—Four P.M.—Off again to sea. What a comfort to breathe fresher air than that which reaches one in a hill-enclosed anchorage. The heat yesterday, and for the two nights at Nagasaki, was very great. It must be a charming place when the temperature is low enough to admit of walks into the country. As it is, we have just passed into the sea, through what Captain O. calls a succession of Mount Edgecumbes. I went ashore yesterday and this morning, chiefly to make purchases. Things here are really beautiful and cheap. The town is wonderfully clean after China. Not a beggar to be seen. The people clean too; for one of the commonest sights is to see a lady in the front of her house, or in the front-room, wide open to the street, sitting in a tub washing herself. I never saw a place where the cleanliness of the fair sex was established on such unimpeachable ocular evidence.

August 6th.—Four P.M.—At anchor off the southernmost point of Japan. It has been blowing hard all day, and our captain proposed that instead of rounding this point and facing the sea and wind, against which we should not be able to make any way, we should creep in under it and anchor. We intend to remain till the gale abates. Nothing can be finer than the coast. We have passed to-day some very high hills, one especially on an island to the right, and a conical-shaped one on the left, on the Japan mainland. I see little sign of population on this coast off which we are anchored. Only one little fishing village. There were a good many junks yesterday. It is very hot though, and I find it difficult to sit at my table and write. . . .

August 7th.—Three P.M.—Still at anchor in the same spot. The storm has not abated, and the wind is dead against us. My time is so short that I cannot well afford to lose any. About three hours after we anchored yesterday, the Retribution arrived with the Emperor yacht in tow, and established herself near us.

August 10th.—Ten A.M.—I wonder if I shall be able to write a few lines legibly. There is still a good deal of motion, but a cool breeze, which is such a relief after the sweltering six weeks we have spent. Ahead of us is a great conical-shaped mountain, the sacred mountain of Fusiama (etymologically the matchless mountain), and somewhere nearer on the long range of bold coast which we are approaching, we expect to find Simoda. But I must tell you of our two past days—days of suffering. At about twelve during the night of the 7th, the wind shifted and began to blow into our anchorage, so as to make it unsafe to stay there, and to promise us a fair wind if we proceeded on our way, so off we started. We have had our fair wind, but no great deal of it; and as the Furious is both a bad sailer and a good roller, we have passed a very wretched time,—every hole through which air could come closed. However, we have made good progress and burnt little coal, which is good for the public interest. We see now in the distance two sails, which we suppose may be our consorts, the Emperor and Retribution. We have travelled some 1000 miles since we left Shanghae, besides spending two days at Nagasaki. I feel much better than when I started, notwithstanding the shaking we have had. *Noon.*— It is a magnificent prospect which we have from the paddle-box. Immediately before us a bold junk, its single large sail set, and scudding before the breeze. Beyond, a white cloud, slight at the base, and swelling into the shape of a balloon as it rises. We have discovered that it rests on a mountain dimly visible in the distance, and which we recognise as the volcanic island of Oosima. Towards the right the wide sea dotted with two or three rocky islets. On the left of the volcano island a point of land rising into a bold and rocky coast, along which the eye is carried till it encounters a mighty bank of white clouds piled up one upon another, out of which rises clear and blue, with a white streak upon the side which seems to tell of perpetual snow, the cone-shaped top of Fusiama. Passing on the eye from the magnificent object to the left still further, the rocky coast is followed till it loses itself in the distance. What is almost more charming than the scene is the fresh breeze which is carrying off the accumulated fever of weeks.

August 12*th.*—At sea again. (Grouse day. I am following different game.) We dropped anchor in the harbour of Simoda on the 10th at about three P.M. I went off immediately to see the American Consul-General, Mr. Harris, the only foreigner resident at Simoda. I found him living in what had been a temple, but what in point of fact makes a very nice cottage, overlooking the bay. As soon as we anchored we began to feel the heat, though not as great as at Shanghae. I found that the Consul had contrived to make a pretty good treaty with Japan, evidently under the influence of the *contrecoup* of our proceedings in China. He had had an interview with the Emperor, but it transpired that he had a letter of credence, which I have not, and that Putiatine not having one, is not permitted to go to Yeddo. I also learnt that there is no way of communicating with the Japanese officials except through the Dutch language. Being without a Dutch interpreter, and without letters of credence, my case looked bad enough. However, I made great friends with the American, and the result is that he has lent me his own interpreter, who is now beside me translating into Dutch a letter from me to the foreign minister of the Japanese Emperor. You see how I was situated. The problem I had to solve was:—How to make a treaty without *time* (for I cannot stay here above a few days), *interpreter*, or *credentials!!* When I say credentials, I do not mean *full powers*. *These* I have; but prestige is everything in the East, and I should not like to be prevented from seeing the Emperor, now that the American has been received. We shall see how we can get out of all this. Another difficulty is, that the American has done the most unjustifiable thing, of extorting from the Japanese authorities a written pledge, that they will not sign a treaty with any other power until thirty days after the signature of his treaty, viz., the 29th of July.[1] We have just passed Uraga; it is rather hazy, and there is a fresh breeze off shore on our left. It seems hardly so bold as on the other side of Simoda. High banks covered with wood, and numerous villages crouching on the sand and in the valleys between them. We see on the right the faint outline of what seem to be lofty hills. The Retribution is at a short distance behind us, lying a little over, with her sails well filled. The Emperor is farther off, and for the present lost in the mist. The agitation of the sea is nothing more than a ripple, so we are moving pleasantly along. Simoda is a pretty place, lying on flat ground at the head of a short bay, with rocky volcanic-looking hills, covered with fine trees and intersected by valleys all around. The people seem the most amiable on earth. Crime and pauperism seem little known. All anxious to do kindnesses to strangers, and steadily refusing pay., There are innumerable officials with their double-swords, but they appear to be on the most easy terms with the people. To judge from the amount of clothing worn by both sexes, it does not seem likely that there will be any great demand for Manchester cotton goods. I cannot say what it may be in winter, but in summer they seem to place a very filial reliance on nature. They are the cleanest people too. The floors of their houses are covered with mats which are stuffed beneath, and which serve for beds, floors, tables, etc. It is proper to take off the shoes or sandals on entering the houses or temples.

[1] This turned out afterwards to be of no moment.

I looked into one or two bathing-houses which are most unlike those I saw at Shanghae;—an inner room which is a kind of steam bath, and an outer room where the process of drying goes on. The difference in China is, that it is only the men that clean themselves there, whereas the rights of the fair sex on this point are fully recognised in Japan, and in order that there may be no inequality in the way they are exercised, all bathe together. I visited some temples. Though Buddhistic, they had not the hideous figures which are seen in the Chinese temples. They were generally prettily situated near the foot of the rocky and wood-covered cliffs, with flights of steps running up to shrines among the rocks. They were surrounded by numerous monuments to the departed, consisting generally of little pilasters, squared on the sides, and bearing inscriptions, surmounted by a coping or ball. On the pedestal, etc., in front of the pilaster, generally, were one or two branches of what looked like myrtle stuck into pieces of bamboo which serve for flower-pots. These monuments, crowded together around the temples and overshadowed by the lofty trees, had a very graceful effect. We have just committed an act of vigour. In place of going into the harbour of Kanagawa where Count Putiatine is at anchor, I have determined to proceed to a point several miles higher up nearer to Yeddo. We completely foil by our audacity all the poor Japanese officials. I have said nothing of the bazaar of Simoda, where there were a great many pretty things, of which I bought some, nor of a visit which the Governor paid to me. He was a very jolly fellow, liked his luncheon and a joke. He made the conventional protests against my going on, etc., but when he saw it was of no use, he dropped the subject. The Japanese are a most curious contrast to the Chinese, so anxious to learn, and so *prévenants*. God grant that in opening their country to the West, we may not be bringing upon them misery and ruin. . . .

August 14*th.—Eight* A.M.—I have just been on deck to enjoy a pleasant cool breeze, and see hundreds of little junks proceeding to sea. They are strangely constructed, with a beautifully shaped sharp prow, and a single sail a great way towards the stern. We moved yesterday to within about one mile of the shore off the suburb of Yeddo. The shore is flat, and the buildings of the town, interspersed with trees and enclosures, seem to stretch to a great distance along the crescent-shaped bay. Immediately in front of the town and opposite to us are five large batteries. Four Japanese men-of-war built on European models are anchored beside us. Three princes came off to see me yesterday. They were exceedingly civil, but very anxious to get me to go back to Kanagawa, a port about ten miles down the bay, from which they said they would convey me by land to Yeddo. Of course I would not agree to this. They were very much puzzled (and no wonder) by my two names. I complimented the prince on the beautiful Fusiama, calling it a high mountain. "Oh!" he said at once, "I have seen a scale of mountains, and I know that there are many much higher than Fusiama." There were persons in the suite taking down in shorthand every word that passed in conversation, and I thought I saw in one of their note-books a sketch of my face. No doubt these were spies also, to watch and report on the proceedings of the officials, for that seems to be the great means of Government in Japan. Still there is no appearance of oppression or fear anywhere. It seems to be a matter of course that every man should fill the place and perform the function which custom and law prescribe, and that he should be denounced if he fail to do so. The Emperor is never allowed to leave the precincts of his palace, and everybody, high and low, is under a rigid rule of *convenances*, which does not seem to be felt to be burdensome. I am afraid they are not much disposed to do things in a hurry, and that I must discover some means of hastening them, if I am to get my treaty before returning to Shanghae. The Lee, my gunboat, arrived this morning. She has had a bad time of it, and was nearly lost in our gale, but her arrival here will, I think, do good.

August 15*th*.—*Sunday, noon*.—I fear that the earlier pages of this letter bear considerable traces of the tossing seas amid which they were written. We have just been at service, and I am now awaiting a second visit from my "princes." Yesterday and the day before it rained torrents, but to-day hitherto it has been fine, and the temperature is perfect, about 72°. Putiatine has reached Yeddo, having come up by land from Kanagawa, where he left his ships. . . .

August 16*th*.—Princes, five in number, arrived on board yesterday at about three P.M. Among them was the Lord High Admiral, a very intelligent well-bred man. It was agreed that I was to land to-day, and some discussion took place as to the house I was to inhabit. They said that they could give me the choice of two, but that they recommended the one farthest from the palace as being in best repair. I chose the one nearest the palace, because one is always obliged to be on one's guard against slights, but it has rained so much to-day that I have sent to say I will not land till to-morrow, and to inquire where I can really be best lodged. I have handed to the authorities a draft of my Treaty. The chief interpreter, by name Moriama (the wooded mountain), a very acute and smooth-spoken gentleman, told one of my party yesterday that the princes who have come off to me are Free Traders, and that this is the spirit of the Government, but that some of the hereditary princes are very much opposed to intercourse with foreigners, and that some little time ago it was apprehended that they would raise a rebellion against the Government, in consequence of the concessions it is making. The official princes are named by the Emperor for life, but the hereditary ones are great feudal chiefs owing rather a qualified allegiance to the Emperor. Moriama pretended that he and his friends had seen the arrival of our ship with pleasure, but of course one never knows whether to believe a word they say. My gentlemen have just returned from their visit to the town of Yeddo. It appears that the authorities had not made the best arrangements for my landing and lodging, so it is just as well I did not land to-day.

Yeddo.—August 18*th, Seven* A.M.—Here I am installed in a building which forms the dependence of a temple. It consists of some small rooms forming two sides of a square, with a verandah running in front of them. From the verandah you step into a garden not very well kept, with a pond and trees, and some appearance of care in laying it out. In the centre is the temple, with a back-door opening into the garden. I entered it yesterday, and found a "Buddha" coming out of the lotus, looking very freshly gilt and well cared for. There were in the temple two or three priests, who seem to live there; at any rate, one was asleep on the matting, which, as I told you, is in Japanese houses laid on the top of a bed of straw. They are charmingly soft and clean, as all shoes are put off on entering. The natives use neither tables, chairs, nor beds. They lie, sit, and feed on this matting. They have made considerable exertions, however, to fit up our house on European principles. We landed yesterday at noon. The day was fine, and the procession of boats imposing. An immense crowd of good-natured, curious people lined both sides of the streets along which we passed. The streets are wide and handsome. We were preceded and accompanied by officers to keep off the crowd, but a blow with a fan was the heaviest penalty that I saw inflicted on any one breaking the line. At every fifty yards, or so, the street was crossed by large gates, which were closed as soon as our procession passed through, which prevented a rush after us. On arriving, as I had nothing else to do, I proposed a ride through the town, to the considerable consternation of our attendants. We set off on saddles made of hard and rather sharp bits of wood, stirrups which I can't undertake to describe, and our knees in our mouths. However, we made our way to the quarter of the Palace or Castle. As we approached it, we passed through streets inhabited by princes. I did not enter any of their houses, but they seem to be constructed somewhat on the principle of the "*entre cour et jardin*" houses in parts of Paris. On the street front the offices, substantially built, and often with very handsome gateways. The "Castle" is surrounded by three concentric enclosures, consisting of walls and moats. They are at a considerable distance from each other, and the Emperor resides in the innermost enclosure, from which he never goes out. The intervals between the enclosures are filled up with handsome houses, etc. We passed over the first moat, and rode up to the second. When we came up to the second, we discovered a spectacle which was really very grand. The moat was some forty or fifty yards wide; beyond it a high bank of grass nicely kept, with trees rather like yews every here and there dropped upon it. The crest of the bank seemed to be crowned by a temple, surrounded by trees. The stone wall was on a grand scale, and well finished. In short, the whole thing would have been considered magnificent anywhere. After China, where everything is "*mesquin*," and apparently "*en décadence*," it produces a great effect. I did not see a single beggar in the streets; as in this ride of yesterday we took our own way, without giving any notice, we must have seen the streets in their usual guise. My poor, dear friends, the Japanese, object to everything and always give way. It is a bad plan, because it forces one to be very peremptory and overbearing. Nothing can be milder than their objections, but they lose time. I have told them that I must see the Foreign Minister to-day, and that I must have another house, as the situation of this one is not sufficiently aristocratic. I do not know, however, whether I shall press the latter point, as it will put myself to much inconvenience. The thermometer is now 72°. Nothing could be more pleasant.

August 19*th.*—Yesterday forenoon, I took a ride to visit some shops, and spent some money in lacquer and silk. The shops were large and handsome, and we were shown upstairs where all the fine things were displayed to us. A great crowd surrounded the shops while we were in them, but they made way for us when we re-mounted. In the evening, I visited the Foreign Minister, or rather, the two Foreign Ministers (I believe there are three, but one is unwell). I took my whole staff, but only my secretary and interpreter remained in the room when we came to talk of business. There has been a change of Government, and the present Foreign Secretaries seem stupid enough. The Government seems to be a sort of oligarchy in the hands of the hereditary princes. Count Putiatine, who has just been with me, tells me that he does not consider the officers with whom we are negotiating princes at all. They have the title of *Kami*, but it is not hereditary, and they are altogether inferior to the others. Both have the title of *Kami*, but the hereditary princes are also called *Daimios*.

August 21*st*.—Count Putiatine had his audience of the Heir-Apparent yesterday, and I send a single line by him to Shanghae, that it may be posted to you, in case *he* should arrive *before* the mail goes and *I after*. On the 19th, the Plenipotentiaries appointed to treat with me came. They are six in number. We exchanged our full powers, and I made some difficulty about theirs, but was satisfied by their explanations. After the *séance*, I went out riding through the streets. I had not given notice, and we went through a densely peopled quarter, which gave me an opportunity of seeing something of the popular feeling. We were followed by immense crowds, among whom some boys took to hooting, and by degrees to throwing stones. This got rather disagreeable, so at length we took to stopping at the gates, turning right about, and facing the mob with our horses, until the gates were shut. It proves to me, however, that it is not prudent to go about without a good Japanese escort. Yesterday we had a most charming expedition into the country. We started at about eleven A.M., rode first to the road I have already described, and which runs along the moat of the second enclosure of the Emperor's domain. We passed alongside of this enclosure. The effect of the domain within, with its dropping trees (not, yews, I see, but pines of some sort, many of them with spreading branches like cedars), being somewhat that of a magnificent English park. This, mind you, in the centre of a city of two or three millions of inhabitants.

Sunday, August 22*d*.—We then passed through the gate of the outermost enclosure on the opposite side, and entered some crowded streets beyond, through which we made our way, passing on our right the palace of the greatest of the hereditary princes, really an imposing mass of building. Beyond, we got into the country, consisting at first of a sort of long street of quaint cottages with thatched or tiled roofs, embosomed in gardens, and interspersed with avenues conducting to temples. Further on were cultivated fields, with luxuriant crops of great variety : rice, sweet potato, egg-plant, peas, millet, yams, taro, melons, etc. etc. At last, we reached a place of refreshment, consisting of a number of kiosques, on the bank of a stream, with a waterfall hard by, and gardens with rock-work (not *mesquin*, as in China, but really pretty and in good taste) opposite. Here we had luncheon. Fruits, and a kind of Julienne soup; not bad, but rather *maigre*, served to us by charming young ladies, who presented on their knees the trays with the little dishes upon them. The repast finished, we set out on our return (for we had overshot our mark), and visited the gardens, which were the object of our expedition. They had the appearance of nursery gardens, with rows of pots containing dwarf-trees and all manner of quaint products; all this, however, in a prettily *accidenté* country, abounding in forest trees and luxuriant undergrowth. We got back at about seven P.M., having met with no mishap. On the whole, I consider it the most interesting expedition I ever made. The total absence of anything like want among the people; their joyous, though polite and respectful demeanour; the combination of that sort of neatness and finish which we attain in England by the expenditure of great wealth, with tropical luxuriance, made me feel that at last I had found something which entirely surpassed all the expectations I had formed. And I am bound to say, that the social and moral condition of Japan has astounded me quite as much as its material beauty. Every man, from the Emperor (who never leaves his palace) to the humblest labourer, lives under a rigid rule, prescribed by law and custom combined; and the Government, through its numerous agents, among whom are hosts of spies, or more properly inspectors (for there is no secrecy or concealment about this proceeding), exercises a close surveillance over the acts of each individual; but, in so far as one can judge, this system is not felt to be burdensome by any. All seem to think it the most natural thing in the world that they should move in the orbit in which they are placed. The agents of authority wear their two swords; but, as they never use them except for the purpose of ripping themselves up, the privilege does not seem to be felt to be invidious. My interpreter, a Dutchman, lent to me by the United States Consul-General, has been two years in the country, and he assures me that he never saw a Japanese in a passion, and never saw a parent beat a child. An inexhaustible fund of good temper seems to prevail in the community. Whenever in our discussions on business we get on rough ground, I always find that a joke brings us at once upon the level again. Yesterday, at a formal audience with the Foreign Ministers (to settle about the handing over of the yacht), they began to propose that, in addition to the Commissioners, I should allow some other officers (probably spies, or inspectors) to be present at our discussions on the clauses of the Treaty. After treating this seriously for some moments, without settling it to their satisfaction, I at once carried the day, by saying laughingly, that as they were six to one already, they ought not to desire to have more chances in their favour. This provoked a counter-laugh and a compliment, and no more was said about the spies. When the Commissioners came yesterday afternoon to go through the clauses of the Treaty with me, I was much pleased with the manner in which they took to their work, raising questions and objections in a most business-like manner, but without the slightest appearance of captiousness or a desire to make difficulties. Their interpreter, Moriama, is a very good Dutch scholar, and, of course, being a remarkably shrewd gentleman withal, has a leading part in the proceedings; but all seem to take an intelligent share. I went into the temple of which this building forms a part, this morning. Two priests came up to me, knelt down, and laid before me two pages of paper, holding out to me at the same time the painting-brush and Indian inkstand, which is the inseparable companion of every Japanese, and making signs which I interpreted into a request that I would write down my name. I sat down on the floor, and complied with their request, which seemed to please them. The priests appear by no means so wretched here as in China, and the temples are in much better case. I have not, however, seen many of them. It is difficult, of course, to speak positively of the political condition of a country of which one knows so little; but there seems to be a kind of feudal system in vigour here. The hereditary princes (Daimios), some 360 in number (I doubt much their being all equally powerful), exercise extensive jurisdiction in their respective domains. A Dutch officer, who visited one of these domains in a Japanese man-of-war, found that the chieftain would not allow even the officers of the Japanese Emperor to land on his territory. The only control which the Emperor exerts over them is derived from his requiring all their wives and families to live at Yeddo permanently. The Daimios themselves spend half the year in Yeddo, and the other half at their country places. The Supreme Council of State appears to be in a great measure named by the Daimios, and the recent change of Government is supposed to have been a triumph of the protectionist or anti-foreign party. There is no luxury or extravagance in any class. No jewels or gold ornaments even at Court; but the nobles have handsome palaces, and large bodies of retainers. A perfectly paternal government; a perfectly filial people; a community entirely self-supporting; peace within and without; no want; no ill-will between classes. This is what I find in Japan in the year 1858, after a 200 years' exclusion of foreign trade and foreigners. Twenty years hence, what will be the contrast?

August 27*th*.—Here I am at sea again. It is nine P.M. I have just been on deck. A lovely moon, nearly full, gliding through cloudless blue, spangled here and there with bright twinkling stars. The square-sails of the foremast of the Furious all set, and such of the mainmast sails as will be serviceable, with a breeze right aft. Very little motion, and a way of about ten knots an hour, at an expenditure of less than one ton of coal. Thus favourably are we moving back to Shanghae, having made a treaty with Japan. I left Shanghae on the 31st ult., without an interpreter, or any compass to steer by. Hardly three weeks have elapsed, and I am actually on my way back; all the work done. I begin to feel as if at last I was really on my way home. Both my treaties are made, and I am steering westwards! Is it so, or am I to meet some great disappointment when I reach China? I feel a sort of terror when I contemplate my return to that place. My trip to Japan has been a green spot in the desert of my mission to the East. . . . But I must tell you how I have been spending my days since the 22d, when I last added a word to this letter. On the afternoon of that day, I had a long sitting with the Japanese Plenipotentiaries, and we went over the clauses of the Treaty which we had not reached on the previous day. On the 23d they returned, and we agreed finally on all the articles. It was also settled that the signature should take place on the 26th (the very day two months after the signature of the Treaty of Tientsin), and that the delivery of the yacht should take place on the same day; the Japanese agreeing to salute the British flag with twenty-one guns from their batteries—a proceeding unheard of in Japan. On the 24th, we took a ride into the country, in the opposite direction to our former ride. We passed through a long suburb on the shore of the sea, and eventually emerged into a rural district, rich and neat as that we had formerly visited; but as the country was flat, it was hardly so interesting. The object of our visit was a temple, far the finest I have seen either in China or Japan. We had some luncheon in a tea-house, and got back at about seven P.M. On the 25th, we went to another temple, through the most crowded part of the city (where we were stoned before). We were followed by large multitudes, but nothing disagreeable took place. At the temple we found a scene somewhat resembling Greenwich Fair. Immense numbers of people amusing themselves in all sorts of ways. Stalls covered with toys and other wares; kiosques for tea; show places, etc. etc. Life seems an affair of enjoyment in Japan. We made some purchases, and got home by about five P.M., in order to receive a party. I had invited the Imperial Commissioners to dine with me, and requested that they would send a juggler to perform before dinner. They tried to fight shy after having accepted; I suppose because they considered it *infra dig.* to attend at the performance of the juggler, but they came at last, and enjoyed the dinner part of the affair thoroughly. The juggler was good, but one particular feat was beyond praise. He twisted a bit of paper into the shape of a butterfly, and kept it hovering and fluttering, lighting here or there, on a fan which he held in his other hand, on a bunch of flowers, etc.,—all by the action on the air, produced by a fan which he held in the right hand. At one time he started two butterflies, and kept them both on the wing. It was the most graceful trick I ever saw, and entirely an affair of *skill*, not *trick*. The juggler was succeeded by the dinner, which I wound up by giving sundry toasts, with all the honours, to the great amusement of my Commissioners. Thursday morning was occupied in paying bills, which was a most difficult matter, as the Government will not allow the people to take money in the shops, and the complication of accounts was very great. The accuracy of the Japanese in these matters is, however, very great. At one P.M. the Commissioners came to sign the Treaty. We have agreed to make the Dutch copy the *original*, as it is the language both parties understand. The Dutch copy, written by their man "Moriama," was so beautifully written, that I have kept it to send to England. After the signature, I lunched on a dinner sent to me by the Emperor; not so bad, after all. At about three P.M. I set off to go on board the Emperor yacht, which I reached at about five; immediately after which the Japanese fort saluted the British flag with twenty-one guns (ten-inch guns); as good a salute as I ever heard, an exact interval of ten seconds between each gun. The Japanese flag was then hoisted on the Emperor, and saluted by the Retribution and Furious with twenty-one guns each. We ended the day with a collation on board the Retribution, and trip in the Emperor; and as I was pacing the deck of the Furious, before retiring to rest, after my labours were over, to my great surprise I observed that the forts were illuminated! Imagine our daring exploit of breaking through every *consigne*, and coming up to Yeddo, having ended in an illumination of the forts in our honour! At four A.M. this morning we weighed anchor, and are now some 140 miles on our way to Shanghae.

August 30*th*.—*Eleven* A.M.—We are now passing by Cape Chichakoff, behind which we took shelter on the 6th. A fine breeze right aft, and an atmosphere clear enough to enable me to scan pretty accurately the outline of the bold coast which protects this extremity of Japan, and to watch the white breakers as they dash against the rocks. We are again plunging into the China Sea, and quitting the only place which I have left with any feeling of regret since I reached this abominable East,—abominable, not so much in itself, as because it is strewed all over with the records of our violence and fraud, and disregard of right. The exceeding beauty external of Japan, and its singular moral and social picturesqueness, cannot but leave a pleasing impression on the mind. One feels as if the position of a Daimio in Japan might not be a bad one, with some two or three millions of vassals; submissive, but not servile, because there is no contradiction between their sense of fitness and their position. To return, however, to my narrative. We glided along pleasantly on the 28th, and I was able to do something to my report for the Government concerning the Japan trip. On the 29th, it blew more strongly; gradually all the ports had to be closed; what made it worse was, that it was very thick and showery, so that when we came off Cape Chichakoff, it was not considered prudent to pass it, and we had to lie off it for some twelve hours, tossing and rolling very unpleasantly, and losing all the time that we had gained by our splendid run. The storm is now over for the present. We have about 500 miles of open sea to Shanghae.

September 1st.—We made another good run up to noon yesterday, when the breeze began to freshen, and about eight P.M. some of our sails were blown away, and we found ourselves in the folds of a typhoon. We were obliged to lie-to, and spent a pretty uncomfortable night, as you may suppose. It was raining torrents; all ports, etc., were closed. . . . We had expected to reach Shanghae to-day, but I hope we may still catch the homeward mail. We have still rather more sea than I like.

September 2d.—We had a fine night, and thanks to the pluck of Captain Osborne and his master, Mr. Court, we went on among the islands. I went on deck early, and found a fresh breeze, in our teeth however. As the dawn ripened into day, we descried a man-of-war screw behind us, which turned out to be the Cruiser, attached to my squadron. She had orders to follow me to Nagasaki, when I was wanted; so her appearance is a proof that I am not much behind my time. Shortly afterwards we met the Yangtze, one of the opium steam-clippers. She tells us that the mail leaves on the 4th. This is so far well.

Shanghae.—September 3d.—We reached this place yesterday at about one P.M. I found Baron Gros and Mr. Reed. The Imperial Commissioners are not arrived. News from Canton favourable. I have your letters to July 9th, and expect a former one to-day, which is on board the Cruiser. . . . On the whole, however, I think that the mist between me and England is clearing a little. By next mail I hope to be able to say something positive about my plans. . . .

Shanghae.—Sunday, September 5th.— . . . I wish to be off for England; but I dread leaving my mission unfinished. . . . I feel, therefore, that I am doomed to a month or six weeks more of China. Still I really begin to feel that we are approaching the wind-up of the affair. I was at church to-day: rather hot; but the climate is very much more bearable than it was when I was last here. . . . I have two letters of yours before me. . . . Poor F. I hope he says truly, " God is helping our papa!"

September 6th.—It is very weary work staying here really doing for the moment little. But what is to be done? It will not do to swallow the cow and worry at the tail. . . . I never saw such a set as this British China community. I have been looking over the files of newspapers, and those of Hong-kong teem with abuse ;—this, notwithstanding the fact that I have made a Treaty which exceeds everything the most imaginative ever hoped for. The truth is, they do not really like the opening of China. They fear that their monopoly will be interfered with. . . .

September 9th.—It is a kind of calm here, however, for the moment. . . . Gros and Reed are both gone to Japan, and the community here are comparatively quiet. It is fine summer weather, clearer and brighter than England. It is a very dull place: all the residents resign themselves to making enormous fortunes, and being bored during the process. However, I have got a whole month of European news to read and digest. . . . I have written to the Imperial Commissioners to hasten their movements. I am quite sure that my wisest course in every point of view is to finish off all my business here, and to call at Hong-kong only on my way home. . . .

September 11th.—I have taken to American bowls, in order to get some exercise beyond walking up and down the Bund. I have also had some people to dine with me. I am amused with the confident way in which the ladies here talk of going home after five years with fortunes made. They live in the greatest luxury,—in a tolerable climate, and think it very hard if they are not rich enough to retire in five years. . . . I do not know of any business in any part of the world that yields returns like this. No wonder they dislike the opening of China, which may interfere with them. This is the secret of the malevolence towards me. . . .

September 14th.—It has been blowing for several days, and there is heavy rain besides. One cannot but be thankful for being on shore. . . . The thermometer continues about 80°, notwithstanding the wind. No news from the South nor from the North, though I hear that my Commissioners are expected to arrive soon. . . . I imagine F. will have arrived in England about this time. What an impression it gives one of the distance by which we are separated! I expect letters replying to my first from Pecheli. At the same moment *he* ought to be arriving in England with the *Chinese* Treaty,—while *I* have already despatched from hence my *Japan* Treaty. I hear from the captains of the Retribution and Lee, who went to Nagasaki on their way back from Yeddo, that neither the Japanese nor the Dutch would believe the report they gave of our performances at Yeddo—our having been in the city, etc. As for the salute to the English flag, that was beyond the swallow of any of them. Baron Osten Sacken, Putiatine's secretary, has just been here. He tells me that they left Kanagawa, in a gunboat, on the 23d. After being out two days their engine went wrong, and they had to return. They then embarked in their frigate, apparently on the same day on which we left Yeddo. They fell in with our typhoon of the 31st, and having run out of coal and lost spars, etc., have been tossing about, not far from the mouth of the Yangtze, till now.

September 15*th.*—Your letter to July 24th reached me this morning. . . . The Government have not even acknowledged my despatches. . . . The news from Canton seems tolerably good, so that I really hope that I may be getting under weigh for home. . . . To-day the storm has passed. It is very hot and calm—the thermometer 88°. . . .

Sunday.—September 19*th.*—We had a melancholy sermon. The clergyman who preached it lost his wife while we were in Japan. Two other leading ladies in this place died while we were in the north. So many deaths make a great blank in so small a society. I hear that there is great excitement at Hongkong about the articles in the *Times* reflecting on the Admiral. There is some talk of an address to him. . . . L. goes home. I have told him to visit you if he goes to Scotland . . .

Shanghae.—September 23*d.*—I am still here in a kind of calm. We get no news from the South except when the fortnightly mails come in, so that I am less worried than I should be at Hong-kong. I am, moreover, in a comfortable house, and the climate is tolerable. . . . I intimated yesterday that to expedite matters I should go and meet the Imperial Commissioners at Soochow, but I was assured that they will not delay there, and will positively be here on the 2d or 3d of next month. . . . I have been reading the debate on the Hudson's Bay Territory. It is amusing to see the wonderful confidence in the permanence of the British Colonial Empire now professed by statesmen, as compared with their language in 1846, and for some years following. . . .

September 26*th.—Sunday.*—This morning brought me your letter to August 7th. . . . It replies to my gloomy letter from the Gulf of Pecheli. . . . Lord M. answers the first letter I wrote after I had heard of the change of Government in England. . . . The Commissioners are hurrying down by forced journeys in consequence of my pressing letters, so I may expect them any day. This is another step in my prospects of homewards. I hear from India that the report of my Treaty was not believed in Calcutta. It was considered too good to be true. You had not seen the telegram from Tientsin when you wrote, but the last *Times* has it, as well as a report of a few words from Disraeli, showing that they think there has been a want of promptitude. . . . I heard yesterday that the Commissioners were near Soochow. . . .

October 3*d*.—I am laid up with a cold. . . . Yesterday the Chinese courier from Soochow was four hours behind his time in arriving here,—the reason given being that the canal was blocked up by the *cortége* of the Imperial Commissioners. . . . I have been reading for the first time, *Vanity Fair*. It is certainly very clever, though one would hardly like to have written it. They are more literary here than in any place out of England where I have found my countrymen and countrywomen. There is a very fair library, of which Mr. Reid (my Dunfermline friend) is at present librarian. I enclose two photographs, done by Jocelyn at Yeddo, of the six Commissioners, etc.

October 4*th*.—I am assured that the Commissioners arrived this forenoon. In a few days I shall know how I get on with them, and how much longer I am likely to be detained here. The favourable monsoon is commencing, so that I may get on quickly when I once start. May it be soon ! . . .

Sunday, October 10*th*.—*Shanghae*.—We have not done much yet, which is the cause of my having written less than usual during the last few days. I have reason to suspect that the Commissioners came here with some hope that they might make difficulties about some of the concessions obtained in the Treaty, with a kind of notion perhaps that they might continue to bully us at Canton. If I had departed I think it probable enough that everything would have been thrown into confusion, and the grand result of proving that my Treaty was waste paper might have been attained. I have thought it necessary to take steps to stop this sort of thing at once, so I have sent some very peremptory letters to the Commissioners about Canton, refusing to have anything to say to them till I am satisfied on this point, etc. I have also through a secret channel had the hint conveyed to them that if they do not give me full satisfaction at once I am capable of going off to Tientsin again,—a move which would no doubt cost their heads to both Kweiliang and Hwashana. I have already extorted from them a proclamation announcing the Treaty, and I have now demanded that they shall remove the Governor-General of the Canton Provinces from office, and suppress the War Committee of the Gentry. If I succeed in this, the Hong-kong press and public will have to invent some new lie, because I shall have done everything which up to this moment they have said I could not do. Mr. Reed is said to have arrived at Woosung (the outward anchorage of this port). Baron Gros is still absent, so I have to fight my battle here single-handed, which is just as well. *Au reste,* beyond this business of the Commissioners, nothing can be more monotonous than our life here. . . . The weather is now tolerably cool, but the sun is hot, and unless one shoots, the country is dull and uninteresting. I play at bowls for exercise about two hours, generally before dinner; the rest of the day I spend in my room, reading, etc. . . . This morning I was at church, and had a sermon from the Bishop. . . .

October 16*th.*—. . . Yes, the report of the conclusion of a Treaty which was conveyed so rapidly overland to St. Petersburg was true, and yet I am not on my way home! . . . Do not think that I am indifferent to this delay. It is however, for the moment, inevitable. Everything would have been lost if I had left China. The violence and ill-will which exist in Hong-kong are something ludicrous. . . . As it is, matters are going on very fairly with the Imperial Commissioners, and I expect an official visit from them this day at noon. The English mail arrived yesterday. . . . The visit of the Commissioners went off very well. I think that they have accepted the situation, and intend to make the best of it. Jocelyn took a photograph of us as we were all sitting together. . . .

October 19*th.*—Unfortunately the photograph has not answered. Yesterday I returned the visit of the Commissioners, going in state, with a guard, etc., into the city. We had a Chinese repast—birds'-nest soup, shark-fins, etc. I tried to put them at their ease, after our disagreeable encounters at Tientsin. They seemed disposed to be conversible and friendly. The Governor-General of this province, who is one of them, is considered a very clever man, and he appears to have rather a notion of taking a go-ahead policy with foreigners. I am interrupted by a missionary who has called to see me.

October 21*st.*—. . . I enclose a letter written to the Bishop's wife by a Chinese scholar at their Hong-kong school, which may amuse you :—

Copy.

St. Paul's College, *October* 7*th,* 1858.

My dear Madam,—I was very sorry to hear that you were driven back to Amoy by a typhoon on the way to Shanghae.

Mrs. Cleverly takes the first class every Saturday from ten to eleven, for a little reading with her in the dining-room. The College goes on very well, but only several boys have been sick lately. Mr. Jones has sent one school-boy away, because he did not come back in the appointed time which Mr. Jones allowed him to go home and see his dying grandfather. I do not know who will buy some winter clothes for Alum the blind boy, who has not a suit of warm clothes for the cold weather. I am very sorry to inform you that my uncle urges me to marry a heathen girl. I have told him that I must marry a Christian girl. I know very well that a Christian boy must marry a Christian girl; it is not proper for me to marry a heathen girl like that; if I do, what will the Bishop and you say to me? I suffer very much from my uncle's and brother's anger against me for refusing them to follow their opinions. Aloi spoke to me the other day, that his uncle has a daughter whose name is called Akom. I dare say you know her by the name. His uncle says if I would like to marry her, he is quite willing to do it. I had a long conversation with him the other day. I have not yet promised him until I receive a letter from you, seeing whether the Bishop and you like it or not; then I can promise him. Her father and brothers are Christians, so that I like to marry her much better than my uncle marries for me. I have no father nor mother to depend upon, therefore I must depend upon the Bishop's and your opinion; will you be kind enough to write me a few lines and let me know all about it? I wish to go to Canton for a few days, so that I ask Mr. Jones' permission to go for a few days; he refuses to let me go; I daresay he supposes that if I go, perhaps I shall not come back again. I do not mean that I wish to leave the College, but I only wish to see my sisters and relations, because I have not seen them for three years. Will you ask the Bishop to let me go for a few days? You need not fear that I shall not come back again; I will come back in the proper time. I hope Miss Alice is gaining strength daily. With my kind regards to you and the Bishop, I remain, my dear Madam, your most humble and obedient servant, S. ASEW.

Shanghae.—November 2d. . . . You will, I am sure, see how necessary it has been for me to protract my stay to this time. The systematic endeavour to make it appear that my work was a failure could be counteracted only by my own presence. The papers, etc., from England are complimentary enough about the Treaty, but some of the accounts which have gone home are somewhat exaggerated, and perhaps there will be a reaction. . . . More particularly, I find a hope expressed that we have plundered the wretched Chinese to a greater extent than is the case. . . . Meanwhile, I have achieved one object, which will be, I think, the crowning act of my mission. I have arranged with the Imperial Commissioners that I am to proceed up the river Yangtze. The Treaty only provides that it shall be open when the Rebels have left it. I daresay this will give rise to comments. If so, I shall have anticipated them, by going up the river myself. I shall take with me my own squadron (what I had in Japan). The weather is beautiful; quite cool enough for comfort. We shall visit a region which has never been seen, except by a stray missionary. I shall lose by this move some three weeks, but I do not think they will be really lost, because it will give so very complete a demonstration of the acceptance of the Treaty by the Chinese authorities, that even Hong-kong will be silenced. . . . You must remember how I am situated; not a person to take my place in whom I can put confidence, and all my work dependent on the tact and judgment with which it is carried out. I got no letters from any one but you. Gros tells me that he has received complimentary ones from all sorts of people; from some with whom he is not even acquainted. . . . Gros returned from Japan a week ago. He had fine weather, and got the same Treaty as I did. It was lucky he returned here when he did, as it enables me to arrange my affairs with the Imperial Commissioners. They came here on Saturday last, but our chief business was photographing them. J. has taken them very well.

November 6th.— I hoped to have started to-day, but am obliged to put off till Monday, as the Tariff is not yet ready for signature. I grieve over every day lost, which protracts our separation. I see that in the very flattering article of the *Times* of September 7th, which you quote, it is implied that when I signed the Treaty, I had done my work, and that the responsibility of seeing that it was carried out rests with others. If this be true—and you will no doubt think so—I might have returned at once, at least after Japan. But is it true? Could I, in fairness to my country, or, in what I trust you believe comes second in the rank of motives with me, to my own reputation, leave the work which I had undertaken unfinished? . . . Besides, I own that I have a conscientious feeling on the subject. I am sure that in our relations with these Chinese we have acted scandalously, and I would not have been a party to the measures of violence which have taken place, if I had not believed that I could work out of them some good for them. Could I leave this, the really noblest part of my task, to be worked out by others? Any one could have obtained the Treaty of Tientsin. What was really meritorious was, that it should have been obtained at so small a cost of human suffering. But this is also what discredits it in the eyes of *many*, of *almost all* here. If we had carried on war for some years; if we had carried misery and desolation all over the Empire, it would have been thought quite natural that the Emperor should have been reduced to accept the terms imposed upon him at Tientsin. But to do all this by means of a demonstration at Tientsin! The announcement was received with a yell of derision by connoisseurs and baffled speculators in tea. And indeed there was some ground for scepticism. It would have been very easy to manage matters here, so as to bring into question all the privileges which we had acquired by that Treaty. Even then we should have gained a great deal by it; because when we came to assert those rights by force, we should have a good, instead of a bad *casus belli*. But I was desirous, if possible, to avoid the necessity for further recurrence to force; and it required some skill to do this. This has been my motive for protracting my stay. . . . You must not be alarmed if the next mail is blank. We shall not probably be able to send letters from up the river, and I fear we shall not be here again before its departure. Beyond Nankin the river is quite unknown, and we shall have to go slowly. . . .

H. M. S. Furious.—November 8th.— . . . I write a line to tell you that I got over the signature of my Tariff, etc., very satisfactorily this morning, and set off in peace with all men, including Chinese Plenipotentiaries, and colleagues European and American, on my way up the Yangtze-Kiang. We are penetrating into unknown regions, but I trust shortly to be able to report to you my return, and all the novelties I shall have seen. . . .

H. M. S. Furious.—River Yangtze, November 8th.--Evening.-- I resume my journal, which fell into a sort of abeyance during my monotonous life at Shanghae. This morning at ten, I went to a temple which lies exactly between the foreign settlement and the Chinese town of Shanghae, to meet there the Imperial Commissioners, and to sign the Tariff. We took with us the photographs which J. had done for them, and which we had framed. They were greatly delighted, and altogether my poor friends seemed in better spirits than I had before seen them in. We passed from photography to the electric telegraph, and I represented to them the great advantage which the Emperor would derive from it in so extensive an empire as China; how it would make him present in all the provinces, etc. They seemed to enter into the subject. The conference lasted rather more than an hour. After it, I returned to the consulate, taking a tender adieu of Gros by the way. I embarked at one, and got under weigh at two P.M. .... The tide was very strong against us, so we have not made much way, but we are really in the Yangtze river. We have moved between two flats with trees upon them; the mainland on the left, and an island (Bush Island), recently formed from the mud of the river, on the right. Though the earth has been uninteresting, it has not been so with the sky, for the dark shades of night, which have been gathering and thickening on the right, have been confronted on the left by the brightest imaginable star, and the thinnest possible crescent moon, both resting on a couch of deep and gradually deepening crimson. I have been pacing the bridge between the paddle-boxes, contemplating this scene, until we dropped our anchor, and I came down to tell you of this my first experience of the Yangtze. And what will the sum of those experiences be? We are going into an unknown region, along a river which, beyond Nankin, has not been navigated by Europeans. We are to make our way through the lines of those strange beings the Chinese Rebels. We are to penetrate beyond them to cities, of the magnitude and population of which fabulous stories are told; among people who have never seen Western men; who have probably heard the wildest reports of us; to whom we shall assuredly be stranger than they can possibly be to us. What will the result be? Will it be a great disappointment, or will its interest equal the expectations it raises? Probably before this letter is despatched to you, it will contain an answer more or less explicit to these questions.

November 9th.—Last night, Capt. W. (of the Dove and Actæon, surveying vessels) came on board, and told me that the Dove gunboat and the Cruiser were aground on a bank ahead of us. The channel of this river shifts about so, that it is difficult to tell to-day what it will be to-morrow. We are now starting; the gunboat Lee ahead; we next; Retribution astern of us. Both sides flat; and on the right, Bung Ming Island. *Ten* A.M. —I was stopped by hearing our anchor drop. I went on deck and found that a man had fallen overboard, and the water had suddenly shallowed. The man was picked up, and the anchor heaved; but it has been dropped again. This is notoriously a bad part of the river.

November 10*th.*—*Eleven* A.M.—Bad report. We got aground at about three P.M. yesterday; it was near high water, so that we have stuck fast ever since. We are now taking everything we can out of the ship to lighten her. .... *Six* P.M.—The tide rose well, and we got off at about two P.M. We then started in the following order: Dove, Retribution, Cruiser, Furious, Lee; rounded the shoal, and are now anchored all together off Harvey

Point, where we are taking on board again our guns, etc., which we were obliged to unship in order to lighten ourselves. We are not above twenty-five miles from Woosung.

November 11*th.*—*Seven* A.M.—I have been about an hour on deck; a fine clear morning; cool enough to make a pretty thick coat agreeable. We are going beautifully along, the two gunboats in front like outriders, the white steam gushing from their cylinders at each stroke of the piston, and curling fantastically as it loses itself in the atmosphere; they are just far enough apart to give us the width of the channel, and far enough in advance to enable us to pull up if they get into a difficulty, before we come to grief. When I came on deck the Retribution and Cruiser were before us. We have now slipped past them, and are next to the gunboats. The land as flat as before. *Noon.*—Going merrily along, Lee first, Furious next, then Dove, Retribution; the Cruiser having little power, dropping far behind. We have passed some mountains at a distance on the left, and are now between three conical hills, with buildings upon them on the right (named Langshan on the chart), and the town of Fooshan on the left. It is nicely situated, with some mounds and forts about it, and apparently, from the junk masts, a canal running through it. It is a hamlet rather than a town. We had just passed this when the Lee signalled us to stop. She has got into shoal water, and is hunting for a channel; the Dove is come up to help her. It is pretty to see them skirmishing in front, hoisting flags to tell their news. The Cruiser is profiting by our stoppage to make up to us.

November 12*th.*—*Noon.*—No progress since this time yesterday. We knew that this was a difficult passage, and have not been able yet to find a channel. The gunboats are far away searching. We begin to feel somewhat anxious. *Six* P.M.—Capt. O. has just returned from surveying in the Lee since five this morning. No channel is to be found. The old ones seem filled up. At present, therefore, it appears probable that the question which I put three days ago, is to be answered by " a great disappointment."

November 13*th.*—*Ten* A.M.—A junk is to be sent to Woosung with sick from the Retribution. I shall take advantage of the opportunity to send you this letter. We have no channel yet; but I can hardly think that we shall have to turn back. . . . Meanwhile the weather continues charming. . . .

Sunday, November 14*th.*—After I had despatched my letter yesterday, Captain O. returned in the Lee, bringing the intelligence that a channel had been found by Capt. W. in the Dove. We were to go back eight miles. At four A.M. we started, passed the Retribution and Dove, and seemed to be having it all our own way; but about eight A.M. we got into difficulties, and the Dove and Retribution are now ahead of us. . . . Unless we make more rapid progress, this expedition promises to be of longer duration than I intended. *Noon.*—We have just passed within about a mile of the place at which we have been lying for two days, separated from it by a shoal, which was impassable, and round which we have been compelled to go. The weather is lovely; the temperature delightful; the sunshine a little scorching. . . . *Six* P.M.—We have just dropped anchor, some eighty miles from Woosung. I wish that you had been with me on this evening's trip. You would have enjoyed it. During the earlier part of the afternoon, we were going on merrily together. The two gunboats ahead, the Furious and Retribution abreast, sometimes one, sometimes the other, taking the lead. After awhile we (the Furious) put out our strength, and left gunboats and all behind. When the sun had passed the meridian, the masts and sails were a protection from his rays, and as he continued to drop towards the water right ahead of us, he strewed our path, first with glittering silver spangles, then with roses, then with violets, through all of which we sped ruthlessly. The banks still flat, until the last part of the trip, when we approached some hills on the left, not very lofty, but clearly defined, and with a kind of dreamy softness about them, which reminded one of Egypt. Altogether, it was impossible to have had anything more charming in the way of yachting; the waters a perfect calm, or hardly crisped by the breeze that played on their surface. We rather wish for more wind, as the Cruiser cannot keep up without a little help of that kind.

November 15*th.*—*Seven* A.M.—The Cruiser has not come up, so we are to run back to her and give her a tow, and the Retribution is to take the gunboats in tow to-day, that they may have time to cool their boilers and make some repairs. I wish to have my fleet together when we pass Nankin, in case the Rebels should be troublesome. After that it will not so much matter. . . . *Noon*—Going on well, Furious towing Cruiser, and Retribution a little astern towing the two gunboats. We have just passed a pretty little town called Kiangyin, nestled among the hills, behind which we anchored last night. We put it under contribution, or rather robbed it to the extent of some £200,000 or £300,000 in the last war, under pain of bombardment. The banks are flat again. Quantities of tall reeds or bulrushes seem to grow on them, and to be cropped for fuel or fencing. *Six* P.M.—We have just come to anchor after a fair day's run, about fifty miles, without an incident, except one, a hurried dropping of the anchor, throwing loose the Cruiser, etc., because of the sudden shoaling of the water. We soon recovered the channel and went on again. It has been really cold, with a stiff breeze from the north-east, although the thermometer was only 53°. I was glad of a thick coat and a warm at the funnel before I came down to write these lines.

November 16*th.—Seven* A.M.—It was very cold on deck, but a beautiful morning. We are going on as yesterday, very near the left bank of the river (our right), which seems fertile, well wooded; great numbers of cottages, and the people in groups in front of them, looking amazedly at us as we pass. On the left, at some distance, is a pretty high hill, with a pagoda or temple on the summit. It is near Chin-kiang Foo, and we shall pass close to it when the river takes its next turn. . . . *Ten* A.M.— We have passed the Choosan hills, which have a fine, bold outline, and are farther from Chin-kiang Foo than I supposed. We are now just below Silver Island, with a town on our left, and barren hills stretching out to the distance, a ruddy purple colour on them like heather hills. We have anchored to land an unfortunate Chinaman whom we took out of a junk two days ago, to act as our pilot. *Noon.*—A bad business. We were running through a narrow channel which separates Silver Island from the mainland, in very deep water, when all of a sudden we were brought up short, and the ship rolled two or three times right and left, in a way which reminded me of a roll which we had in the Ava immediately after starting from Calcutta. On that occasion we saw beside us the tops of the masts of a ship, and were told it had struck on the same sand-bank, and gone down about an hour before. Our obstacle on this occasion is a rock —a very small one— for we have deep water all around us. However, here we are. I hope our ship will not suffer from the strain. It is curious that in this narrow pass, where fifty ships went through and returned in 1842, this rock should exist and never have been discovered. *Six* P.M.—The sun has just set among a crowd of mountains which bound the horizon ahead of us, and in such a blaze of fiery light that earth and sky in his neighbourhood have been all too glorious to look upon. Standing out in advance on the edge of this sea of molten gold, a solitary rock, about a quarter of the size of the Bass, which goes by the name of the Golden Island, and serves as the pedestal of a tall pagoda. I never saw a more beautiful scene, or a more magnificent sunset; but alas! we see it under rather melancholy circumstances, for after six hours of trying in all sorts of ways to get off, we are as fast aground as ever. We are now lightening the ship. Silver Island is a kind of sacred island like Potoo, but very much smaller. I went ashore, and walked over it with a Bonze, who conversed with Lay. He told us that the people in the neighbourhood are very poor, and will be glad that foreigners should come and trade with them. The Bonzes here are much like their brethren of Potoo, the most wretched-looking of human beings. Our friend told us that they have no books or occupation of any kind. Four times a day they go through their prayers. He had twelve bald spots on his head, which were the record of so many vows he had taken to abstain from so many vices, which he enumerated. I gave them five dollars when I left the island, which seemed to astonish them greatly. I asked him what would happen if he broke his vows. He said that he would be beaten and sent away. If he kept them he hoped to become in time a Buddha.

November 17*th*.—*Ten* A.M.—Still on our rock; thermometer 43° at seven A.M.; yesterday at the same hour it was 37°. In my morning's stroll on deck I saw two or three Bonzes in their ample wrappers — yellow, grey, or brown — sitting by the side of the path which runs round Silver Island, and gazing at us listlessly. Our master (Court) tells me we have taken already 100 tons out of the ship, and can take 200 more. The tide behaved shabbily, and we did not rise an inch during the night. He is greatly annoyed at this accident. I said to him that though I thought time precious, I considered the ship's keel, etc., more so, and would rather have some of the former expended than the copper taken off the latter. This sentiment, uttered with due emphasis, seemed to lighten his heavy heart, and on the strength of it he set to work with redoubled energy to perform the same office for his ship. *Six* P.M.—After taking 150 tons out of the ship, we have just made an attempt to get her off—in vain. The glorious sun has again set, holding out to us the same attractions in the west as yesterday, in vain! Here we remain, as motionless as the rock on which we are perched. I have not been quite idle, however. I landed about noon on the shore opposite Silver Island, and walked about three miles to the town of Chin-kiang. It was taken by us in the last war, and sadly maltreated, but since then it has been captured by the Rebels and re-captured by the Imperialists. I could hardly have imagined such a scene of desolation. I do not think there is a house that is not a ruin. I believe the population used to be about 300,000, but now I suppose it cannot exceed a few hundreds. The people are really, I believe, glad to see us. They hope we may give them free trade and protection from the Rebels. A commodore and post-captain in the Chinese navy came off to us this afternoon. They were very civil, offering to do anything for us they could. They tell us we can go in this ship to Hankow and the Poyang Lake. We have found another rock beside us, and only think that this should not have been known by our Navy! . . .

November 18*th.*—*Eight* P.M.—At about six P.M. I was crossing on a plank over a gully, on my return from an expedition to Golden Island, when three rounds of cheers from the Furious, about a mile off, struck my ear. Three rounds of cheers, followed by as many from the other ships. She was off the rock! Some 250 tons were taken out, and when the tide rose she came off—nothing the worse! and our time has not been quite lost, for this is an interesting place, if only because of the insight which it gives into the proceedings of the Rebels. Golden Island is about five miles from here. It was a famous Buddhist sanctuary, and contained their most valuable library. Its temples are now a ruin. Its library burnt. In returning I had another view of the devastated city of Chin-kiang Foo. . . .

November 19*th.*—*Seven* A.M.—As you may suppose, we are in a most filthy state, having discharged a quantity of coal, and being now engaged in taking it on board again. I fear we can not get away to-day. . . .

November 20*th.*—*Noon.*—Going along at a good pace, in the usual order; a finer day, if possible, though somewhat hazy. On the left some high bold hills at a little distance; on the right a well-wooded plain. We have got rid of the accumulated coal and dust. Nankin is about twenty miles ahead. I have just written a memorandum for Captain B. as to the conduct he should observe towards the Rebels. . . . Yesterday I took a long walk, not marked by any noteworthy incidents. We went into some of the cottages of the small farmers. In one we found some men smoking opium. They said that they smoked about 80 cash (fourpence) worth a day. That their wages when they worked for hire were 120 cash (sixpence). The opium was foreign (Indian). The native was not good. I asked how they could provide for their wives and families if they spent so much on opium. They said they had land, generally from two to three acres a-piece. They paid about a tenth of the produce as a tax. They were very good-humoured, and delighted to talk to Wade and Lay. They appear to welcome us more here than in other places I have visited in China. *Eight* P.M.—We have been under fire. The orders given on our approach to Nankin were, that the Lee should go in advance; that if fired on, she should hoist a flag of truce; if the flag of truce was fired on, she was not to return the fire until ordered to do so. It was a lovely evening, and the sun was sinking rapidly as we approached Nankin; the Lee about a mile in advance. I was watching her, and saw her pass the greater part of the batteries in front of the town. I was just making up my mind that all was to go off quietly, when a puff of smoke appeared from a fort, followed by the booming of a cannon. The Lee on this hoisted her white flag in vain; seven more shots were fired from the forts at her before she returned them. Then, to be sure, we began all along the line, all the forts firing at us as we came within their range. I was on the paddlebox-bridge till a shot passed very nearly over our heads, and Captain O. advised me to go down. We were struck seven times; one of the balls making its way into my cabin. In our ship nobody was hit; but there are one killed and two badly wounded in the Retribution. We have passed the town; but I quite agree with the naval authorities, that we cannot leave the matter as it now stands. If we were to do so, the Chinese would certainly say they had had the best of it, and on our return we might be still more seriously attacked. It is determined, therefore, that tomorrow we shall set to work and demolish some of the forts that have insulted us. I hope the rebels will make some communication, and enable us to explain that we mean them no harm; but it is impossible to anticipate what these stupid Chinamen will do.

November 21*st.*—*Eleven* A.M.—We had about an hour and a half of it this morning. We began at six A.M. at the nearest fort, and went on to two or three others. We pounded them pretty severely, and very few shots were fired in return. They seemed to have exhausted themselves in last night's attack. As soon as my naval chiefs thought that we had done enough for our honour, I begged them to go on, as I did not want to have to hand over the town to the Imperialists, who are hemming it round on every side. I am sorry that we should have been forced to do what we have done; but I do not think we could have acted with greater circumspection. . . . A set of Imperialist junks set to work to fire at the town as we were leaving off, throwing their shot from a most wonderfully safe distance. . . . I should think that these wretched Rebels must give in soon, for the town seems invested all round. We are now passing into a part of the river which is little known. One American vessel (the Susquehanna) went up in 1854 as far as Woohoo, about sixty miles above Nankin; but beyond that no foreign vessel has, I believe, ever been. At present the river is magnificent, wider and deeper than below Nankin. The wind is fair, and we are going on rapidly; on our left are hills; on the right flat ground. *Six* P.M.—We have come to anchor near a town called Taiping, in the hands of the Rebels. Two or three miles back some of those idiots came down to a fort on the shore, and fired gingalls, etc., at us, which did not reach us by many hundred yards. We threw a few shot into them in passing. The navigation throughout the day has been magnificent; a fine broad river and deep channel. Nothing remarkable in the appearance of the country; the only crop at present visible being the bulrush, which the people are now gathering. The river seems entirely deserted; since we parted from the Imperialist war-junks at Nankin, we have hardly seen a sail.

November 22*d.*—The Retribution got aground behind us at about nine A.M., and we are engaged in trying to get her off. Last night a letter came off from our " humble younger brother" (the Rebel chief), praying us to join them in annihilating the " demons" (Imperialists). I sent them in reply a sort of proclamation which I had prepared in the morning, intimating that we had come up the river pacifically; had punished the Nankin forts for having insulted us, from which persons repeating the experiment would learn what they had to expect. Later at night a present of twelve fowls and two pieces of red bunting came to the river bank, from some villagers, I believe. We are now approaching Woohoo. Beyond all is unknown, except from the records of Lord Amherst's Embassy, which ascended the river in junks. *Six* P.M.—We have lost this day, but the Retribution is off at last. When Captain W. was on shore surveying, two Chinamen came to him, stating that an express had come from Nankin to say that the attack on us was a mistake, that we were taken for Imperialists, etc. etc. I hope therefore that we shall have no more trouble of this description.

November 23*d.*—*Noon.*—We have just passed the Eastern and Western Leangshan (Pillar Hills), two fine bold hills on either side of the river, with fortifications upon them, which seem to be in Rebel hands. No flags, however, have been hoisted, nor guns fired, so I presume orders have been sent up not to molest us. . . . We only got off at eleven A.M., the Retribution having anchors to get up, etc. It is proposed that she shall not go beyond Woohoo. . . . *Six* P.M.—Arrived off Woohoo at about three P.M. We passed the town, and anchored just above it. It is in the hands of the Rebels, but no hostility was shown to us. Wade has been on shore to communicate with the chiefs, who are very civil, but apparently a low set of Cantonese. The place where he landed is a kind of entrenched camp; the town about three miles distant. An Imperialist fleet is moored a few miles up the river. I sent Lay to communicate with the commanding officer, and he recommends the Retribution to go a little farther on to a place in the possession of the Imperialists. . . .

November 24*th.*—*Ten* A.M.—We set off this morning at about six A.M. In passing the fleet we begged from the commander the loan of a pilot. He proves to be a Cantonese, so that the active spirits on both sides seem to come from that quarter.

We asked him why the Imperialists do not take Woohoo. He says they have no guns of a sufficient size to do anything against the forts, but that about twice a month they have a fight on shore. They cut off the heads of Rebels, and *vice versâ*, when they catch each other, which does not seem to happen very often. The war, in short, seems to be carried on in a very soft manner, but it must do a great deal of mischief to the country. While I was dressing I was called out of my cabin to see a fight going on, on the right bank of the river. The Rebels occupied some hills, where they were waving flags gallantly, and the Imperialists were below them in a plain. We saw only two or three cannon shots fired while we passed. As things are carried on, one does not see why this war should not last for ever. The day, though fine, is hazy as yet. *Three* P.M.—We have left the Retribution at a small place called Kiewhein, where a detachment of the Imperial fleet is stationed. It is in the immediate vicinity of a range of mountains, and we have since passed the finest scenery we have yet met with in the Yangtze. Hills really lofty, and as they approach the river well wooded and coloured, so as to remind one of a Canadian autumn. This on our left—(the right bank). The left bank continues flat. My friends, the Commissioners, seem to have acted in good faith towards me, for the Chinese naval authorities all inform me that they had been forewarned of our coming, and ordered to treat us with every courtesy. As we approached Kiewhein we observed long strings of peasants hastening along with their cattle, etc., and we fancied it implied that they feared a Rebel attack. We are now reduced to three vessels: for the Dove—I know not why—has gone back to the Retribution. *Five* P.M.—We have anchored in a fine, wide, deep stream: after making fifty miles or so, both sides now flat, but we see mountains in the distance. . . .

November 25*th*.—*Ten* A.M.—The Dove rejoined us in the night. We have just passed a bit of scenery on our left, which reminds me of Ardgowan,—a range of lofty hills in the background, broken up by deep valleys and hillocks covered with trees; dark-green fir, and hard-wood tinted with Canadian autumn colours, running up towards it from the river. With two or three thousand acres—what a magnificent situation for a park! There are so many islets in this river that it is not easy to speak of its breadth, but its channel still continues deep, and, with occasional exceptions, navigable without difficulty. *Eleven* A.M.—I was interrupted by the information that two Mandarin boats were coming off to us, and the inquiry whether I would wait for them. I determined to do so, and it proved that they were sent off with cards of compliment by the commanding-officer of the district of Tatong. The Rebels are among the hills, but not in the river bank here. They are in occupation of Nganching, about forty miles ahead, but surrounded by Imperialist forces,—so say our Mandarin friends. Meanwhile the weather continues beautiful,—in the morning so misty that we had some difficulty in getting on, but rainless and cloudless. They have just begun to repair the mainstay, which was cut by the ball that passed so closely over our heads off Nankin. Curiously enough it was cut over at almost the same point at Sebastopol! *Noon.*—We have a great number of trading junks about us, for the first time for many days. Chefoo is not far off. *Four P.M.*—We have passed over a shallowish part of the river; and one gets nervous when the gunboats mark five, four, and three fathoms. We have now, however, got back to seven and eight; so we may breathe freely. The scenery is very striking. . . . Fine ranges of hills on both sides and on the left bank,—a rich flat running up to them, chequered with trees and apparently well cultivated. The sun is powerful, but the air cool; thermometer 49° at seven A.M.; add to this water as smooth as a mirror, and you have an idea of our day's yachting. *Six P.M.*—A very pretty spectacle closed this day. The sun was dropping into the western waters before us as we approached a place called Tsong-yang, on the left bank. We knew it was the station of an Imperial fleet, and as we neared it we found about thirty or forty war-junks, crowded with men and dressed in their gaudiest colours. Flags of every variety and shape. On one junk we counted twenty-one. You cannot imagine a prettier sight. We anchored, supposing that the authorities might come off to us. As yet, however, they have shown no disposition to do so. I presume, however, that the display is a compliment. Figure to yourself the gala I have described at the mouth of a broad stream running at right angles to the river Yangtze, and up which the town lies, about two miles off—the river, plains, town and all, surrounded by an amphitheatre of lofty hills—and you will have an idea of the scene in the midst of which we are anchored, and from which the golden tints of sunset are now gradually fading away.

November 26th.—Noon.—We have just had another sample of this very unedifying Chinese warfare. About an hour ago we came off the city of Nganching, the capital of the province of Aganhoei—the last station (so we are assured) in the hands of the rebels. As we neared a pagoda, surrounded by a crenulated wall, we were fired upon two or three times. We thought it necessary to resent this affront by peppering the place for about ten minutes. We then moved slowly past the town, unassaulted till we reached the farther corner, when the idiots had the temerity to fire again. This brought us a second time into action. It is a sorry business this fighting with people who are so little a match, but I do not suppose we did them much harm, and it was, I presume, necessary to teach them that they had better leave us alone. O., who was aloft, saw from that point a curious scene. The Imperialists (probably taking advantage of our vicinity) were advancing on the town from the land side in skirmishing order, waving their flags and gambolling as usual. The Pagoda Rebels ran out of it as soon as we began to fire, and found themselves tumbling into the arms of the Imperialists. For a moment they were in considerable perplexity, but when we moved on they resumed their place in the Pagoda. Nganching is prettily situated; but the day is so hazy, though fine, that we can see little of the distance. We passed this morning a narrow rocky passage, otherwise the navigation has been easy. *Six* P.M.—Anchored off Tunglow, a walled town, nicely situated on the river. The sun is sinking to his repose through a mist, red, and round, like a great ball of fire. The pilot is the most vivacious Chinaman I have seen,—inquiring about everything, proposing to go to England, like a Japanese. It was from the naval commander at Kiewhein that we got him. Lay was present when the commodore sent for him. He fell on his knees. The chief informed him that he must go up the river with us, and pilot us. "That is a public service," says the man, "and if your Excellency desires it I must go; but I would humbly submit that I have a mother and sister who must be provided for in my absence." "Certainly," said the chief. "Then," answered our man, "I am ready;" and without further ado he got into the boat with Lay and came off to us.

November 27th.—Eight A.M.—We started well, but there is such a fog that we are obliged to stop till it clears. Our pilot ashore last night at Tunglow, and has returned with the front part of his head cleanly shaved. I asked him what the people had thought of our appearance. He answered that they were greatly afraid lest we should fire upon them, and their hearts at first went pit-a-pat; but when they heard from him how well we treated him, and that we were no friends to the Rebels, they said "Poussa" (that's Buddha's doing," or "thank God"). *Ten* A.M.—Aground again, not very firmly, I hope. . . . 4.30 P.M.—Just off.

November 28th. —Eleven A.M.—The morning began as usual: calm, fair and hazy. At about nine it began to blow, and gradually rose to a gale, causing our river ripple to mimic ocean waves, and the dust and sand to fly before us in clouds, obscuring earth and sky. About ten we approached a mountain range, which had been for some time looming on the horizon. We found we had to pass through a channel of about a quarter of a mile wide; on our left, a series of barren hills, bold and majestic-looking in the mist; on the right, a solitary rock, steep, conical-shaped, and about 300 feet high. On the side of it a Buddhist temple, perched like a nest. The hills on the left were crowned by walls and fortifications built some time ago by the Rebels, and running over them in all manner of zig-zag and fantastic directions. I have seldom seen a more striking bit of scenery. When we had passed through we found more hills, with intervals of plains, in one of which lay the district city of Tongtze, enclosed by walls which run along the top of the hills surrounding it. The inhabitants crowded to the shore to witness the strange apparition of foreign vessels. I mentioned a rocky passage on the morning of the 26th. Ellis, in his account of Lord Amherst's Embassy, speaks of it as a place of great difficulty. A series of rocks like stepping-stones run over a great part, and the passage is obtained by sticking close to the left bank. Our pilot tells us that it is named the "Hen Barrier," and for the following reason: Once on a time, there dwelt on the right bank an evil spirit, in the guise of a rock, shaped like a hen. This evil spirit coveted some of the good land on the opposite side, and proceeded to cross, blocking up the stream on her way. The good spirits, in consternation, applied to a Bonze, who, after some reflection, bethought himself of a plan for arresting the mischief. He set to work to crow like a cock. The hen rock, supposing that it was the voice of her mate, turned round to look. The spell was instantly broken. She dropped into the stream, and the natives, indignant at her misdeeds, proceeded into it and cut off her head. I have been skimming over a Chinese book, translated by Stanislas Julien: the travels of a Buddhist. It is full of legends of the character of that which I have now narrated. . . . This is our third Sunday since we started. The trip has been a slower operation than I expected; but in point of incident it has not fallen short as yet of my expectations.

November 29th.—12.30 P.M.—I had just come down with a heavy heart to tell you we were again aground, when we began to swing, and, hurrah! we are off again. We prudently buoyed a narrow channel yesterday, and passed through it this morning without accident. Soon after, we neared the entrance of the Poyang Lake, the finest bit of scenery which we have yet passed. The lake is connected with the river Yangtze by a stream of about two and a half miles in length, on one side of which, as one moves up the river, one sees a range of low hills, the Jagged Hills by name, terminating in a bluff, with a fortress on its summit, on the other a row of lofty mountains. The stream in question flows into the right bank of the Yangtze, at right angles to its general direction; but when we came nearly opposite, we steered sharp to our right, so as to turn our backs upon it. After proceeding merrily for about an hour, we came to a shallow bar, and grounded. But our mishap here has only cost us about two hours' delay. The weather is fine, but very cold. We had ice on deck early this morning, and the thermometer marked 31°. We have been very near the bank this morning. I see more cattle on the farms than in other parts of China. They are generally buffaloes, and for agricultural purposes; and when out at pasture, a little boy is usually perched on the back of each to keep it from straying. *Six P.M.*—No progress since we got afloat. It has been determined to drop anchor in all difficult places, and wait till the channel has been buoyed, and our emissaries are now exploring another branch of the river. I went ashore to pass the time, and got into conversation with some of the peasants. One man told us that he had about three acres of land, which yielded him about twenty piculs (1½ ton) of pulse or grain annually, worth about forty dollars. His tax amounted to about three-fourths of a dollar. There was a school in the hamlet. Children attending it paid about two dollars a year. But many were too poor to send their children to school. We went into another cottage. It was built of reeds on the bare ground. In a recess screened off were two men lying on the ground, with their lamp between them, smoking opium. In June and July the river rises to the top of the bank, and floods the land; now it is from twenty-five to thirty feet below it. No doubt this is one cause of the difficulty we experience. In compensation we have a cool and healthy climate.

November 30th.—Late last night our master returned from his exploration, we had got into the wrong channel, and this morning we had to go a mile back, no very easy matter with this large ship, and we took the middle channel. At about nine A.M., we had to anchor and buoy another passage. I have just been watching our progress through it. It is rather nervous work when the gunboat ahead and the sailors in the chains are telling that we have less than three fathoms. We are now in waters which no Englishman, as far as is known, has ever seen: Lord Amherst passed into the Poyang Lake through the channel I described yesterday, and so on to Canton. We are proceeding up the river Yangtze. Huc came down this route, but by land. I mentioned the sand-drifts two days ago. Some of the hills here look like the sand-hills of Egypt, from the layers of sand with which they are covered. What with inundations in summer and sand-drifts in winter, this locality must have some drawbacks as a residence. *Noon.*—Anchored again. We have before us in sight the pagoda of Kew-kiang; one of the principal points which we proposed to reach when we embarked on this expedition. . . . We have not much to hope for from our Chinese pilot. Our several mishaps have disheartened him. He said to-day with a sigh, when reminded that we had found no passage in the channel he had specially recommended: "The ways of waters are like those of men, one day here, another there, who can tell!"—a promising frame of mind for one's guide in this intricate navigation. *Five* P.M.—We found a channel in about an hour, and came on swimmingly to Kew-kiang. From the water it looked imposing enough. An enclosing wall of about five miles in circuit, and in tolerable condition. I landed at three P.M. What a scene of desolation within the wall! It seems to have suffered even more than Chin-kiang Foo. A single street running through a wilderness of weeds and ruins. The people whom we questioned said the Rebels did it all. The best houses we found were outside the city in the suburb. We were of course very strange in a town where the European dress has never been seen, but the people were as usual perfectly good-natured, delighted to converse with Lay, and highly edified by his jokes. We did some commissariat business. We had with us only Mexican dollars, and when we offered them at the first shop the man said he did not like them as he did not know them. Lay said, "Come to the ship and we will give you Sycee instead." "See how just they are," said a man in the crowd to his neighbour; "they do not force their coin upon him." This kind of ready recognition of moral worth is quite Chinese, and nothing will convince me that a people who have this quality so strongly marked are to be managed only by brutality and violence.

December 1st.—*Ten* A.M.—Court returned at about eight this morning from an exploration about twenty miles up without encountering any serious difficulty. We started and have been going on pleasantly in a fine river about three-fourths of a mile wide, with flat banks. The weather is milder and the water of a glassy stillness, reflecting the bright sunshine. 1.30 P.M.—We have just anchored. About an hour ago, we turned sharply to our left, and found on that hand a series of red sand-bluffs leading to a range of considerable blue hills which faced us in the distance; the river, as has been the case since we left the Rebel country, was covered with small country junks, and here and there a mandarin one, covered with flags, and with its highly-polished brass gun in the prow. The scene had become more interesting but the navigation more difficult, for the gun-boats began hoisting "3" and "4," and all manner of ominous

K

numbers. So we had: "Hands to the port anchor," "slower," and "as slow as possible," "a turn astern," and after a variety of fluctuations, "drop the anchor." *Six* P.M.—We had to go a short way back, and to pass, moreover, a very shallow bit of the river; that done we went on briskly, and bore down upon the mountain range which we descried in the forenoon. At about four we came up to it and turned to the right, with the mountains on our left and the town of Wooseuh on our right, while the setting sun, glowing as ever, was throwing his parting rays over one of the most beautiful scenes I ever witnessed. The whole population crowded to the river bank to see this wonderful apparition of the barbarian fire-ships. The hills rising from the water had a kind of Loch Katrine look. We have made some thirty-five miles to-day, but have still I fear about 100 to go.

December 2d.—*Eleven* A.M.—A very prosperous forenoon. Mountains soon rose to the right, similar to those on the left. We cut our way through deep calm water, amid these hills of grey rock and fir woods, for some three hours, and might really have imagined ourselves in the finest loch scenery of the Highlands. Numbers of little boats dotted the river, and moved off respectfully to the right and left as we approached. At about ten we passed out of the mountain range, and soon after neared Chechow, from which the population seemed to be moving, as we inferred from the numbers of small-footed women hobbling along the bank with their household effects. We were boarded by a mandarin-boat, the officer of which informed me that he had been sent by the Governor-General to pay his respects. He said that the Rebels were at no great distance, and the people were flying for fear of their attacking the town. He added, however, that they (the Imperialists) had a large force of cavalry in the neighbourhood, and that they would check the exodus of the inhabitants. Between Imperialists and Rebels, the people must have a nice time of it. His best piece of news was that we are only about fifty miles from Hankow. I trust that it may be so, for, despite my love of adventure, I shall be glad when we are able to turn back and proceed homewards. The reason which the pilot assigns for the destruction of the temples by the Rebels is the following: "At present," says he, "the rich have a great advantage over the poor. They can afford to spend a great deal more in joss-sticks and other offerings, so that, of course, the gods show them a very undue allowance of favour. The Rebels, who do not approve of these invidious distinctions, get rid of them by destroying the temples altogether." This is evidently a popular version of the religious character of the Rebel movement. A Buddhist priest, whom I saw at Kew-kiang, said that the Rebels had destroyed some forty temples there. "They do not worship in temples," he said, "but they have a worship of their own." The room in which Mr. Wade saw the Rebel chief at Woohow was said to be their place of worship. It had no altar, or anything to distinguish it as such. *Six* P.M.—We anchored at noon, but only for half an hour, for the channel was then recovered, and we went on for a short time between flat banks, bearing down on a bold bluff which jutted into the river on our left. Beyond it we found another magnificent site for a Highland deer forest; rugged grey hills, some rising to 2000 feet, and at their base a trout stream, through which the Dove, Lee, Furious, and Cruiser were rushing at full speed; the leadsmen reporting "no bottom" at ten fathoms! Some way ahead we descried the small town of Hwang-shih-kiang, unwalled, and we resolved to anchor off it, though at four P.M., having made fifty miles—altogether our best day. I have just returned from a stroll. We found a wondering, good-humoured population, busily engaged in exporting and manufacturing cotton and hemp. The day was cloudy, and I think about six drops of rain fell,—the first I have seen since the 21st of October.

December 3d.—*Ten.* A.M.—Just anchored in what looks to me a very awkward place. The river has widened considerably, and the water suddenly shallowed near the left bank where we are steering. We are near a small town called Lanshih. *Noon.* —We have just got over our difficulty,—the most touch-and-go case we have yet encountered. It was very nervous work; the leadsmen for some twenty minutes calling out three fathoms, and less. Just ahead is a town called Pâho. *Five* P.M.—After another short stoppage at one P.M., we got on and passed between two considerable towns—on the left, Woochang; on the right, Hwang-chow Foo. There was a good deal of bustle about them, and both had fine pagodas, which seemed to have also suffered from the Rebels. After a few miles more, we were stopped for the night in another shallow place, after making about thirty miles in the day.

December 4th.—*Six* P.M.—Anchored again for the night, not half a mile farther than yesterday. An island in process of formation, covered at high water, separates the two anchorages. We had to go back, etc., and ended the day's work by getting through a very tight place in a most masterly manner; leadsmen sounding at the bow and stern, as well as at the two paddles, and the Lee and Cruiser stationed as pivots at the edges of the shoal. We had to perform a sort of letter S round them, and we passed by the latter so near, that we might have shaken hands with the crew. I should be amused with these triumphs, were it not for the reflection that we have to repeat them all in returning, with a favouring current, which will make our task more difficult. The day has been raw, but no rain.

December 5th.—One P.M.—Going on well, having had twice to buoy the channel. It is raining, and we should be the better of a few feet more water for our return. 5.30 P.M.—Anchored, after making thirty-five miles. We ought not to be more than fifteen from Hankow. The river has had an excellent depth lately. We are off a town called Yang-lo.

December 6th.—Three P.M.—At Hankow; four weeks, almost to a minute, since we left Shanghae. We have brought this ship to a point about 600 miles from the sea,—a feat, I should think, unprecedented for a vessel of this size. We have reached the heart of the commerce of China. At first sight, I am disappointed in the magnitude of the place. I am anchored off the mouth of the river Han, which separates Hankow and Han-yang on the left bank of the Yangtze. On its right bank is Ouchang Foo. I do not see room for the eight millions of people, at which rumour puts the population of these three towns. The scene is very animated. We are surrounded by hundreds of boats, and the banks are a sea of heads. My gentlemen are gone ashore. I think I shall get through the streets more conveniently to-morrow morning. This day's sail was very prosperous, with abundance of water, and we passed through a rich country, densely peopled on either side. We did not start till nine A.M., owing to a heavy fog; but when it lifted, the weather became fine.

December 7th.—Four P.M.—I have just returned from a walk through Hankow. Like all the places we have visited on this trip, it seems to have been almost entirely destroyed by the Rebels; but it is recovering rapidly, and exhibits a great deal of commercial activity. The streets are wider and shops larger than one generally finds them in China. When "foreign" parties landed yesterday, they were a good deal pestered by officious mandarin followers, who, by way of keeping order, kept bambooing all the unhappy natives who evinced a desire to see the foreigners. In order to defeat this plan, which was manifestly adopted with the view of preventing us from coming in contact with the people—I landed near Han-yang, on the side of the river Han, opposite to Hankow, and walked in the first instance to the top of a hill where there is a kind of fortress, from which we had a good view of Ouchang, Han-yang, and Hankow. The day was rather misty, but we saw enough to satisfy us that there must have been great exaggeration in previous reports of the magnitude of these places. Some of the mandarin satellites tried to accompany us on our walk, but we soon sent them about their business. After seeing all we wished of the view, we descended and crossed the river Han in a sanpan to Hankow, where we walked about for some hours, followed by a crowd of perfectly respectful people. As some hint was conveyed to me implying that it was hoped we would not go to Ouchang, I have sent a letter to the Governor-General of the Two Hoo, who resides there, informing him that I intend to call upon him to-morrow. I shall go with as large an escort as I can muster. These Chinamen are such fools that, with all my desire to befriend them, I find it sometimes difficult to keep patience with them. They are doing all they can to prevent us from having any dealings with the people; refusing our dollars, sending us supplies as presents, etc. I have sent back the presents, stating that I must have supplies, and that I *will* pay for them.

December 8th.—Eleven A.M.—An officer has been off from the Governor-General, proposing that my visit should take place to-morrow, in order that there may be sufficient time for the preparations. He was very profuse in his protestations of good-will, but as usual there were a number of little points on which it was necessary to take a half-bullying tone. I could not have a chair with eight bearers; such a thing had never been seen at Ouchang. There were not thirty chairs (the number for which we had applied) in the whole place. "Lord Elgin won't land with less, do as you please," was the answer given. Of course, the difficulties immediately vanished. Considerable indignation was expressed at the fact that some of our officers had been prevented from entering the town of Ouchang yesterday. A hope was expressed that nobody would land on the Ouchang side to-day; all would be arranged by to-morrow to our satisfaction, etc. etc. So, after an interview, in which there was the necessary admixture of the bitter and the sweet, the officer was sent back to his master. Supplies are coming off in abundance to the ships. In short, the people are most desirous to buy and sell, if the authorities will only leave them alone.

Six P.M.—I have had a long walk on the same side of the river as yesterday. We first went through the whole depth of Hankow, on a line parallel with the river Han. We estimated our walk in this direction at about two miles, but a good deal of it was along a single street flanked on both sides by ruins. We then embarked in a sanpan and came down the Han, passing through a multitude of junks of great variety in shape and cargo. We landed near its mouth on the Han-yang side, and walked to that town, which is a Foo or prefectoral city, and walled. It contains the remains of some buildings of pretension, triumphal arches, etc., which imply that it must have been a place of some distinction, but it has been sadly maltreated by the Rebels.

December 9th.—Four P.M.—The day is rainy, and the purser complains of difficulty in making his purchases yesterday, and that coal is not coming off to us as promised, etc. So I thought it expedient to do a little in the bullying line to keep all straight. When the Governor-General therefore sent off this morning to say that he was ready to receive me, I despatched Wade and Lay to inform him in reply that the day was too bad for me to land, and that I had to complain of the difficulties put in my way about money, etc. He received them in person, and was very gracious; said that he had been at Canton; that he understood all about us; that if he had been there, Yeh would never have behaved as he did; that in former days the Chinese Government had bullied us; that we had bullied them of late years; that it was much better that henceforward we should settle matters reasonably; that he was desirous to show me every attention in his power; that when the port should be open he would do all he could to promote commerce and good understanding. In short, he spoke very sensibly. It is exceedingly probable that if he had not got a little check, he might have kept us at as great a distance as possible; but, be that as it may, it is just another proof of how easy it is to manage the Chinese by a little tact and firmness. We are now loading coal, flour, etc., as fast as we can take it on board. I went on shore for an hour, but it was disagreeable to paddle about the dirty, wet streets. This town is, however, less pestiferous than the other towns I have visited in China. I observe in it neither temples nor domestic altars in the shops, as at Canton.

December 10th.—Six P.M.—This day broke fine and clear, so I sent off to the Governor-General to tell him that if he would receive me I would visit him at two P.M. We went with considerable pomp. A salute going and returning. A guard of eighty marines and sailors, and a party of about thirty in chairs. We passed through about a mile of the town of Ouchang Foo, and were received by the Governor-General and his suite, dressed in their best. The ceremony was as usual; conversation and tea in the first room, followed by a more substantial repast in the second. I have never, however, seen a reception in China so sumptuous, the authorities so well got up, and the feeding so well arranged. The Governor-General is a good-looking man, less artificial in his manner than Chinese authorities usually are. He is a Mantchoo. It is rather hard to make conversation when one is seated at the top of a room surrounded by some hundred people, and when, moreover, one has nothing to say, and that nothing has to be said through an interpreter.

However, the ceremony went off very well. After it, I got rid of my ribbon and star, and took a stroll *incog.* through Hankow, where we bought some tea. Ouchang seems a large town with some good houses and streets, but sadly knocked about by the Rebels. We are getting all our supplies, etc., on board, and hope to start to-morrow evening.

December 11*th.—Six* P.M.—This day the Governor-General paid me a return visit. We received him with all honour; manned yards of all four ships, and gave him a salute of three guns from each. It has been a beautiful day, and the scene was a striking one when he came off in a huge junk like a Roman trireme, towed by six boats, bedizened by any number of triangular flags of all colours. A line of troops, horse and foot, lined the beach along which he passed from the gate of the city to the place of embarkation; quaint enough both in uniform and armament, but still with something of a pretension to both about them. I have seen nothing in China with so much display and style about it as the turn-out of the Governor-General of the Two Hoo, both to-day and yesterday. We showed him the ship, feasted him, photographed him, and entertained him one way or another for upwards of three hours. After he had departed, I landed on the Ouchang side, and walked through the walled city. Some objection was made to our entering, as we went through a side instead of the main gate, but we persevered and carried our point. The city is a fine one, about the size of Canton, but much in ruins. To-morrow at six, please God, we set forth on our return. I may mention as an illustration of the state of Ouchang, that in walking over a hill in the very centre of the walled town, we put up two brace of pheasants!

December 12*th.—Eleven* A.M.—We are on our way back to Shanghae. I am very glad of it, because we have accomplished all the good we could possibly expect to effect at Hankow, and I am becoming very tired of the length of time which our expedition has lasted. It is a feat to have reached this point with these big ships at this season of the year, and I think the effect of our visit will be considerable. The people evidently have no objection to us, and the resistance opposed by the authorities can always be overcome by tact and firmness. I am afraid you will consider a great deal of this journal very tiresome. Unless some novelties occur I shall now confine it to the record of the success with which we pass the difficulties we discovered on our way up. We have already got over two. We are now passing the White or Benevolent Tiger Mountains. The day has been gloomy, but it is clearing up, and the thermometer was 50° this morning. *One* P.M.—We have passed successfully two places which I mentioned on the 5th. The last is a very awkward bit of navigation. The gunboat leading marked *seven feet*, at a distance of apparently not more than two ships'-lengths from the bank, and signalled to us to stop, but our master, who is certainly very skilful, persevered, and picked up his channel between the position of the gunboat and the land. . . . *Six* P.M. —Anchored near Woochang above a bad place. I have taken a walk ashore, along a line of hamlets, the people of which seem to have comfortable farms of their own, and to be well off, if they were not so dirty. As usual they were delighted to be talked to.

December 13*th.*—*Nine* A.M.—At about eight we heaved anchor, having carefully buoyed this very awkward passage. The current ran about four miles an hour, and at some points where the leadsmen were calling out sixteen and seventeen feet, the channel was not much greater than the width of the ship, and we draw about fifteen and a half feet of water, so it was a nervous matter to get through. To make the vessel obey the helm it was necessary to go faster than the current, and difficult to do this without proceeding at such a rapid rate as would, if we had chanced to take the ground, have stuck us upon it immovably. We skirted our several buoys in a most masterly manner, and are now anchored till they have been picked up. . . . *Six* P.M.— . . . "Where we had eighteen feet as we came up, we cannot find fourteen now," are the ominous words which Captain O. has just addressed to me as he reached the deck from a surveying expedition. . . . It looks a little serious, for I fear there is a worse place beyond.

December 14*th.*—*Six* P.M.—We have got over our bad place of yesterday, and hope to find a passage through the " worse place beyond," a place which I mentioned on the 3d as a most touch-and-go case. . . . I went on shore this morning when there was no prospect of moving. When a channel was found, the Dutch ensign was to be hoisted at the main. We took a long walk, conversing with the peasants who live in a row of cottages with their well-cultivated lands in front and rear of their dwellings; the lands are generally their own, and of not more than three or four acres in extent I should think, but it is difficult to get accurate information from them on such points. We found one rather superior sort of man, who said he was a tenant, and that he paid four out of ten parts of the produce of his farm to the landlord. They gave me the impression of being a well-to-do peasantry. Afterwards I walked through the country town of Pâho, which is built of stone, and seemingly prosperous. The Rebels had destroyed all the temples. By this time I was about five miles from the ship, and it was past three P.M. I had begun to despair of our moving, when suddenly I saw through my glass the wished-for Dutch ensign. I hurried to my boat, and we weighed anchor soon after four P.M. We were conveyed by Mr. Court with great skill through a very narrow winding channel. The leadsman once called out 14½ feet, and we draw 15½. . . . Here we are, however, safe for the night, having left behind one difficulty more. . . .

December 15*th.*—*Eleven* A.M.—We are over the " worse place." . . . It reminded me sometimes of the river St. Lawrence rapids. . . . *Four* P.M.—At about one we had passed the village of Hwang-shih-kiang, and were entering that part of the river I described as a fine site for a Highland deer forest, when the Lee hoisted the " negative" (the signal to stop). She had got on a rock, where, on our way up, we had found no bottom at ten fathoms. I landed immediately, and found the people engaged in quarrying and manufacturing lime from the hills on the right bank. We had a pleasant walk; the day being beautiful, and the scenery very fine. They sell their lime at about 17s. per ton (200 cash a picul), and buy the small coal which they employ in their kilns at about 25s. (300 cash a picul). I wish I could do as well at Broomhall!

December 16*th.*—*Ten* A.M.- The Lee got off her rock at about four P.M. yesterday; but as she had been lightened, we could not get off till eight this morning. It was fortunate for us that she got aground; for if she had missed the rock we should almost certainly have hit it; and what would have happened it is difficult to conjecture. . . . *Two* P.M.—We have passed over a shoal place, where we anchored on the 2d, and have left behind us Kichow. Since then we have been going through the fine mountain scenery. The day is cold and rainy, but the mountains are more distinct. *Five* P.M.—A short stoppage at two o'clock, and since then we have been proceeding smoothly, . . . passed the town of Wooseuh, and anchored for the night above a bad place. . . .

December 17*th.*—*Ten* A.M.—The gunboats are hunting for a channel. . . . I am going ashore. On this day last year I em barked on board this ship for the first time. What an eventful time I have spent since then! *Four* P.M.—I have returned from my walk, but, alas! no good news to greet me. Only eleven feet of water, where we found seventeen on the way up. . . . Our walk was pleasant enough, though it rained part of the time. Some of the gentlemen shot, for the whole of China is a preserve, the game hardly being molested by the natives. We went into the house of a small landowner of some three or four acres; over the door was a tablet to the honour of a brother who had gained the highest literary degree, and was therefore eligible for the highest offices in the State. The owner himself was not so literary, and had bought the degree of *bachelor* for 108 taels (about £35). If he tried to purchase the degree of *master* he would have, he said, 1000 taels to pay, besides passing through some kind of examination. We asked him about the Rebels. He said that when they visited the rural districts, they took whatever they pleased, saying that it belonged to their Heavenly Father. Before meat they make a prayer to the Heavenly Father, ending with a vow to destroy the " demons" (Imperialists). " But," added our informant, " they are poor creatures, and their heavenly father does not seem to do much for them." We also visited a manufactory where they were extracting oil from cotton seed.

December 18*th*.—*Nine* A.M.—It rained all night, and the wind is ahead; but, alas! the water has not risen an inch. *Six* P.M.— We are to try a channel, such as it is, to-morrow morning. I landed for a walk. Wade took a gun with him. We saw quantities of water-fowl of all kinds. The plain on the left bank of the river is bounded on the other side by a pretty lake. The plain is subject to inundations, and seems to be covered by a bed of sand of about five feet in thickness. The people cultivate it by trenching for the clay beneath, and mixing it with the sand.

December 19*th*.—10.30 A.M.—The Cruiser went through this bad passage safely. We followed, and are now aground. Anchors are being laid out in hopes of dragging the ship over.

December 20*th*.—*Eleven* A.M.—Our difficulty yesterday was not unexpected, . . . but we were compelled to make the attempt. The mud was very soft, and as we pressed against it, kept breaking away; but the difficulty was, that as we moved the shoal, the tide was forcing us towards it, and preventing our getting clear of it. At night we fixed the ship securely by three anchors, and left it to make its own way, which it did so effectually, that at four A.M. we slipped into deep water. We did not get off till ten A.M., and the first thing we had to do was to turn in a channel which was exactly the length of the ship, and not a foot more. This very clever feat we performed with the help of an anchor dropped from the stern, and are now in the main river. . . . *Two* P.M.—We have anchored below Kew-kiang, at the spot where we anchored on November 30th. The Dove met us an hour ago with the ominous signal, " Afraid there is no passage." *Six* P.M.—Captain O. has returned from an exploration, which will be continued to-morrow. . . . It would be very sad if the Furious had to be left behind. Meanwhile I landed and took a walk. It is a pretty country, on the right bank, consisting of wooded hillocks with patches of cultivated valley, and sometimes lakes of considerable size. Cosy little hamlets nestle in most of the valleys; the houses built of sun-dried bricks, and much more substantial than those we saw yesterday, etc., where the walls generally were made of matting, probably because of the inundations.

December 21*st.—Ten* A.M.—The water has fallen about seven feet since we were here on our way up. The river branches off into three channels, separated by flat islands. . . . We must pass from one to the other, and are now endeavouring to find some deep enough crossing-place; on this our hopes rest. Captain Ward has been to tell me that his coal is exhausted. . . . *Six* P.M.—Very bad news; no more than eleven feet of water on any part of the crossing. There is still the north branch of the river. . . .

December 23*d.—Noon.*—Yesterday was very cold and rainy, and I did not land. At about six Captain O. returned from an exploration of the north channel, which he found rocky, and twelve feet of water the utmost that could be found. Captain B. was disposed to try and lighten the Cruiser; but I at once determined that I would run no risk of the kind. As yet no harm has happened to any of our ships, and the delay at this point of some of the squadron for three months, is more an inconvenience to me than a disadvantage in any other way. On public grounds it will even be attended with benefit, as it will insure the Yangtze being kept open; for supplies will be sent up to them from Shanghae, and they will have an opportunity of examining the Poyang Lake besides. If any of the vessels were lost or seriously injured, it would be a very different matter. I have therefore resolved that we shall all pack into the Lee (the Dove being crammed already), and with the aid of two junks for servants and baggage, make our way to the Retribution. We shall have to pass Nganching, but it is to be hoped that the Rebels will not repeat the experiment they made when we were on our way up. " *Au reste, Dieu dispose.*" . . .

December 24*th.—Noon.—On board the Lee.*—We have just passed the shallow behind which we were anchored for three days; but we have passed it only by leaving our big ships behind us. At ten A.M. I had all the ship's company of the Furious on deck, and made a short farewell speech to them, which was well received by a sympathetic audience. The whole Mission is on board this gunboat, pretty closely packed as you may suppose. The servants in a Chinese boat astern, and the effects in another astern of the Dove. The Dove leads, and we follow. It is raining and blowing unpleasantly. I am very sorry to have left the Furious. . . . If the Rebels let us pass them unattacked, it will be well; if they do not, we shall be obliged in self-defence to force a passage through their lines, in order to carry supplies to our ships. Either way, the object of opening the Yangtze will be attained. Yesterday the Prefect of Kewkiang came on board the Furious. He was very civil, undertook to supply Captain O. with all he wanted. . . . In the little cabin where I am now writing, five of us are to sleep!

Christmas Day.—Many happy returns of it to you and the children! . . . It is the second since we parted. . . . We are now (three P.M.) approaching Nganching. I have resolved to communicate with the authorities to express my indignation at what happened when we passed up the river, and tell them that if it is repeated I shall be obliged reluctantly to take the town. This may seem rather audacious language, considering that my whole force now consists of two gunboats. However, I think it is the proper tone to take with the Chinese. We anchored last night near the Orphan Rock, which we passed on the 28th of November. The day so miserable, raining and blowing, that we could not enjoy the scenery. We spent the night very sociably, reclining on shelves and all sorts of places. The Dove had such bad coal that we have been obliged to give her some, and to take her junk in tow. However, we get on pretty well, and have certainly gained in speed by changing our conveyance. It is cold and gloomy, but with no rain to-day, which is a comfort, with our limited accommodation.

December 26th.— *One* P.M.—It grew so dark before we anchored near Nganching last night, that we abandoned the idea of communicating till this morning, and found, when day broke, that we were nearer the town than we had anticipated. It was raining heavily, with a slight admixture of sleet, and some of the heights in rear of the town were covered with snow. We heaved anchor at about seven, and dropped it again at about half a mile from the wall of the city. Wade went off in a boat. He steered to a point where there was an officer waving a flag somewhat ominously, and a crowd behind him, generally armed with red umbrellas. When he got to the shore, he was informed that the officer was third in command, and a Canton man, as the other chiefs also appeared to be. He told them that it was our intention to pass up and down the river; that I had come with a good heart (*i.e.*, without hostile intentions); that nevertheless we had been scandalously fired at, etc. etc. They at once, in the manner of Chinamen, confessed their error, and said that the firing had been a mistake; that it was the act of some of the local men, who did not know the ships of " your great nation ;" that it should not happen again, etc. Wade told them that the same thing had occurred at Nankin, and that we had destroyed the peccant forts. They answered that they were aware of what had happened then. He added, that we did not wish to interfere in their internal disputes, but that they must know, if we were driven to it, we should find it an easy matter to sweep them out of the city. They admitted the truth of all he said, offered presents, begged him to go into the city and see their chief (both which proposals he declined); in short, they were contrite and humble. On his return to the Lee, she and her consort lifted their anchors, and we steamed quietly past the city, under the very walls, and within easy gingall shot, for so we were compelled to do by the narrowness of the channel. We have since gone on smoothly; we have just passed the Hen Rocks, and are giving some of our coal to the Dove. . . . How different is the scene on this gloomy day from the gala which greeted us when we anchored here on the 25th November. Wade says that the Rebels at Nganching had a more respectable look than those he met at Woohoo.

December 27th.—*One* P.M.—We are now very near Kewhein, where we left the Retribution. We are in the mountain scenery, and it is raining heavily. *Three* P.M.—Reached Kewhein at about two, and were rejoiced to find " no Retribution." Wade went ashore, and came back with a memorandum from Captain B. dated the 18th, and saying, that as the river had fallen nine feet, he intended to go to Woohoo on the 20th, and to cross the shoal at Taiping if an unexpected rise of the tide took place. . . .

December 28th.—*One* P.M.—It rained heavily yesterday afternoon. About six we anchored, it being pitch dark, when suddenly we saw ahead of us lights, and shortly afterwards heard cheers. It was the Retribution welcoming us on our return. The cheers were not very gratifying to me, as they proved to us that she had not crossed the shoal. We moved down to her, and Captain B. came on board. He had one piece of good news to communicate. The Rebels had sent from Nankin most pacific letters, promising an amicable reception for the future, etc. This morning I sent for Captain W. of the Dove, pressed upon him the importance of our getting the Retribution over the shoals, etc. He went to that ship, and returned to inform me that Captain B. could not start till one P.M. I saw that this involved the loss of a day, with the chances of falling water, etc., so I proposed that we in the Lee should go on immediately, and try to find a channel. This we are now doing. *Four* P.M. —Retribution over, all right. We found our channel, buoyed it, and when she arrived, led her over without the loss of a moment. This is a great comfort, for if we had been obliged to leave her behind, it would have been a serious annoyance. Just before the shoal, we passed the " Pillar Hills," and are now off Taiping.

December 29th.—Eleven A.M.—We passed, at five P.M. yesterday, the scene of our second action of November 21, and anchored at about six. We are now approaching Nankin. I have sent O., Wade, Lay, and a Mr. W. (a missionary) ahead in the Dove, to land, if possible, at the first fort, with the view of going into the town and calling on the authorities. The Dove will then proceed past the other forts to an anchorage on the farther side of the city, to which point the Lee and Retribution will follow her. My emissaries will inform the Nankin authorities that I am pleased that they should have apologized for their scandalous conduct towards us on our way up; that we have no intention of meddling with them if they leave us alone; but that we intend to move ships up and down the river, and that they must not be molested. They have sent me a letter written on a roll of yellow silk, about three fathoms long. It seems to be a sort of rhapsody, in verse, with a vast infusion of their extraordinary theology. It is now snowing heavily, so we cannot see far ahead. It would, I think, be awkward for me to have any intercourse with the Rebel chiefs, so I do not, as at present advised, intend to land. My position on board this ship is a very amusing one. We are packed close, and it has been raining or snowing ever since we set out; but we all get on very well. . . . *One* P.M.—Off Nankin; between two forts above the town, one being on each side of the river. We seem to be about 400 or 500 yards from each, so that the river here is well commanded. My emissaries sent to request that we would await their return here. The scene is a good deal changed from what it was when I last saw it. Then, we were pouring shot and shell into the forts; now we are lying listlessly under their guns; a few idlers with umbrellas being alone visible. The ravages which we did, however, seem repaired, and the forts again pretty much in the degree of efficiency in which we found them; sufficient against their Chinese adversaries, though useless as against us. . . .

December 30th.—Eleven A.M.—We waited yesterday till dark, when Captain B. said he could remain no longer, and we moved on a few miles, and anchored in the midst of an Imperialist fleet. About seven P.M., the Dove rejoined us with the emissaries. It appears that they had a long way to go on horseback, some seven or eight miles before they reached the Yamun of the chief, who received them. They do not seem to have learnt much from him. He professed to be third in the hierarchy of the Rebel Government of Nankin, but was a rather commonplace person. He said that our bombardment had killed three officers and twenty men, and that they had beheaded the soldiers who fired at us! Arrangements were made for the free passage of vessels communicating with the Furious. They describe their ride through Nankin as if it had been one through a great park,—trees, and the streets wider than usual in China; but no trade is allowed, and the place seems almost deserted. There was not quite so much appearance of destruction, but more of desolation, than in any town previously visited by us. The officer who guided them to the Yamun asked Wade to take him away with us, and on being told that was impossible, applied for opium, saying that he smoked himself, and that about one in three of the force in Nankin did the same. Whether the original Taiping chief, "Hung-Seu-Chuen," is still alive or not, we have not been able to discover. Some say he remains shut up with about 300 wives. At any rate he is invisible. One of the Imperialist fleet (a steamer) telegraphed that she had letters for us, but we found only some newspapers. From the latest *Times*, of the 25th September, I gather that the Treaty is well received, and that F. went to Balmoral. . . . The country was covered with snow this morning, the thatched cottages and fir-woods peeping picturesquely out of the white landscape. It is calm and fair, however, and we are going at full speed. *Four* P.M.— We reached Chin-kiang Foo at about one. I begged Captain W. to take me on board the Dove; and while the Lee was coaling from the Retribution, we went down to Silver Island and buoyed the channel, while I walked up to the top of the island to look again at the magnificent view from the summit. In about an hour we had completed our work, went back to the Retribution, got her under weigh, and now we are already past the danger. We have also taken on board the Lee all the luggage which we had in our junk; so we are packed and laden like a Dover packet, but gett'ing on famously; and with one of Captain W.'s surveyors to pilot us, we shall make a push to reach Shanghae to-morrow. The only thing remarkable which I have observed to-day is the quantity of wild-fowl. I saw one flock this morning which was several miles long. It literally darkened the sky. I suppose the cold weather is driving them inwards from the sea.

December 31*st*.—We weighed anchor at about 5.30 A.M. Soon after, the Retribution consented to take our junk in tow, and we have been going on rapidly, leaving the other vessels nearly out of sight. At seven we passed our anchorage of the 15th November, at about eleven that of the 14th; but I fear we shall not reach Shanghae to-night. . . . I wish that some of the great men who consider gunboats useless for any purpose except doing little jobs for big ships, could see the Lee at present, conveying the whole *personnel* and *matériel* of this mission, servants and all, down an unknown river-navigation of 500 miles in length, and running the gauntlet of hostile forts on the way. *Five* P.M.

—I hardly expected to have to record another grounding, but so it is. We have been going on gallantly all day, leaving the other ships some ten miles behind us. We had passed the Lunshan Hills, off which we spent two days, and from which I sent you my last letter. We were abreast of Plover Point, when suddenly the water shoaled so much that we had to drop anchor. Alas! the ebbing tide was too strong for us, and drove us on a bank, where we are now sticking. If we get off before morning it will not matter much; but if the Retribution comes down and finds us here, we shall look horribly small.

January 1st, 1859.—Many, many returns of the New Year. It is a beautiful day, and we are just anchoring at Shanghae, at three P.M. As soon as the tide rose (about midnight) it lifted us off our shoal. We had to go cautiously sometimes to-day; but we have closed this eventful expedition successfully. I find that poor Gros was wrecked on his way to Hong-kong, and his wounded ship is now in this harbour, saluting me. I find no less than three mails awaiting me from home.

P.S.—January 6th.—Before midnight a fourth mail arrived. I have hardly had time to read my letters. I fear I cannot till next mail send you a map, to make this interminable letter intelligible. I trust and hope, too, that next mail will take you some specific intelligence respecting my return home. . . .

Shanghae.—January 17th.—The Furious and Cruiser arrived here safely on the 10th. . . . I have just accomplished the herculean task of looking over a two-months' supply of newspapers, and this occupation, interlarded with a certain number of letters and visits to and from the Imperial Commissioners, and to-day, an address from the British community of Shanghae, has pretty fully occupied my time. The home mail is due to-day, and I am anxiously waiting to learn from it what the Government intends to do about relieving me. . . . I trust that your many disappointments as to my return may have been somewhat relieved by the conviction that I am following the right course. This opening up of the East is not a light matter. . . . The comet was most magnificent here. Did I ever mention it in my letters? During the whole period of its visit in this quarter it had night after night a clear blue cloudless sky, spangled with stars innumerable, to disport itself in. . . . Canton is coming round to tranquillity as fast as we ever had any right to expect; but the absurd thing is that these funny people at Hong-kong are beginning to praise me! . . .

January 20th.—I had hardly written the words "Canton is coming round to tranquillity," when I heard that there had been fighting there again. It is a good thing in my opinion, as it will enable us to demonstrate our superiority to the Braves, if the General and Admiral improve the opportunity properly; not by a great deal of slaughter, that is quite unnecessary, but by promptitude, and striking a blow at the right moment. The Chinese do not care much about being killed, but they hate being frightened, and the knowledge of this idiosyncrasy of theirs is the key of the position. I have just written a letter to my friends the Imperial Commissioners here, which will, I think, shake their nerves considerably, and bring them to a manageable frame of mind. . . . Alas! no English letters. The mail had not reached Hong-kong when the steamer left. Yesterday I took a walk through the town of Shanghae with a missionary who is a very good *cicerone*. We went into a good many *ateliers* of silversmiths, ribbon-makers, tobacco manufacturers, carvers in wood, and the like. The Chinese are skilful manipulators, but they are singularly uninventive. Nothing can be more rude than their labour-saving processes. We visited also a foundling establishment. There was a drawer at the entrance in which the infants are deposited, as is, I believe, the case at Paris. The children seem tolerably cared for, but there were not many in the house. The greater portion are given out to nurse. We went also into a large inn or lodging-house, frequented by a respectable class of visitors—silk merchants, etc. The rooms seemed comfortable, quite as good as the accommodation provided for commercial travellers at an English inn. A good many books seemed to form part of the luggage of the occupant of each room that we entered. . . . It is very curious that I should have been engaged in so many enterprises of rather an out-of-the-way character since I have been out here. I confess that in my own opinion the voyage up the Yangtze is not the least important one. . . .

January 22*d.*—Mail arrived. F.'s appointment is very satisfactory, and I am sure it is the best the Government could have made for the public interest. It is a great comfort to me to know that he will wind up what I cannot finish. . . . I enclose a map, and an impromptu by your relative, Lieut. D. (a very nice fellow), sung at a jollification which the Staff, etc., had on the eve of our leaving the Furious behind at Kew-kiang. . . .

SONG.
IMPROMPTU BY LIEUTENANT D. OF H. M. S. FURIOUS.

To the swells of the squadron the noble Earl said,
The Furious is jammed for the river is sped;
Then gather around me, my Mission, and we
Will go down to Shanghae in the dark little Lee.
Come fill up the cup, come fill up the can,
We've polished off Yeh and we've polished off Tan;
Kweiliang and Hwashana have set their ports free,
And allowed us a trip up the glorious Yangtze.

> There are dangers by rocks, there are dangers by shoals,
> But the Lee down the yellow stream fearlessly bowls,
> And the Rebels, douce men, they just let her be,
> For they don't like the looks of the dark little Lee.
>   Come fill up the cup, etc.
>
> With dread and dismay they already have seen
> How we settled their hash at the walls of Nankeen,
> And the Furious and Cruiser ready will be
> To avenge any insult that's offered to she.
>   Come fill up the cup, etc.
>
> There are hills beyond Pentland and lands beyond Forth,
> Oft we'll think of our Chief in his home in the North;
> Sunny memories with him connected will be,
> Of Canton, the Peiho, and the Gulf Pecheli.
>   Come fill up the cup, etc.
>
> We brought you up safe both in body and bones,
> But we can't take you down, so we leave you to Jones,[1]
> And the folks at Shanghae will surprised be to see
> That the Mission are stowed in the dark little Lee.
>   Come fill up your cup, come fill up your can,
>   We got to Hankow, but we stuck at Kewkang;
>   But it will indeed be amazing to me
>   If we don't manage somehow to beat the Yangtze!

Shanghae.—January 25th.—After full consideration I have resolved to go at once to Hong-kong, and take the Canton difficulty in hand. A variety of circumstances lead me to the conclusion that the Court of Pekin is about to play us false. Ho, the Governor-General of the Two Kiang; the Tautai of this port; and the Treasurer of the district, all well-disposed to foreigners, have been gradually removed from the councils of the Commissioners. Some papers which we have seized also indicate that the Emperor is by no means reconciled to some of the most important concessions obtained in the Treaties. This row at Canton is therefore very opportune. I have taken a high tone, informed the Commissioners that I am off to the South to punish disturbers of the peace there, and that when I have taught them to respect treaties, I (or my successor) will return to settle matters still pending here, pacifically or otherwise as the Emperor may prefer. It is to be hoped that this language will bring them to their senses, or rather bring the Court to its senses, for I do not suppose that the Commissioners are so much to blame. I had already asked all the society here to a party for this evening, so it will be a farewell entertainment, and I shall embark as soon as it is over. I hope to catch the mail at Hong-kong. . . .

January 27th.—Four P.M.—We are off from Woosung. We

[1] Commander of the Lee.

started immediately after the party on the 25th, but after proceeding about fifty miles we met the Inflexible with stores for this ship, and I was obliged to agree to Captain O.'s proposal to turn back for them. This has lost us a day and a half. . . . I was not very well yesterday, and the day was rough. To-day I am better, and the weather is fine though very cold. The Inflexible is going to Jeddo, . . . and I have taken it on myself to authorize the Captain to offer to bring to England a couple of Japanese Ambassadors, whom the Yankees wish to catch and to carry across the Pacific to Yankee Land, in the hope of persuading them that their country whips all creation. I do not know that I shall succeed, but the experiment is worth making.

January 30*th.—Sunday.*—We are going on well, with a fair wind. I suppose we are about half-way to Hong-kong. . . . Eleven months have passed since we steamed up this sea on our way to Shanghae. What a busy eleven months!

February 1*st.*—Another month begun. On the 2d of March 1858 we left Hong-kong for the North. We shall probably anchor in that harbour again on the 2d February 1859. We have had fair wind but too much motion for writing. . . . There is a wonderful change of temperature. Last night late I stayed some time on deck inviting the breeze, which was balmy though strong, to beat upon me. Two war-steamers and a gunboat have just passed us on some expedition after pirates. It may be all right, but I fear we do some horrible injustices in this pirate-hunting. The system of giving our sailors a direct interest in captures is certainly a barbarous one, and the parent of much evil; though perhaps it may be difficult to devise a remedy. The result, however, is that not only are seizures often made which ought not to be made at all, but also duties are neglected which do not bring grist to the mill. B. once said to me in talking of the difficulty of exercising a police over even English vessels which carry coolies to foreign ports :—" Men-of-war have orders to seize vessels breaking the law, but as they are not prizes, and the captain if he seizes them wrongfully is liable to an action for damages, how can you expect them to act?" . . .

February 3*d.*—We reached Hong-kong at about eleven A.M. yesterday. The scenery is, I must say, striking, after some months' absence. The Admiral called on me. I called on Sir J. B. Both visits passed off well enough. . . . Having nothing to do at Hong-kong, I set off again this morning up the river to Canton. I hope that we may be able within the next fortnight to bring matters to a satisfactory state in that neighbourhood. I propose then to return, and await the mail of the 25th of

January, which will I think give me definite information respecting F.'s movements. The Hong-kong papers are still labouring hard to prove that I have done nothing since I came out here. . . . Your last letters are gone to Shanghae. . . .

Canton.—February 6*th.*—*Sunday.*—I have just returned from service on deck. . . . It has rained since we came here, but I landed both on Friday and yesterday. On the former day I went to the General's quarters. . . . He seems disposed to carry out my policy here. . . . A great number of houses in the vicinity of the military lines have been destroyed, but otherwise I do not see much change in the appearance of Canton. . . .

February 10*th.*—My letters to the 9th December have arrived. . . . I have nothing either from F. or the Government. . . . It is only by the last mail that I heard of F.'s appointment, and until then I knew nothing of what the Government intended to do, and nothing of what they expected me to do. . . .

February 11*th.*—I was interrupted yesterday by two merchants who came to call. I ought to tell you that on the 8th, a body of troops about 1000 strong started on an expedition into the interior, which was to take three days. I accompanied or rather preceded them on the first day's march, about twelve miles from Canton. We rode through a very pretty country, passing by the village of Sheksing, where there was a fight a fortnight ago. The people were very respectful, and apparently not alarmed by our visit. At the place where the troops were to encamp for the night, a cattle fair was in progress, and our arrival did not seem to interrupt the proceedings. I am not without hope that the Canton Government arrangements will be ultimately justified. . . . I do not think I shall now go to Manilla or Borneo, but proceed straight home when I can get away. . . .

February 13*th.*—The mail of the 25th December is come, but with no letter for me except one from L., written after his visit to you, which ought to have reached me by the mail before. . . . The military expedition into the country was entirely successful. The troops were received everywhere as friends, considering what has been of yore the state of feeling in this province towards us. I think this almost the most remarkable thing which has happened since I came here. Would it have happened if I had given way to those who wished me to carry fire and sword through all the country villages ? Or if I had gone home, and left the winding-up of these affairs in the hands of others? . . . I say all this because I am anxious that you should appreciate the motives which have made me prolong my stay in this quarter. . . .

February 14*th.*—This letter must be despatched to-day. I

await anxiously the next mail. The next mail! Always the next mail, you will say; but really I think this next mail must make my way clearer. . . .

H.M.S. Furious.—Passing Whampoa.—February 15th.—. . . .
I started this forenoon with the intention of joining the General in an expedition which he is about to make up the West River, towards the interior of the Kwan-tung province. I found, however, on inquiry that I should be obliged to go a great part of the way in this ship alone, as the gunboats and the force take a short cut, and although I am not much afraid either of Chinamen or shoals, yet, if I went aground or had to fight, the world of my critics might say that I had exposed myself needlessly, etc. etc. . . . In short I felt that to get into a scrape by following the General up the West River, was a different thing altogether from getting into difficulty on such an expedition as that of the Yangtze. So I changed my plan of operations, sent back the gunboat attached to me, and resolved to visit instead the port of Hainan, the southernmost port opened by the new Treaty. This expedition, if no accident happens, ought not to occupy more than eight or ten days. I shall be again at Hongkong before the next mail from England arrives, and meanwhile I shall be more usefully employed in visiting a place which others are not going to, than I should be in accompanying a military expedition.

February 17th.—We reached Macao yesterday morning, and I landed to visit the Portuguese Governor and M. de Bourboulon. The former was absent. From the latter I gathered that nothing had been received from the French Government as to their intentions respecting an Ambassador for Pekin. I visited the Garden of Camoëns, and wandered among the narrow up-and-down streets, which with the churches and convents, and air of quiet *vétusté*, remind one of a town on the continent of Europe. After some hours I re-embarked, and this morning we started for Hainan, and are now going through a calm sea, with a number of bleak hilly islands on our right. . . . The only thing I have heard of F. is a rumour that he was to leave England early this month. The Magicienne goes to Singapore to meet him. . . .

February 19th.—Yesterday morning we reached the island of Hainan, a sandy flat-looking coast. At 9.30, as we were at breakfast, we came to a sudden stop, and put about, having discovered shallow soundings and a coral rock, an unpleasant hint. . . . In short Captain O. was of opinion that with the wind blowing on shore and very imperfect charts, it would not be wise to go on to the port of Hainan, and we put about, steering to the coast of the Kwan-tung province. It was rough, and

I felt otherwise out of sorts. . . . This morning we sighted the coast, and have been going along it all day. It is bold and hilly, but the hills, as is the case generally in this part of China, are sadly in want of trees. We have now anchored for the night in a quiet harbour named Hailing-shan. I did not land, as there does not seem to be anything to see. There are a good many fishing-boats, and two junks heavily armed, which some of my friends would be glad to vote pirates. . . .

February 20th.—Sunday.—We have just anchored in a quiet harbour, on the island of St. John, or Sancian, as Huc calls it; the first place in China where the Portuguese settled. Here, too, St. François Xavier died. I should land and look at his tomb if I thought it was in this part of the island, but it is late (five P.M.), and a long way to pull. It has been blowing all day. . . . We have never been far from the shore, which has the same character as yesterday, perhaps even bolder.

February 22d.—Seven A.M.—We are starting from our anchorage off Luntoo Island, and may reach Hong-kong about ten. I trust that this visit may be the wind-up of my affairs, and that the English mail may decide me to start at once for home. I cannot expect much satisfaction at Hong-kong, where the people are ill disposed, and where the business I have to transact, the indemnity and the factory site, is essentially so troublesome. Nevertheless, these disagreeables must be faced. . . . This morning is almost cold, but we cannot count on any continuance of cool weather now in this quarter.

February 23d.—Hong-kong.—We arrived yesterday at about noon. I have paid the usual visits of ceremony, and to-day a great number of merchants, etc., have been off to call on me. . . . Meanwhile I have good news from the North. As I was walking on the deck this morning at eight A.M., Mr. Lay suddenly made his appearance. He had come by the mail-packet from Shanghae, with a letter from the Imperial Commissioners, announcing that the seal of Imperial Commission had been taken from Hwang, the Governor-General of this province, and given to Ho, the Governor-General of the provinces in which Shanghae is situated. Lay further states that his friend the Taoutae informed him that they are prepared to receive the new ambassador peacefully at Pekin, when he goes to exchange ratifications. If so, I think that I shall be able to return with the conviction that the objects of my mission have been accomplished.

February 26th.—No mail yet from England, and this letter goes to-morrow. It is very vexatious. . . .

Canton River.—March 3d.—I am really and truly off on my way to England, though I can hardly believe that it is so. The last mail brought me not a word either from F. or about his plans; only, what was very satisfactory, the approval of Government of my arrangement respecting the residence of the British Minister in China. I have, however, determined to start, and to take my chance of him somewhere *en route*. Unless I were to go back to Shanghae, I could not do much more here now; and if I put off, I shall have the monsoon against me, and great heat in the Red Sea. Having resolved on this course, I invited the Hong-kong merchants to come up with me to Canton, to look at the several factory sites. In their usual arrogant way, they have been dictating the choice of a site to me, abusing me for not fixing upon it; and I found out that very few of them had even taken the trouble of looking at the ground. In short, I found that in my short visits, I had seen a great deal more of the sites than they had done, who live constantly on the spot, and are personally interested in the matter. I started from Hong-kong yesterday morning, and to-day I went over the ground with them. The rain poured, and I got a good wetting. . . . As I was starting from the town in a gunboat to rejoin my ship, I met the military and naval expedition, which has been absent for more than two weeks, returning. I had not time to communicate with the officers, but they seemed in good spirits. It is a curious wind-up of this most eventful mission, that as I am starting from China, I should meet an Anglo-French force returning from a pacific invasion into the very heart of the province of Kwan-tung!—the *pépinière* of the Canton braves, of whom we have heard so much. I was not comfortable at Hong-kong. . . . The weather, too, was most oppressive, hot and muggy, so that I am glad to get away, independently of the fact of its being *homewards*. . . . On the 1st of this month, I was invited to dine at the mess of the Royals, and to attend an amateur theatre afterwards. The play was put off, however, in consequence of the very shocking death of an engineer officer, who blew out his brains with his revolver —accidentally it is hoped. *Six* P.M.—We have anchored, on account of the thickness of the weather. . . . I have two letters from you, one of which ought to have reached me by a previous mail. . . .

March 4*th.*—*Eleven* A.M.—We are going on at a good pace. A cool day. I have been calculating that if F. does not leave England till the mail of the 25th February, I may, by pushing on, catch him at Galle. This would be a great point, . . . but as I am left in the dark, I must push on and take my chance. . . .

Sunday, March 16*th.*—We have been making about nine knots, which is as much as the Furious is good for. It has been roughish till this afternoon, when it is charming. All our sails are set. The heat tropical, but bearable in the breeze. . . .

March 8th.—We are passing Pulo Lapata, a bald, solitary rock, standing in the midst of the China Sea, the resort of sea-fowl, as is indicated by its guano-like appearance. There it stands day after day, and year after year, affronting the scorching beams of this tropical sun. All ships pass by it between Singapore and China. So I am looking at it for the fourth time—the last time, we may hope. We have made fully 200 miles a day —a great deal for this ship. . . .

March 10th.—We are now very near the Line, and the breeze has nearly failed us; so you may imagine we are not very cool, but we hope to reach Singapore to-morrow. These Tropics are very charming when they do not broil one; and I passed a pleasant hour last night on the top of the paddle-box, with a balmy air floating over my face from the one side, a crescent moon playing hide-and-seek behind a cloud on the other, and right above me a legion of bright stars, shining through the atmosphere as if they could pierce one with their glance. . . .

March 11th.—We have passed the Horsburgh lighthouse, and entered the Straits. Wooded banks on either side, diversified by hillocks, and a ship or two, give some animation to the scene. It is very hot, and I have been on the paddle-box getting what air I can, and watching a black wall of cloud covered with fleecy masses, which rests on the bank to our right, and seems half inclined to sweep over us with one of those refreshing pelts of which we had a succession last night. It is this habit of showers which renders the vicinity of the Line more bearable than the summer heat of other parts within the Tropics. However, the cloud sticks to the shore, so I have come down to write this line to you. . . .

Singapore.—*Sunday, March* 13*th.*—*Seven* A.M.—This place looks wonderfully green and luxuriant after China. The variety of costumes and colours too, Malay, Indian, Chinese, etc.; and the pretty villas perched on each hillock among flowering trees, give it a festival air. Heavy showers of rain also keep the temperature down. I have missed the mail of January 25th, and am hurrying on to Penang in the hope of getting that of February 9th there. . . . 3.30 P.M.—I went to church and embarked immediately after; and here we are, about ten miles from Singapore, going well through a calm sea, with a slight breeze rather against us. Twenty months ago I left this place at about the same hour with poor Peel for Calcutta. . . .

Penang.—*March* 15*th.*—*Noon.*—Arrived here half an hour ago. The steamer from England not yet come. It is pleasant to look upon this hilly island, covered with cocoa-nut trees and other tropical vegetation, and there is a breeze to temper the heat. . . .

March 16*th.*—*Ten* A.M.—Mail arrived at three P.M. yesterday. No letters from you; no papers but a few old ones. It is evident that my bag is entirely neglected. . . . The Queen's speech, etc., I have seen through the civility of others. After I had received my bag, it was rumoured that somewhere or other there was a despatch marked "Malmesbury" and "immediate," to my address. At last it was brought to me. It proved to be a telegram forwarded by the Marseilles Consul, saying, that "Lord M.'s letter to me had not been sent, and that if this telegram reached me before I had left China, I was to wait F.'s arrival at Canton." . . . At any rate, I am going on to Galle. If I miss him it will not be my fault. . . . I went up to the top of Penang Hill, to sleep there, last night. It is a beautiful ride through the most luxuriant jungle growth. Trees of all sizes; leaves of all dimensions; flowers of all colours. From the top a magnificent view. But I have told you of it before. We did not dine till after nine P.M., and had to get up at five A.M. this morning. I walked down the hill; rather hard work for the knees. I did not find it as cool on the top of the hill as I expected. . . . .

March 19*th.*—*Two* P.M.— . . . We have accomplished fully our 200 miles a day since we left Penang, and hope to reach Galle on the 22d, where I may have to wait for F. . . . We are now crossing the Bay of Bengal. Sea on all sides. . . .

March 20*th.*—*Sunday.*—*Eleven* A.M.—Captain O. thinks we may reach Galle to-morrow. . . . I have just returned from our ship church. It was rather hot, and too much rolling motion to be quite pleasant. . . .

March 21*st.*—*Six* A.M.—On the starboard side we have a high hill, popularly known as the Elephant's Hill, and out to sea not far from it the "Basses" Rocks. So we are actually off Ceylon, about seventy miles from Galle. It is by far the fastest run ever made by the Furious. . . . I have been an hour on deck watching the great bright stars eclipse themselves, and the sun break through the clouds right astern of us. It is a lovely day, and we are a little bent over by a breeze from the shore of Ceylon, along which we are now running. *Noon.*—Just anchored at Galle, after a run of about 270 miles in twenty-four hours. The English mail of February 25th not yet in. . . . We are surrounded by curious boats about two feet wide, prevented from capsizing by *outriggers*—beams of wood *floating* on the water on one side of them, and attached to them by poles of about eight feet in length. I believe these boats are wonderfully fast and safe. It is *very* hot, and I shall go on shore if I can. . . .

March 25*th*.—The mail came yesterday, Sir C. Trevelyan on board. A letter from Lord Malmesbury dated February 3d (this being the mail of February 25th), which seems to say that F. was to leave by the second packet in February. Nothing later from the F. O. or from F. . . . I was very nearly embarking in despair for Suez, when I found in the *Home News* that places were taken for the 4th March for F. I must therefore remain here till that mail arrives. I have two letters from you, one ought again to have arrived by the last mail, and the newspapers are generally a month old! You have borne your long period of suspense, while I was up the Yangtze, very courageously, and I hope my letters received since will have cheered you. . . . But this one more, as I end it by begging you to write to Paris, . . . to say whether you will meet me there. I think I shall be obliged to go on to Suez by the Furious, for the steamers are all crammed. . . . I finish this to-day, as I intend to go to Colombo to-morrow, to visit Sir H. Ward, and see something of this island. . . .

Colombo.—*Sunday, March* 27*th*.—I found I could send my letter from here. We came yesterday to this place. A drive of seventy-two miles through an almost uninterrupted grove of cocoa-nut trees, interspersed with bread-fruit, jack-fruit, and other foliage, with occasional gleams of the *Gloriosa superba*. The music of the ocean waves hissing and thundering on the shore accompanied us in all our journey. The road was good and the coach tolerable, so it was pleasant enough. To-day the heat is very great; hardly bearable at church. All Sir H. Ward's family are on the hill—Newra Elyia—some 6000 feet above the sea; this being the hottest season in Ceylon. My writing is not very good, for I cannot sit still for the heat. I am walking about the room in very light attire, taking up my pen from time to time to indite a few words.

March 28*th*.—There is a great dinner here to-night. To-morrow I go to Kandy, and remain there till Saturday, when I return to Galle, so as to meet the mail from England. . . .

H. M. S. Furious.—*At Sea, April* 9*th*.—Will this letter be delivered to you by the post or by the writer in person? *Chi sa!* . . . You will like to have a complete record of my experiences during my long absence. I am now again at sea, and I cannot say how this fact rejoices me. I was tired of Ceylon; and my longing to get home increases as the prospect of my doing so becomes more real. I was ill, too, at Ceylon. The heat was very great; and under O.'s guidance I was, I fear, somewhat imprudent. On the day after I despatched my last letter to you from Colombo, I started for Kandy, a pretty little country town seated in the centre of a circle of hills. I reached it at five P.M., time enough to walk about the very beautiful grounds of the "Pavilion," the Governor's residence. Next day, after seeing the shrine which contains the famous tooth of Buddha, I set off for the mountains, and reached a coffee estate of Baron Delmar's at about six P.M. We found ourselves in a fine cool climate, at about 3000 feet above the sea. That night, however, I felt a shiver as I went to bed. I had a bad headache next morning, and when I arrived at Newra Elyia, the famous sanatarium, 6000 feet above the sea, I was obliged to go to bed, and send for the doctor. I could not remain quiet, however, as the packet from England might be at Galle on the 3d; so I had to hurry down on Friday from the mountain to Kandy and Colombo, where I arrived on Saturday evening more dead than alive. Sir H. Ward's doctor declared me to be labouring under an attack of jungle fever. . . . I sent for the Furious, which conveyed me from Colombo to Galle on Monday the 4th. F. did not arrive till the 6th; so all ended well. It was an unspeakable comfort to me to meet F. at last. We had a day to talk over our affairs, as he did not proceed till the afternoon of the 7th. . . . I am pleased with Ceylon, notwithstanding my mishaps. For a tropical climate it is healthy and bearable; but we happened to be there at the very hottest season. At Newra Elyia it is really cold, and at the height of the coffee estates, very tolerable to vegetate in.

April 15*th.*—We have been getting on very well, over a sea as smooth as glass; but it is very hot, and I have found writing out of the question. Besides which, I have not quite got over my Ceylon attack. . . .

April 18*th.*—The most wonderful weather; a dead calm all the way between Asia and Africa. We sighted Cape Guardafui yesterday, soon after noon, and passed it before dark. In truth, however, it is never dark, for the moon has just passed the full, and the nights are glorious. The heat is, however, too great for me, and I am not yet well. To-day is cooler, with a breeze into my cabin. We are within 200 miles of Aden. . . .

April 20*th.*—*Four* P.M.—Just passed Perim, and the entrance of the Babelmandeb Straits! A fine breeze right aft. We reached Aden yesterday, just within our ten days from Galle. I found there my captain of the Ava, in charge of the P. and O. coal; so I secured his good graces, and our coaling was accomplished in a few hours. We started again this morning at five. I found a mail, with your letters to March 25th. . . . Your patience was beginning to be nearly exhausted! This morning as we were starting, the mail to Bombay from England arrived with news to April 4th. I learn from it that the Government is beat, but nothing more. . . . I landed yesterday on that most barren of rocks, Aden, and dined with the Commandant. He was living in a sort of extensive hut, near the landing-place, on an eminence. I found it wonderfully cooler than it was about three weeks later, in 1857. Then, however, he was living at the Cantonment. Hearing that Captains Speke and Burton, who have been making an exploratory journey into the interior of Africa, were at Aden on their way home, I offered them a passage in the Furious. The former accepted. He gave us interesting accounts of his journeyings, where no foreigner had ever been before. He went from Zanzibar to a lake about 600 miles in the interior, out of which he supposes the Nile to flow.

Easter-day.— . . . We are sensibly passing out of the Tropics. There is already something bracing in the air, which will, I trust, set me right again. We have been progressing with our usual good fortune, and there is every probability that we may reach Suez in two days.

April 26th.—It blew a good deal yesterday—a head wind. We passed Mount Horeb with the light of the setting sun upon it. This morning there is less sea. We may reach Suez to-night. . . .

SECOND MISSION TO CHINA.

1860.

Peninsular and Oriental Steamer Valetta.—Sunday, April 29th, 1860.—*Off the coast of Sardinia.*—I embarked, with a heavy heart, from the Dover pier, after leaving you, at eleven P.M. . . . Captain Smithett took great charge of me, and deposited me on a sofa in a cabin from which the rest of the world was excluded. It was very cold, and blowing, and a good deal of sea, so I thought it best to remain until I was roused by being told that we were entering the port of Calais. I went on deck, and found that we were threading our way, under a bright starlit sky, between two piers, so close to each other that we had some difficulty in passing clear of the fishing-boats we met, which were sallying forth for their morning's work. The custom-house officials were very civil, informed us that they had received orders from Paris to facilitate our progress in every way. We got a compartment to ourselves, and reached Paris, without any adventure, at the proper time. There, at the station, were A., etc., and a *facteur* from the Embassy. I went off at once with A. to the Lyons Station. . . . There I breakfasted, and some of my Staff joined us; and I had a few minutes' conversation with O. and with Wm. G. . . . We were magnificently lodged on the Lyons Railway, having two compartments reserved for us. We dined at Dijon, supped at Lyons, and reached Marseilles soon after six next morning. The Consul there gave me the telegram from the Foreign Office, telling me that nothing had arrived by the mail of Friday to stay my progress. From Marseilles we started at about eight A.M. We rolled a great deal all day, so that any attempt at writing was out of the question. During the night we entered the Straits of Bonifacio, and when I got up this morning I found Sardinia on our right, and a perfectly calm sea. We had prayers at eleven, and I am now writing to you at one P.M. The sea still calm, but a few drops of rain are falling from time to time. So much for my chronicle; but I write it with a certain feeling of repugnance and self-reproach. It was very well on the occasion of my first voyage, when I wished to share with you whatever charm the novelty of the scenes through which I was passing might supply to mitigate the pain of our separation. But this time there is no such pretext for the record of our daily progress. I am going through scenes which I have visited before, on an errand of which the issue is almost more than doubtful. When I see my friend Gros I feel myself doubly guilty, in having consented to undertake this task, and thus compelled him to make the same sacrifice. And F.—What will he think of my coming out? It is a dark sky all around. There is only one bright side to the picture. It is very unlikely that my absence can be of long duration. If such ideas were to prevail in England as those which are embodied in an article on China, which is to appear in the forthcoming *Blackwood*, of which I believe Captain O. is the author, I might be detained long enough in that quarter; but these are not the views of the public or the statesmen of England. What is desired is a speedy settlement, on reasonable terms,—as good terms as possible; but let the settlement be speedy. This, I think, is the fixed idea of all. Gros tells me that when he took leave the Emperor grasped both his hands, thanked him with effusion, and said that not one man in fifty would make such a sacrifice as he (Gros) was doing. I do not think that we shall hear in Egypt anything to arrest our progress, but it is possible we may do so at Aden. The ultimatum was sent to Pekin on the 8th of March. The mail, which we met in Egypt, will have left Shanghae about the 20th of March. I do not think that an answer to the ultimatum will have been received by that time; but we may meet a later mail at Aden. If the ultimatum has been accepted, shall we be able to turn back at once? This is doubtful. I think that we must assure ourselves that it is not only accepted in terms but actually carried out in practice, before we can consider our mission closed. Under the most favourable circumstances I think that we shall have to go on to Galle or Singapore. I believe that there is uninterrupted telegraphic communication now between Alexandria and Galle *viâ* India. If so, a telegram from England to Marseilles repeated at Alexandria ought to reach Galle in about seven or eight days. This is worth remembering. The consul at Marseilles offered to forward any telegram from you, . . . or I daresay they would send me a message through the Foreign Office,—if only to tell me how you all are. . . .

Monday, 30th.—I do not know whether I shall do much more

to this letter before I reach Malta, for we are both rolling and pitching, which is not favourable to writing. The climate has now changed. It is very near perfection in point of temperature. If we could only keep it so all the way! We expect to reach Malta this evening, and remain about four hours. Where are you now? . . . Have you returned to your desolate home? I think I see B. looking up to you with his thoughtful eyes, and dear little L. putting pointed questions, and, in her arch way, saying such kind and tender words! . . . You must continue to write, as you did last time, all you are doing and thinking, that I may reproduce, as faithfully as I can, the life which you are living. I do the same by you, though it is with a more leaden pen than formerly. . . . Poor Gros has retired to his cabin in order to take a horizontal position. Many of my companions are in the same way. I must finish this later. . . . *One* P.M.—We have had a most disagreeable day, and, to crown our misfortunes, the Vectis, with the homeward mails, which we expected to have met at Malta, has just passed us. This letter will not, therefore, reach you till much later than I had hoped; perhaps too late to enable you to profit by my suggestion about telegraphing. . . .

May 3*d*.-- . . . We are to reach Alexandria to-night or early to-morrow; and if the Simla has had a good passage, she will be in waiting for us at Suez, and we shall proceed at once to join her. In that case I shall have to post this letter to-night or to-morrow morning. As we reached Malta at nine P.M. on the 30th, I did not attempt to visit the authorities, but contented myself with a stroll through the streets and a supper at the hotel; re-embarking at about midnight; soon after which we were off again. There was a good deal of sea at first, and Tuesday was not comfortable; but the weather improved yesterday, and to-day it is a dead calm, the thermometer about 80° in the shade. The only person I saw at Malta was Charles Elliot, and the only news we heard was that the Sardinian fleet had visited Palermo, an important incident if it be true. What shall we hear at Alexandria? Shall we find any intelligence from China which will enable me to surprise you by a sudden return? I hardly think so. . . . Are you still shivering in the cold, while I am gliding through the calm sea under an awning, and going against a breeze sufficiently light to do no more than fan us pleasantly? If it would never go beyond this, there is certainly something very delightful in such a climate. The clear atmosphere, bright stars, light nights, and soft air; and to be wafted along through all this, as we now are, at the rate of some twelves miles an hour, with so little motion that we hardly know that we are making progress. It will be a different story,

I fear, when we get into the Red Sea, where we may expect a wind behind us, and around us the hot air of the Desert! . . . *Six* P.M.—We are still making twelve knots an hour, and are sure to arrive at an early hour to-morrow. I shall therefore put up this letter to be posted at Alexandria. . . . I have been employing myself for a good part of to-day in a sad work. I took with me a number of letters of very old date, and have been looking over them, and tearing up a great part of them, and throwing them overboard. I thought it would be an occupation suited to this heavy tropical sea-life. I cannot sit in my cabin, for it is too hot, and I have only a small port-hole out of reach; so I have been obliged to instal myself in a quiet nook on the deck for my work. I shall be sorry when it is over, as it is also soothing, and brings back many pleasing memories which had nearly faded away. . . . Some few I keep, because they are landmarks of my past life. . . .

May 4th.—Six A.M.—*Alexandria.*—Nothing at all from China, so we proceed in an hour or two to Cairo *en route* for Suez. . . .

Cairo, May 4th.—Five P.M.—Just arrived here after a very hot and dusty drive of seven hours, Baron Gros and I installed *tête-à-tête* in a magnificent carriage of the Pacha's. As I have seen Cairo, and as I consider it a sort of crime to pass through Egypt thrice without visiting the Pyramids, I have resolved to set off to-night at nine o'clock, sleep there, and see the sunrise from the top of the great Pyramid to-morrow. I shall sleep in a tomb, with a mummy for a pillow.

On board the Steamer Simla, off Suez.—May 5th.—Five P.M.— We are about to start in a few moments. Our night at the Pyramids was, beyond anything I could have anticipated, impressive. I cannot attempt to give you an account of it now; but the drive across the Desert to-day was the hottest experience I ever made. The south wind was literally like a blast from a furnace, and although Gros and I had the Pacha's carriage to ourselves, it was hardly possible to endure. This seems a magnificent ship, and not many passengers in proportion to its size. This letter will go by the first chance from Alexandria. . . .

Steamer Simla.—May 9th.—I had only a few moments to write before we left Suez, and my writing, such as it was, I performed under difficulties, as the bustle of passengers finding their cabins, and conveying to them their luggage, or such portions of it as they could rescue from its descent into the hold, was going on all around me. I had, therefore, only time to tell you that our visit to the Pyramids had been a success. It was one of the greatest which I ever achieved in that line. It came about in this way: When Baron Gros and I, accompanied by a gentleman called *Betts Bey* (he is the chief director of the railway, and all such officials are *Beys* in Egypt), were journeying in our Pachalic state-carriage from Alexandria to Cairo, a question arose as to how we were to spend the few hours which we should have to remain at the latter place. I expressed a desire to see the Pyramids, as I had witnessed all the other lions of Cairo. But Betts Bey observed, that to go there during the day, at this season of the year, was a service of considerable danger, the risk of sunstroke being more than usually great. We were, in fact, traversing Egypt during the period (of about six weeks' duration) when the wind from the south blows, and the only air one receives is like the blast of a furnace heavily charged with sand. He added, however, that it was not impossible to go to the Pyramids at night, remain there till dawn, see the sunrise from the summit, and return before the great heats of the day. When I found myself at Cairo I proposed to my *entourage* that we should undertake this expedition. My proposal was eagerly accepted, especially by "Our own Correspondent," Mr. Bowlby, who is a remarkably agreeable person, and has become very much one of our party. It was arranged that we should dine at the *table-d'hôte* at seven P.M., start at nine, in carriages to the crossing of the Nile (about four miles), and on donkeys from Gieja (about six miles). The Pasha's state-coach came to the door at the appointed hour; we started, our own party, Mr. Bowlby, Captain F., and M. de B., Gros' secretary; Gros himself, having twice seen the Pyramids, declined going with us. The moon was very nearly full, and but for the honour of the thing we might have dispensed with the torch-bearers, who ran before the carriage and preceded the donkeys, after we adopted that humbler mode of locomotion. Our row across the river to the chant of the boatman invoking the aid of a sainted dervish, and our ride through the fertile borders of the Nile, covered with crops and palm-trees, were very lovely, and after about an hour and a half from Cairo we emerged upon the Desert. The Pyramids seemed then almost within reach of our outstretched arms, but lo! they were in fact some four miles distant. We kept moving on at a sort of ambling walk; and the first sign of our near approach was the appearance of a crowd of Arabs who poured out of a village to offer us their aid in various ways. We had been told before we started that a party who had visited the Pyramids the night before, had been a good deal victimized by these Arabs, who, alas! in these degenerate days, have no other mode of indulging their predatory propensities than by exacting the greatest possible amount of "backshish" from travellers who visit the Pyramids. We pushed on over the heaps of sand and *débris*,

M

or probably covered-up tombs, which surround the base of the Pyramids, when we suddenly came in face of the most remarkable object on which my eye ever lighted. Somehow or other I had not thought of the Sphinx till I saw her before me. There she was in all her imposing magnitude, crouched on the margin of the Desert, looking over the fertile valley of the Nile, and her gaze fixed on the east as if in earnest expectation of the sunrising. And such a gaze! The mystical light and deep shadows cast by the moon, gave to it an intensity which I cannot attempt to describe. To me it seemed a look, earnest, searching, but unsatisfied. For a long time I remained transfixed, endeavouring to read the meaning conveyed by this wonderful eye, but I was struck after a while by what seemed a contradiction in the expression of the eye and of the mouth. There was a singular gentleness and hopefulness in the lines of the mouth, which appeared to be in contrast with the anxious eye. Mr. Bowlby, who was a very *sympathique* inquirer into the significancy of this wonderful monument, agreed with me in thinking that the upper part of the face spoke of the intellect striving, and striving vainly, to solve the mystery—(What mystery? the mystery shall we say of God's universe or of man's destiny?)--while the lower indicated a moral conviction that all must be well, and that this truth would in good time be made manifest.

We could hardly tear ourselves away from this fascinating spectacle to draw nearer to the Great Pyramid, which stood beside us, its outline sharply traced in the clear atmosphere. We walked round and round it, thinking of the strange men whose ambition to secure immortality for themselves had expressed itself in this giant creation. The enormous blocks of granite brought from one knows not where, built up one knows not how; the form selected solely for the purpose of defying the assaults of time; the contrast between the conception embodied in these constructions, and the talk of the frivolous race by whom we were surrounded, and who seemed capable of no thought beyond a desire for daily "backshish,"—all this seen and felt under the influence of the dim moonlight was very striking and impressive. We spent some time in moving from place to place along the shadow cast by the Pyramid along the sand, and observing the effect produced by bringing the moon sometimes to its apex and sometimes to other points on its outline. I felt no disposition to exchange for sleep the state of dreamy half-consciousness in which I was wandering about; but at length I lay down on the shingly sand, with a block of granite for a pillow, and passed an hour or two, sometimes dozing, sometimes wakeful, till one of our attendants informed me that the sun would shortly rise, and that it was time to commence to ascend the Pyramid, if we intended to witness from its summit his first appearance. We had intended to spend the night in the tombs, but it was so hot that we were only too glad to select the spot in which we could get the greatest amount of air. A very soft and gentle breeze, wafted across the Desert from an unknown distance, fanned me as I slept. The ascent was, I confess, a much more formidable undertaking than I had anticipated, and our French friend, M. de B., gave in after attempting a few steps. The last words which had passed between him and me before we retired to rest, were interchanged as we were standing in front of the Sphinx, and were characteristic: *Ah que c'est drôle!* was the reassuring exclamation which fell from his lips while we were then transfixed and awestruck. As far as the ascent of the Pyramid was concerned, I am not sure but that I was sometimes tempted to follow his example, when I found how great was the effort required to mount up, in the hot air, the huge blocks of granite, and the unpleasantness of feeling every now and then with what facility one might topple downwards. This sensation was most disagreeably felt when, as generally happened at any very critical place, my Arab friends, who were helping me up, began to talk of "backshish," and to insinuate that a small amount given at once, and before the ascent was completed, would be particularly acceptable. However, after awhile the summit was reached. I am not sure that it repaid the trouble; at any rate, I do not think I should ever wish to make the ascent again. We had a horizon all around tinted very much like Turner's early pictures, and becoming brighter and more variegated as the dawn advanced, until it melted into day. Behind, and on two sides of us, was the barren and treeless Desert, stretching out as far as the eye could reach. Before us, the fertile valley of the Nile; the river meandering through it, and, in the distance, Cairo, with its mosques and minarets, the highest, the Citadel Mosque, standing out boldly upon the horizon. It was a fine view, and had a character of its own, but still it was not in kind very different from other views which I have seen from elevated points in a flat country. It does not stand forth among my recollections as a spectacle unique, and never to be forgotten, as that of the night before does. Very soon after the sun rose, the heat became painful on our elevated seat, and we hastened to descend—an operation somewhat difficult, but not so serious as the ascent had been. We mounted our donkeys, and after paying a farewell visit to the Sphinx, we returned to Cairo as we had come, all agreeing that our expedition was one of the most agreeable and interesting we had ever made. I confess that it was with something of fear and trembling that I returned to the Sphinx that morning. I feared that the impressions which I had received the night before might be effaced by the light of day. But it was not so. The lines were fainter, and less deeply marked, but I found, or thought I found, the same meaning in them still. When I determined to visit the Pyramids, I took advantage of Betts Bey's offer (on behalf of the Pacha), that we should have a special train to take us to Suez. We started from Cairo at noon, after having had baths and breakfast, and submitted to the hands of an Egyptian barber, for all our luggage had been sent on before us. I also received a visit from the Consul-General, Mr. Colquhoun, who came from Alexandria to see me. . . . The journey through the Desert was tremendous. It was impossible to let the air in, or at least to sit in the draught; it was so heated. We embarked at five, and sailed at eight; since which time till now (one P.M., May 10th), we have had a perfectly smooth sea, with enough head-wind to temper the heat a little. There is a little more wind and movement to-day, but not enough to speak of. We are now passing some islands, and are nearly opposite to Mocha; to-morrow at an early hour we shall probably reach Aden. Shall we find any Chinese news there? And if we do, what will be its character? We have not yet heard a syllable to induce us to think that matters will be settled without a conflict, but then we have seen nothing official. . . . We met, at the station-house on the Nile, between Alexandria and Cairo, the passengers by the last Calcutta mail-steamer. There were some from China among them, but I could gather from them nothing of any interest. It was a curious scene, by the way, that meeting;—260 first-class passengers, including children, pale and languid looking, thrown into a great barn-like refectory, in which were already assembled our voyage companions (we ourselves had a separate room), jovial looking, and with roses in their cheeks, which they are doubtless hastening to offer at the shrine of the sun. These two opposing currents, bearing such legible records of the climes from which they severally came, met for a moment on the banks of the Nile, time enough to interchange a few hasty words, and then rushed on in opposite directions. As I am not like the Englishman in *Eöthen*, who passes his countryman in the Desert without accosting him, I had as much talk as I could with all the persons coming from China whom I could find, though, as I said, without obtaining any information of value.

May 11*th.*—*Seven* A.M.—We are approaching Aden, and the day is hot and sultry and calm, as days at Aden always are. Before I retired last night, I saw, through the starlight (we have little moon now), Perim. We passed it on the opposite side from that on which I had on a former occasion passed it,—on the right of the island, instead of the left. On the right is an excellent safe channel, eleven miles wide; so that it will be impossible to command the entrance of the Red Sea from Perim. There is a good anchorage on this side; so says our captain; but of course we could not see it. I am sorry we passed it so late, as I should have liked Gros to have seen it, in order that he might calm the susceptibilities of his Government in respect to its formidable character. Before nightfall we saw the place where the Alma was wrecked. I enclose a little bit of a plant which I gathered on my return from the Pyramids. The botanist on board says it is a species of camomile. It is a commonplace plant, with a little blue flower, but I took a fancy to it, because it had the pluck to venture further into the Desert, and to approach nearer the Pyramids than any other which I saw.

On Shore at Aden.—Noon. I am at the house of Captain Playfair, who represents the Resident during his absence. A very pleasant breeze is blowing through the wall of reeds or bamboo, which encloses the verandah in which I am writing. I am most agreeably disappointed by the temperature; and, strange to say, both Captain P. and his wife do not complain of Aden! So it is with all who live here. And yet when one looks at the place, dry as a heap of ashes, glared upon by a tropical sun, without a single blade of grass to repose the eye, or a drop of moisture from above to cool the air, save only about once in two years, when the sluices of Heaven are opened, and the torrents come down with a fury unexampled elsewhere, one feels at first inclined to doubt whether it can be possible for human beings to live here. I suppose that it is the reaction, produced by finding that it is not quite so bad as it appears, that reconciles people to their lot, and makes them so contented. We have got some scraps of China news; and what there is, seems to be pacific. I still think it possible that I may be arrested before I reach my destination. I could not send a telegraphic message to Galle, I find, and get an answer before we sail to-night, so I suppose we must go on to that point at least. The Calcutta mail is due to-day, but not arrived or in sight. It would be a very happy consummation if I could return to you some months before the time fixed by our most sanguine hopes. . . . As yet I have kept my health very well; better than I did on the last occasion up to this point. The journey through Egypt was hotter; but owing to the head wind, that through the Red Sea has been cooler. We may hope to get on pretty well to Galle; but if we should have to return at once, the heat will, I apprehend, be terrific then. . . .

However, there will be the hope of seeing you again to enable me to bear it. . . . *Nine P.M.*—I am on board again. . . . My next letter will probably be from Galle. Our fate will be, I think, finally determined there. . . .

At Sea.—May 15*th.*—We are getting on slowly, though every thing is in our favour—a smooth sea, and a breeze, if there be any, slightly ahead. The captain lays the blame on the coal, as he says that when he went up to Suez in this ship as a passenger, she then went so well, that it was necessary from time to time to make the engineer reduce the force of steam, lest she should reach her destination too soon. In the last twenty-four hours we have only made 210 miles, whereas we ought to have approached 300. It will make no great difference to us, for the Bombay vessel is not likely to reach Galle before us, and we cannot go on till it arrives there. But shall we go on at all? That is the question. Gros, who is a wise man, declines to discuss it. He says it is his plan never to come to speculative decisions on such points, but to wait until circumstances arise on which his resolutions have to be based. . . . I believe he is right, but it is difficult to abstain altogether from conjecture on a matter so important. . . . On the whole, I lean to the opinion that there will be no war, and no cause for the appearance of our special embassies on the scene. At the same time I am of course quite aware that accidents may occur, etc., which may lead to a different result. . . . As to ourselves, if we are not to reach China, the sooner we reach home the better. It will be a pity to prolong this undertaking, in which the ridiculous will have been so largely mixed with the sublime. But if we go on to China, if we take the matter in hand, then I think, *coute qu'il coute*, we must finish it, and finish it thoroughly. I do not believe that it will take us long to do so; but the indispensable is, that it should be done. This is my judgment on the matter, and I tell it to you . . . as it presents itself to my own mind; but how much wiser is Gros, who does not peer into the dim future, but awaits calmly the dispersion of the mists which surround it! . . . He has been reading the book on Buddhism (St. Hilaire's), which I got on your recommendation, and have lent him. I have myself read Thiers, the *Idylls* over again; some other poems of Tennyson's, etc. etc. The first of these is very interesting. The passion of the French nation for the name of Napoleon seems more and more wonderful when one peruses the record of the frightful sufferings which he brought upon them; and yet, at the time when his reign was drawing to its close, the disgust occasioned by his tyranny seemed to be the ruling sentiment with all classes. As to the *Idylls*, on a second perusal I like "Enid" better than on the first; "Vivien" better; "Elaine" less; and "Guinevere" still best of all. Nothing in the volume can approach the last interview between Arthur and the Queen.

May 19*th.*—A steamer in sight, and I have asked the captain to signalize that I wish to communicate; so we shall be able to send letters by her. We have gone almost as smoothly as when I began this letter. It is very sultry, and some nights were suffocating; but yesterday afternoon we had a tremendous tropical shower, and more rain to-day, which has a little cooled the air. Not quite such a shower as that which I heard of at Aden, where I was told that the last shower which took place, thirteen months ago, had lasted two hours, and swept away 200 houses, drowned any number of people, etc. T. has just come to tell me I must make up my letter, as the boat is going off. We are to reach Galle to-morrow or next day. . . . I think of you and the dear small ones, to whom I feel myself drawn more closely than ever; for in spite of my pre-occupations, I became better acquainted with them during my last eleven months at home, than ever before. Dear B.'s full and thoughtful eye; L.'s engaging and loving ways. Oh that I could be at home and at peace to enjoy all this! . . .

Ceylon, May 21*st.*—The steamer by which I sent my last letter turned out to be one of the Australian packets. Last night was black and stormy, and when I came on deck this morning, I was told that we did not know exactly where we were; that we had turned our ship's head homewards, and were searching for Ceylon. We found it after a while, and landed in a pelt of rain at about noon. Sir H. Ward had come to meet us, and Sir H. Rose was in the Queen's House, having come from Bombay on his way to Calcutta, to take the command of the army in India. On landing, I asked eagerly for China news. Hardly any to be obtained; little more than vague surmises. Nothing to justify an arrest of our movements, so we must go on. I do not know how it is, but I feel sadder and more depressed than I have felt before. I cannot but contrast my position when in this house a year ago, with my present position. Then I was returning to you, looking forward to your dear welcome, complete success having crowned my mission to China. I am now going from you on this difficult and unwelcome errand. . . . I feel as if I knew every stone of the place where I passed so many weary hours, waiting for F., with a fever on me, or coming on. Gros is in the next room bargaining for rubies and sapphires; but I do not feel disposed to indulge in such extravagances. . . . The steamer in which we are to proceed to-morrow looks very small, with diminutive portholes. We shall be a large party, and, I fear, very closely packed.

May 22*d*.—There has been incessant thunder and lightning, accompanied by heavy tropical showers. I got a regular ducking yesterday before dinner; however, I am none the worse, for I was able to change my clothes immediately. The air is now cooler. . . . Have you read Russell's book on the Indian Mutiny? I have done so, and I recommend it to you. It has made me very sad; but it only confirms what I believed before respecting the scandalous treatment which the natives receive at our hands in India. I am glad that he has had courage to speak out as he does on this point. Can I do anything to prevent England from calling down on herself God's curses for brutalities committed on another feeble oriental race? Or are all my exertions to result only in the extension of the area over which Englishmen are to exhibit how hollow and superficial are both their civilisation and their Christianity? . . . The tone of the two or three men connected with mercantile houses in China whom I find on board is all for blood and massacre on a great scale. I hope they will be disappointed; but it is not a cheering or hopeful prospect, look at it from what side one may. We are to sail at two P.M. It is now thundering and pouring. We must expect this sort of weather for some time, till we get nearer the line. . . . As you know, I never much expected that our fate would be decided before we reached Singapore. Even here, China is a very secondary interest; but at Singapore it must necessarily be the first. . . . I so hoped to have had a few words from you here!

Galle, May 23*d*.—*L'homme propose, mais*—. I ended my letter yesterday by telling you that I was about to embark for Singapore amid torrents of rain and growlings of thunder; but I little thought what was to follow on this inauspicious embarkation. We got on board the Peninsular and Oriental steamer Malabar with some difficulty, there was so much sea where the vessel was lying, and I was rather disgusted to find, when I mounted the deck, that some of the cargo or baggage had not yet arrived, and that we were not ready for a start. I was already half wet through, and there was nothing for it but to sit still on a bench under a dripping awning. About twenty minutes after I had established myself in this position, the wind suddenly shifted, and burst upon us with great fury from the north-east. The monsoon, now due, comes from the south-west, and therefore a gale from the north-east was unexpected, though, I must say, that as we were being assailed by constant thunder storms, we had no right, in my opinion, to consider ourselves secure on any side against the assaults of the wind. Be this however as it may, the gale was so violent that I observed to some one near me that it reminded me of a typhoon. I had hardly made this remark, when a severe shock, accompanied by a grating sound, conveyed to me the disagreeable information that the stern of the vessel was on the rocks. Whether we had two anchors out or one; whether our cables were *hove taut* or not; whether we had thirty fathoms out or only fifteen, are points still in dispute; but at any rate we had no steam; so, after we once were on the rock, we had for some time no means of getting off it. During this period the thumping and grating continued. It seemed, moreover, once or twice, to be probable that we should run foul of a ship moored near us. However, after a while the engines began to work, and then symptoms of a panic manifested themselves. The passengers came running up to me, saying that the captain was evidently going to sea,—that there were merchant captains and others on board who declared that the certain destruction of the ship and all on board would be the consequence, and begging me to interfere to save the lives of all, my own included. At first I declined to do anything,—told them that I had no intention of taking the command of the ship, and recommended them in that respect to follow my example. At last, however, as they became importunate, I sent C. to the captain, with my compliments, to ask him whether we were going to sea. The answer was not encouraging, and went a small way towards raising the spirits of my nervous friends around me. " Going to sea," said the captain, " why, we are going to the bottom." The fact is that we were at the time when that reply was given going pretty rapidly to the bottom. The water was rising fast in the after-part of the ship, and to this providential circum stance I ascribe our safety. The captain started with the hope that he would be able to pump into his boilers all the water made by the leak. If he had succeeded, the chances are that by this time the whole concern would have been deposited somewhere in the bed of the ocean. The leak was, however, too much for him, and he had nothing for it but to run over to the opposite side of the anchorage, where there is a sandy bay, and there to beach his ship. We performed this operation suc cessfully, though at times it seemed probable that the water would gain upon us so quickly as to stop the working of the engines before we reached our destination. If this had happened we should have drifted on some of the rocks with which the harbour abounds. When we had got the stern of the vessel into the sand we discovered that we had not accomplished much, for the said sand being very loose, almost of the character of quicksand, and the sea running high, the stern kept sinking almost as rapidly as when it had nothing but water below it. The cabins were already full of water, and the object was to land the passengers. As usual, there was the greatest difficulty in launching any of the ship's boats, and none of the vessels in the harbour, except one Frenchman (and one English I have since heard, but its boat was swamped, and therefore I did not see it), saw fit to send a boat to our assistance. In order to prevent too great a rush to the boats, I thought it expedient to announce that the women must go first, and that, for my own part, I intended to leave the ship last. This I was enabled to do without unnecessary parade, as the first boat lowered was offered to me,—and no doubt the announcement had some effect in keeping things quiet and obviating the risk of swamping the boats, which was the only danger we had then to apprehend. With two exceptions the passengers behaved well. The first exception was a Yankee, who has been our fellow-passenger from Marseilles, and a subject of frequent comment and observation. He is a little vulgar-looking man, with a black beard, who never speaks to any one. It was the joke to consider him an American diplomatist, but, diplomatist or no, he had a notion of self-preservation, for when the boat with the women was shoving off, he jumped into it, at the risk of crushing the inmates or swamping the craft. He had even the effrontery to ask that his box might be thrown after him; but this gratification was denied him. The other exception, I am sorry to say, touches us more nearly. I had objected to luggage being carried on shore before the passengers were saved, and I had particularly desired that nothing of mine should be rescued until then. I was therefore rather annoyed when C. announced that a portmanteau of mine had gone ashore in a native boat, which seemed to be carrying nothing else. On landing, I found my servant S. at the jetty. This did not surprise me, as most of the passengers were on shore by that time. When I arrived at the Queen's House I asked whether a portmanteau with my name on it, which I saw in the verandah, was mine, as I was wet through and anxious for dry clothes. Judge of my astonishment when I was informed by S. that this (as well as other articles from the ship) was his, and when, on farther inquiry, I learned that he had hailed the first native boat he could see, put himself and his own personal effects on board of it, and made for the shore, leaving not only my effects, which were under his charge, but myself and all my suite, on board. I expressed my opinion of this singularly mean proceeding in somewhat strong language, and desired L. to inform him that I had no further occasion for his services. . . . The other servants behaved very well. . . . Such were our adventures of yesterday afternoon. I had a presentiment that something would happen at Galle, though I could hardly have anticipated that I should be wrecked, and wrecked within the harbour! A telegram was sent by Mr. Bowlby to the *Times* last night. He put in very emphatically the assurance that we were all safe, so I thought it unnecessary to send you a separate message, which could only have been to the same effect. Moreover, the line is interrupted, and it is doubtful when the message may reach its destination. *Five* P.M.—I have just been on the beach looking at our wreck. The stern, and up to the funnel is now all under water. A jury of "experts" have sat on the case, and their decision is that nothing can be done to recover what is in the after part of the vessel (passenger's luggage and specie) until the next monsoon sets in—some five or six months hence! A wardrobe which has spent that period of time under the sea will be a curiosity!

May 24th.—I telegraphed to the Foreign Office last night to say that my letter of credence, full powers, etc. etc., were lost, and to request that duplicates may be supplied. Gros is in the same predicament. Besides this he has lost a quantity of plate and money. But if the ship holds together he will probably recover both eventually. I have no doubt you will see a full account of our adventure in the *Times*, for "Our Own" intends to make this occurrence the starting-point of his correspondence. C. has done some capital sketches of our adventures in Egypt. They are very clever.

May 26th.—A mail from China arrived last night. I can get little out of the passengers and newspapers, and that little by no means good or promising, and I have resolved to open the mail-boxes and get at F.'s despatches. . . . The Peninsular and Oriental people here are doing little or nothing either to rescue our effects from the sea, or to provide for our progress. . . .

Sunday, May 27th.—Seven A.M.—The fifth Sunday since we parted, and not a happy one to me, because my hope of seeing you very soon again is at an end. It is clear now that we must go on to China. I opened F.'s despatches yesterday. . . . The Peninsular and Oriental agent has agreed that we shall take back to China the vessel which arrived from thence yesterday, and which would otherwise have gone on to Bombay. None of our things are recovered yet from the hold of the Malabar, and I have lost my stars and badges, but they may still be fished up. The fact is, the Company cares nothing for our luggage. All they think about is the cargo and specie. The steamer from Calcutta which will take this letter home arrived this morning, and will sail again to-morrow. My telegram to Bombay was too late for the mail from there to Suez, so I suppose this letter will be the first report of our disaster which reaches you. I have fortunately saved my uniform, and most of my summer clothes. They were in the cabin. All our books are lost, which is a great distress. *Five* P.M.—I have resolved to wait here for the next regular packet, instead of taking the Bombay one out of her turn. I hear that her boilers are in bad condition, etc. . . . We have now got divers, and they are to begin work to-morrow, so that we shall know in a few days whether we are to recover our effects or no. It will only make the difference of a week in our arrival in China. . . . Gros is strongly in favour of staying. I confess I am rather more doubtful as to our having come to a right decision.

May 28*th*.—*Seven* A.M.—I enclose a sketch by C. of the harbour, and our adventure in it. Sir H. Ward has been here all this time. He goes to-morrow to Colombo, and wishes me to go with him, but I do not like leaving this place till I see what we can save. Besides which I have had enough of travelling in Ceylon. My young gentlemen wish to make a tour. . . . This will be a sad letter to you, and I write it with a heavy heart, though we have much to be thankful for in the issue of this adventure. . . . I trust that Providence reserves for us a time of real quiet and enjoyment. I go to China with the determination, God willing, to bring matters there to a speedy settlement. I think that this is as indispensable for the public as for my own private interest. Gros is of the same opinion. I still hope, therefore, that with the change of the monsoon we may be wending our way homewards. *Nine* A.M.—The divers, who are now *beginning* their operations, seem to think that they will be able to fish up most of the boxes, but it is probable that the contents will be in a sad condition. . . .

May 30*th*.—*Galle*.—. . . Sir H. Ward is gone to Colombo. Most of my party are on a visit to Kandy. I am here alone with W. I wish to be on the spot to press on operations for saving our effects, at least for rescuing them from the water, that we may know what we have lost. As yet I have got nothing but some cases of champagne, and a box of linen. Gros' plate has been recovered. All the silver is black, and his knives with ivory handles destroyed, but the gilt plate looks as well as ever. He had a great apparatus for photography, etc., all entirely destroyed. The only excitement in this dull existence is the report of what is fished up from the wreck. I assisted at the operations the evening before last, and saw the diving dress for the first time. I think on the whole that we did well to wait here for one week. We can communicate by telegraph with Calcutta to obtain what is indispensable for our use on board a man-of-war. . . . At the same time I admit that I regret even this delay. . . .

June 3*d*.—Nothing has occurred to mark the lapse of time

except a visit we paid two days ago to a place called Ballagam, some ten miles from here. It is a missionary station, built by the money of the Church Missionary Society, or by funds raised through the Society. It is situated on rising ground, and consists of an excellent bungalow for the missionary, a church, and a school. A good part of the building is upon an artificial terrace supported by masonry, and must have cost a great deal of money. It appears that at one time, while the work was going on, and cash was abundant, the congregation of so-called Christians numbered some 400. It is now reduced to thirty adults and about fifty children. The European missionary has left the place, and it is in the hands of a native missionary. It gave me a lively idea of the way in which good people in England are done out of their money for such schemes. We were received with honour, a number of natives, dressed in fantastic attire, and wearing hideous masks and beating drums, accompanying us up the river, along which we were punted during the latter part of our expedition, and white cloths being laid down for me to walk upon as I ascended the hill which led to the bungalow. Last night, too, the crew of H.M.S. Cyclops favoured us with some dramatic representations, at which I assisted. . . . The proceeds of the entertainment were to go to the school for orphan children of seamen. As to our fishing, it has gone on slowly. The agents of the Peninsular and Oriental Company hold the doctrine that they have done all that we are entitled to claim at their hands when they have deposited us and our effects under water in Galle harbour, and that we have no right to any exertions on their part to save our goods. I believe they even deny our claim to be carried on to Hong kong. I have, however, got up the box which contained my decorations, and, by the aid of a jeweller here, they are now as good as ever. The Full Powers have also been recovered, and are legible. The letter of credence is destroyed. . . . I got a telegram from Canning two days ago, asking me to go to Calcutta and thence to China, but I told him I must take the direct route. I have been reading a good deal. Among other things Emerson Tennent's book on Ceylon, which is interesting, though the residents open their eyes wide at some of his wonderful tales.

June 4th.—This morning I was awakened by the appearance of L. in my room, carrying a bag with letters from England. I jumped up and opened yours, ended on the 10th of May. . . . Your letter is a great compensation for our shipwreck and delay, and it is at once a strange coincidence and contrast to what happened on the last occasion. Then your first letters to me were shipwrecked, and delayed a month in reaching me. This time I have been shipwrecked myself almost in the same place, and I have got your dear letter a month sooner than I had anticipated. How differently do events turn out from our expectations! . . . I think dear L.'s photograph pretty, though, of course, it does not give the delicacy of her features. R.'s too is very good. F.'s hardly gives his bright look; and E.'s looks heavy. . . . I suppose we shall get off to-morrow, though the steamer for China is not yet arrived. We shall probably be crowded and uncomfortable. . . . I have saved a considerable portion of my effects, some a good deal damaged. But some of my staff have lost much more, as they travel with a greater quantity of clothing, etc., than I do. . . . I have never received your telegram, but I have your letter. . . . It will be long before I hear again. Most probably we shall not remain at Hongkong, but press on to the North. . . . *Three* P.M.—I have just been told that the Bombay steamer is in sight, and will be in this harbour to-night, and we shall, I presume, start to-morrow. . . .

June 5th.—I have spent the last few days with Mr. F., the Government Agent, who inhabits a small bungalow at the top of a hill about 200 feet high, with a beautiful view, a great sea of waving cocoa-nut tree tops stretching out below, and surging up the sides of the hillock. It was wonderfully cooler there than in the fort where the Queen's House is; especially to me, who have the good fortune to be lodged in a room which faces the sea breeze. . . . *Noon.*—We *propose* to sail this afternoon. I leave a telegram in the hands of Mr. F. to be sent to Bombay when we are off. The Foreign Office will surely let you know the contents. . . .

Steamer Pekin, Straits of Malacca.—June 12*th.*— . . . I am beginning this letter under difficulties, for the heat is very great, and I have not yet succeeded in procuring a *wallah* to pull the *punkah*. We reached Penang yesterday morning, after a fair passage. The first three days from Galle were rather rough. The wind favourable, with a good deal of rolling. The smell of opium very distressing; but I have a cabin on deck, so I have not suffered from it as much as many. . . . After those three days the sea fell a little, and as it continued tolerably cool, we got on pretty well, but it was not weather suited to writing operations, so I have not taken my pen in hand until to-day, when we have a dead calm, and heat to match. At Penang, I did nothing, but spent the five hours of delay at the Government House. Nothing had been heard of our shipwreck, but our non-appearance had given rise to all manner of conjectures. The Chinese said that it was quite natural and right that we should be drowned, as we were coming out to attack their country. You may perhaps remember that when I first visited Penang in 1857, the Chinese established there mustered in force to do me honour. There was a sketch in the *Illustrated News*, which portrayed our landing. No similar demonstration took place on this occasion; whether this was the result of accident or design, I cannot tell. I obtained little China news. It is said that the troops have moved northwards. . . . The captain of this ship is from the Cape, by name Cloete. He is a superior man. . . . He tells me that the first notice of our shipwreck which reached Bombay was my telegram to Lord John Russell, asking for fresh full powers. . . . The Hong-kong papers, to judge by the samples which have fallen into my hands, have already recommenced their system of abuse. . . . I have every inducement to labour to bring my work to a close; to reach sooner that peaceful home-life towards which I am always aspiring. . . . I think that I have a duty to perform out here; but as to any advantage which will accrue to myself from its performance, I am, I confess, very little hopeful. . . . It is terrible to think how long I may have to wait for my next letters. If we go on to the North at once, we shall be always increasing the distance that separates us. It is wearisome, too, passing over ground which I have travelled twice before. No interest of novelty to relieve the mind. Penang and Ceylon are very lovely, but one cares little, I think, for revisiting scenes which owe all their charm to the beauties of external nature. It is different when such beauties are the setting, in which are deposited historical associations, and the memories of great deeds or events. I do not feel the slightest desire to see again any even of the most lovely of the scenes I have witnessed in this part of the world. Indeed, so tired am I of this route, that I sometimes feel tempted to try to return by way of the Pacific, if I could do so without much loss of time. . . . This is only a passing idea, however, and not likely to be realized. . . . We are to reach Singapore to-morrow morning, and I shall leave this letter there. . . . It will reach you about the 20th of July. . . .

June 13*th.—Singapore.—*We arrived at about noon. I find a new Governor, Colonel Cavanagh. . . . I am to take up my abode at the Government House. Not much news from China, but a letter from Hope Grant, asking me to order to China a Sikh Regiment, which has been stopped here by Canning's orders, and I think I shall take the responsibility of reversing C.'s order, with which the men were very much disgusted.

June 14*th.—*I have ordered the Sikh regiment to proceed We embark at two P.M. My next will probably be from Hong-kong. . . . There are rumours of differences between the French and English admirals, generals, etc., but nothing authentic. . . . When you receive this, you will be thinking of dear B.'s school plans. Would that I could share your thoughts and anxieties ! . . . I have been reading a rather curious book—the *Life of Perthes*, a Hamburg bookseller. It reveals something of the working of the inner life of Germany during the time of the first Napoleonic Empire. It might interest you. . . .

June 17*th*.—Another Sunday. How many since we parted ? I cannot count them. It seems to me as if a good many years had elapsed since that sad evening at Dover. But here I am going on farther and farther from home ! We hope to reach Hong-kong on Thursday next ; but that is not the end of my voyage, though it is the beginning of my work. I am still comparatively idle, ransacking the captain's cabin for books. The last I have read is Kingsley's *Two Years Ago*. I do not wonder that you ladies like Kingsley, for he makes all his women guardian angels. . . .

June 18*th*.—I was told yesterday that perhaps there would be no steamer to carry the next mails from Hong-kong. I hope, however, there may, for I fear you would be anxious, and think that something had gone wrong with us again. . . . I have just finished the third part of Ruskin's *Modern Painters*. Some of it is very eloquently written, though there is a dogmatism about it which sometimes sets one against him. We are getting on well, with a wind sufficiently strong to keep us tolerably cool ; and as I have a cabin on deck, I am not obliged to shut my windows, as occasionally is the case below. . . . I am told that the Sikh soldiers said to their officers that they would rather die at Hong-kong than live at Singapore. A very bad effect might have been produced on the Sikhs as a body, if I had not interfered to allow them to proceed to China; they were so dreadfully distressed at being prevented.

June 19*th*.—It is pouring, only a shower, but we have had several such. The windows of heaven opening. It makes the deck very wet, and the cabins below close, but I am tolerably comfortable in mine, and trying to write, but under difficulties, as I have no table and my blotting-book is on my knee. I have read Trench's *Lectures on English* since yesterday. I think you know them, but I had not done more than glance at them before. They open up a curious field of research if one had time enough to enter upon it. The monotony of our life is not broken by many incidents. Tennyson's poem of the "Lotus-Eaters" suits us well, as we move noiselessly through this polished sea, on which the great eye of the sun is glaring down from above. We passed a ship yesterday with all sails set. This was an event ; to-day a butterfly made its appearance. In two days I may be forming decisions on which the well-being of thousands of our fellow-creatures may be contingent. . . .

June 20th.—. . . Still it is sad, sometimes almost overwhelming to think of the many causes of anxiety from which you may be suffering, of which for months I can have no knowledge, and with which these letters when you receive them may seem to have no sympathy. . . . I can only pray that you may have in your troubles a protection and a guidance more effectual than any which I could afford when I was with you. . . . As to my own particular interests, I mean those connected with my mission, I can hardly form any conjectures. . . . I am glad that the time for work is arriving, though I cannot but feel a little nervous anxiety until I know what I shall learn at Hongkong respecting our prospects with the Chinese, etc. etc. . . . It is rumoured that I am not to have a Queen's ship, but an Indian vessel, which has been employed in carrying the Governor-General of India. . . .

June 21st.—Five A.M.—The land of China in sight. We are approaching a pass between two projecting points of an island, which bear the name of the "Asses' Ears." . . .

Hong-kong.—Two P.M.—I am established here in the Government House, much as I was three years ago. I have letters from F. which show that he is generous and magnanimous as ever. All the authorities I am to act with are gone from this place, Admiral, General, etc. I hope to get off on Saturday. I find that we shall have room enough in my Indian ship. . . . Meanwhile the news from Shanghae gives me some hope of there being an opening for diplomacy, and a chance of settling matters speedily. God grant that it may be so! . . .

June 22d.—I called yesterday on Lady Grant, who is at my old abode, Head-quarters' House. I gather from her that Hope Grant is anxious for my arrival, that he wishes to get on, that the French are dilatory, and in short, that he is well-disposed. . . . I do not, however, think that I am after my time, for the monsoon has been unusually late in setting in, and the transports are getting on towards the north very slowly. . . . Sir H. Robinson is now Governor here, and the tone of the community has undergone a great change for the better. So I am told by my young men, who are in the market-place picking up opinions and news. . . . The real source of my troubles last time was not so much annoyance at having my own plans checkmated, as my disgust at the manner in which the public interest and the public money were sacrificed. . . . I must not err in this way again—if I can help it. . . .

June 23d.—We all start to-day: this letter to England,—

we to the North. . . . "Our Own" is, I hear, writing a very long letter. . . . I have offered him a passage in my ship to Shanghae. . . . On the whole I think the prospect of an early settlement of our affairs here is better than I expected to find it. . . .

Steamship Ferooz.—*At sea.*—*Sunday, June* 24*th.*—I am off again. The ship is comfortable and the sea smooth, barring the heat, therefore we have little to complain of. I am sailing without my "Flag" (which I used to have last time), the Admiral not having given the necessary orders. The change will be noticed, and lower my position both in the estimate of our own people and of the Chinese. However, we shall see. . . .

June 25*th.*—The wind is against us, but it is now cool, and there is little motion, though we do not go very fast, and shall probably not reach Shanghae before Thursday. I am low. . . . Somehow or other I feel as if I was fifty years older than when I entered on my last mission. . . .

June 27*th.*—We are rolling a great deal and very uncomfortably,—a more disagreeable passage than I made last time in the month of March. So much for all the talk about the monsoon. . . . Writing is no easy matter; and I shall probably also have little time after reaching Shanghae to-morrow, as the mail is likely to leave on Saturday next, and I may have despatches to send which will occupy my time. . . . I cannot go much farther, for already I am separated from you by nearly one-half of the globe. I sometimes think of how I am to return, for a change,—by the Pacific, by Siberia. It would be rather a temptation to take this overland route. T. it appears has already written to St. Petersburg to ask leave for himself and C. to return through Russia. Alas! these are castles in the air, very well to indulge in before we reach Shanghae and the stern realities of the mission. . . .

June 28*th.*—Such a surprise! . . . When I ascended the deck soon after five A.M. in light attire to find myself cool, almost cold! The sea had gone down a good deal, but the wind as usual dead ahead, and the sun under a cloud. I do not expect so cool a day again for some time. We are not to reach Shanghae to-day. . . . Mr. Bowlby is a very pleasant companion, full of anecdote, without being oppressive. What his letters to the *Times* will be, I know not. . . . *Three* P.M.—We are going through the muddy water near the entrance of the river Yangtze, having passed several islands. It is still cool, and the wind pertinaciously heads us, however much we change our course. . . .

June 29*th.*—*Eight* A.M.—Off Woosung, waiting for a rise in the tide to cross the bar. Many ships are visible at the anchorage, supposed to be French. A gunboat (English) passed us, going to the South. It is already hotter. . . . I looked over some old letters yesterday, and found a memorandum from my tutor, stating my studies between eleven and fourteen years old. I enclose it for B.'s edification. . . .

Shanghae.—June 30th.—F. is a noble-hearted man; perhaps the noblest I have ever met with in my experience of my fellows. . . . He has had a most difficult task here to perform, and to the best of my judgment has performed it with great ability. . . . I believe that the *flag* difficulty will be set right. Luckily Gros has an order from his Government to hoist his flag, so mine cannot be refused. . . .

Shanghae, July 1st.—The more one learns of the unfortunate affair at the Peiho last year, the more complete is the demonstration of the fact that on the Admiral, and on the Admiral alone, does the whole responsibility for this disaster rest. . . . But there is no doubt of the fact, that he redeemed his strategical blunders by gallantry of the highest order. . . . F., partly from generosity of character, and partly from sympathy with the Admiral and admiration of his valour, abstained from stating in his own justification all the circumstances of the case. Moreover, F.'s policy at the mouth of the Peiho was one which required success to justify it in the eyes of persons at a distance. After the failure, no matter by whose fault, he could not have escaped invidious criticism, however clear might have been his demonstration that for that failure he was not directly or indirectly responsible. Therefore I think it probable that the result will prove that in following the dictates of his own generous nature, he adopted the course which in the long-run will be found to have been the wisest. . . . What happened has indeed proved a heavy blow to both of us. . . . I do not like to speak too confidently of the future. Of course their victory of last year has increased the self-confidence of the Chinese Government, and rendered it more arrogant in its tone. Nevertheless I am of opinion that the result will prove that I estimated correctly their power of resistance; that we have spent in our armaments against them three times as much as was necessary, and that if we have difficulties to encounter, they are likely to be due not to the strength of the enemy, but to the cumbrous preparations of ourselves and allies, and the loss of time and hazards of climate, and other embarrassments which we are creating for ourselves. My last remark to Lord Palmerston was, that I would rather march on Pekin with 5000 men than with 25,000. . . .

July 5th.—I am off to the North to-day. I hope to catch the mail there; but to make sure that you will receive something, I leave this here. . . .

On board the Ferooz.—July 5th.—Four P.M.— . . . We have passed out of the Shanghae river into the Yangtze-kiang. It is delightfully cool, and the wind which is now against us will be with us when we get out to sea, and direct our course to the North. I received at Shanghae an address from the merchants. As it will probably appear in the *Times* with my answer, I need not send you a copy. . . . F.'s conduct has won for him, and most justly, general admiration. A hint was given to me before I started, that an ambassador would meet me at the mouth of the Peiho as soon as I arrived. If a proceeding of this nature on the part of the Court of Pekin precedes our capture of the forts, it will be a great embarrassment to me. Gros, as usual, gives me two days' start. The poor old Furious was lying at anchor at Shanghae. To see her, brought back many feelings of "auld lang syne." This ship is very comfortable, but I do not think I like her better. Shanghae altogether excited in my mind a good deal of a home feeling. It was the place at which, during my first mission, I had enjoyed most repose. . . . F. remains there until I have completed my work in the North, and I think he is right in doing so, although I should have been glad of his company and assistance. I hope that "Our Own" is taking a just view of Chinese affairs, and that in so far as in him lies, opinion in England will be guided aright. I have him still on board; so we are now a pretty large party; for Wade has joined us, and one of F.'s staff, Mr. de Norman. I have also sent for Parkes. I do not take Lay, because I hope that he may be employed as the adviser of the other party. He is a Chinese official, and when they are thoroughly puzzled, I hope that they may look to him for counsel. This would go far to secure a satisfactory settlement of our difficulties. . . . The French Admiral called on me, and was very civil. The General did not come near me. . . .

July 6th.—We anchored last night, as the pilot did not like to take us at night across the bar at the mouth of the Yangtze river. The night was cool, and we started again at about four A.M. I did not sleep much. . . . When we came to our anchorage, we found there some French ships, one of them the Admiral's. He honoured me with a salute, which is the first-fruit of my flag. . . . It does not do to be sanguine in this world, still I have cause to hope that our business in the North will be speedily settled, if we can only get the French to begin at once. What I have to consider is how best to prevent my mission from impairing in any degree F.'s authority and prestige. As regards his own countrymen there is little danger of this result, he already stands so high in their esteem. With the Chinese there may be more fear of this result; but it is so much in accordance with their notions that an elder brother should take the part which I am now doing, that I do not think the risk is great, and were it so, even, I should find some means of counteracting the evil.

July 7th.—The movement was rather too much for me yesterday, and I was stopped when I arrived at this point in my letter. To-day is calm and cool.

July 8th.—Sunday.—A little warmer. It was very hot while the captain read prayers on deck, the sun piercing through a single awning; but still it is beautiful weather. We are now nearly abreast of the Shantung Promontory, and shall soon change our course, and strike over to Talien-Whan Bay, the anchorage of the English fleet. We have met one or two transports and steamers going southwards, from which we conclude that there may be a want of provisions at the place of rendezvous of the British force. . . . This is the eleventh Sunday since we parted, and I have only once heard from you. . . .

July 9th.—Eight A.M.—It is a calm sea and scorching sun, very hot, and it looks hotter still in that bay, protected by bare rocky promontories and islets, and backed by hills, within which we discover a fleet at anchor. What will this day bring forth? How much we are in the hand of Providence, rough-hew our ends as we may! In little more than an hour we shall probably be at our journey's close for the time. *Three* P.M.—I have received visits from the General and Admiral. I am to go out riding with the former at five o'clock. The latter speaks very fair, assures me that he will carry out my policy, etc. He did *not* salute me, and raised the question of my flag, objecting to it, etc. . . . I told him he was mistaken; that my ship was the seat of my embassy for the time; that on this ground the French Government had authorized Baron Gros to carry a flag, etc. . . . Finally, he agreed to leave things as they are till he can refer home. . . . I have just heard a story of the poor country people here. A few days ago, a party of drunken sailors went to a village, got into a row, and killed a man by mistake. On the day following, three officers went to the village armed with revolvers. The villagers surrounded them, took from them the revolvers (whether the officers fired or not is disputed), and then conducted them, without doing them any injury, to their boat. An officer, with an interpreter, was then sent to the village to ask for the revolvers. They were at once given up, the villagers stating that they had no wish to take them, but that as one of their number had been shot already, they objected to people coming to them with arms. . . .

July 10*th.*—What will the House of Commons say when the bill which has to be paid for this war is presented? The expense is enormous: in my opinion, utterly disproportionate to the objects to be effected. The Admiral is doing things excellently well, if money be no object. . . .

July 12*th.*—We are in a delightful climate. Troops and all in good health. I shall not, however, dilate on these points, because I am sure you will read all about it in the *Times*. " Our Own" is in the next cabin to me, completing his letter. I dare say that he will have a shy at me before long, because he has complained to me dreadfully of the difficulty which he experiences in discovering anything to find fault with. I leave it to him to tell all the agreeable and amusing things that are occurring around us. My letters to you are nothing but the record of incidents that happen to affect me at the time; trifling things sometimes; sometimes things that irritate; things that pass often and leave no impression, as clouds reflected on a lake. . . .

Talien-Whan Bay.—*July* 14*th.*—I begin this letter to-day, although it will be long before I send it. . . . Yesterday, at an early hour, the French Admiral and General arrived. It was agreed that they should go over to the cavalry camp on the other side of the bay, some ten miles off, and that I should accompany them. No doubt you will see in the *Times* a full account of all that took place on the occasion. Nothing could be more perfect than the condition of the force, both men and horses. The picturesqueness of the scene; the pleasant bay, with its sandy margin and back-ground of bleak hills, seamed by the lines of the cavalry tents; the troops drawn up in the foreground in all their variety of colour and costume, from the two squadrons of H.M.'s dragoon guards on the right, to the two squadrons of Fane's light blue Sikh irregulars on the left; the experiments with the Armstrong guns—from one of which a shell was fired which went over the hills and vanished into space, no one knows whither;—will all be described by a more graphic pen than mine. The weather was excellent. Enough covering over the sky to prevent the rays of the sun from striking us too fiercely, and yet no rain. The proceedings of the day terminated by some *tours de force* of the Sikh cavalry and their officers; wrenching tent-pegs from the ground with their lances, and cutting oranges with their sabres when at full gallop. Everything went to confirm the favourable opinion of the state of the army here which I expressed in my last letter. Hope Grant seems very much liked. It can hardly be otherwise, for there is a quiet simplicity and kindliness about his manner which, in a man so highly placed, must be most winning. I am particularly struck by the grin of delight with which the men of a regiment of Sikhs (infantry) who were with him at Lucknow, greet him whenever they meet him. I observed on this to him, and he said: "Oh, we were always good friends. I used to visit them when they were sick, poor fellows. They are in many ways different from the Mohammedans. Their wives used to come in numbers, and walk over the house where Lady Grant and I lived." The contrast with what I saw when I was in China before, in regard to the treatment of the natives, is most remarkable. There seems to be really no plundering or bullying. In so far as I can see, we have here at present a truly model army and navy: not, however, I fear, a cheap one. . . . The Admiral told me last night that he had written to the Admiralty to say that (looking to the future) he believed there were two distinct operations by which the Pekin Government could be coerced,—either by a military force on a large scale such as this, or by a blockade of the Gulf of Pecheli, undertaken early in the year, etc. I was glad to hear him say this, because I recommended the latter course immediately after we heard of the Peiho disaster, with a view to save all this expenditure, and I still think that if the measures which I advised had been adopted, including the sending up to the north of China two or three regiments (enough, with the assistance of the fleet, to take the Taku forts), much of this outlay might have been spared. . . . Baron Gros did not come here yesterday. He had been told I was not at this place. I therefore intend to go over to him on Monday next. The French commanders-in-chief have not yet fixed a day for moving, but it is believed that we may commence operations on the 25th.

Sunday.—July 15*th.*—I have been on board the Admiral's ship for church. Afterwards I had some talk with him in regard to future proceedings. . . . The problem we have to solve here is a very difficult one; for while we are up here for the purpose of bringing pressure to bear on the Emperor, as a means of placing our relations with China on a proper footing, we have news from the South which looks as if the Government of the Empire was about to pass out of his feeble hands into those of the Rebels; who have upon us the claim that they profess a kind of Christianity. . . . I am going to start for Chefoo (the French rendezvous) to-night, in order to arrive in good time to-morrow. . . .

July 16*th.—Two* P.M.—We could not get off last night, for a sudden mist came on before nightfall, which wrapped us in darkness. At about three A.M. there was a violent gust of wind with thunder, which nearly drove us from our moorings. It lasted a very short time, and we started at about 4.30 A.M. We are now in sight of the French anchorage—a long range of coast, studded by not very high hills. The sea has been calm during our passage. About two hours after starting we saw a despatch vessel, making her way to the bay of Talien-Whan. It probably carries the mail, which we shall not receive till we return. . . . I shall most probably curtail my visit to Chefoo, and endeavour to return to-morrow, in consequence.

July 18*th*.— . . . Yesterday morning your letters to the 26th of May arrived. The Admiral sent them over. . . .

July 20*th*.— . . . I know that you will not forget this day, though it can only remind you of the declining years and frequent wanderings of one who ought to be your constant protector, and always at your side. It is very sad that we should pass it apart, but I can say something comforting upon it. The Admiral and General came here yesterday, and agreed with the French authorities that the two fleets are to start for the rendezvous *on* the 26th. Ignatieff, the Russian, who made his appearance here to-day, said, "After your force lands, I give you six days to finish everything." If he says what he thinks, it is a promising view of things. Six days before we start, six days to land the troops, and six days to finish the war! Eighteen days from this, and we may be talking of peace. Alas! what resemblance will the facts bear to these interpretations?

July 21*st*.—I have said nothing to you of Chefoo, and here I am again at Talien-Whan. We started at seven last night, and arrived here at about eight this morning. A quiet passage, though during the night we had one of the sudden and short squalls which seem so common here. The captain was called out of his bed, and told that his ship would not steer! Now for a word about Chefoo. I had agreed to dine with the General, Montauban, on the night of my arrival, so after visiting Gros, I went to his head-quarters. I found him in a very well-built, commodious Chinese house. I must tell you that as we were entering the bay, we descried a steamer ahead of us, and it turned out to be a vessel sent by the French to examine the spot (south of the Peiho Forts), which had been selected for the place of their debarkation, when the attack comes off. On the evening of our dinner, the General did not enter into particulars, but gave me to understand that the result of the exploration had been very unsatisfactory, and that his scheme for landing was altogether upset. I heard this with considerable dismay, as I feared that it might be employed as a reason for delay. Before we parted that night, I agreed to land at seven next morning, to see his artillery, etc. It was a pour of rain at that hour, and soon after the letters arrived, so that I did not reach the shore till ten. I then told him that if he pleased, I would send back the Roebuck, which had brought the letters, to Talien-Whan, with a request that our General and Admiral would come over to Chefoo to talk over with him this difficulty, and endeavour to remove it. He thanked me for this offer, and then read me the unfavourable report of his exploring party, which was headed by Colonel Schmid, a great friend of the Emperor's, and the best man (so they say) they have got here. He contends that all along the line of coast there is a band of hard sand, at a considerable distance from low-water mark; that the water upon it is very shallow; and that beyond, there is an interval of soft mud, over which cannon, etc., could not be carried. . . . I am glad that our chiefs have now agreed to a combined landing, instead of at two separate places; for if they had not done so, we should have gone on exploring for ever. The French are no doubt very much behind us in their preparations, but then it is fair to say that they have not spent a tenth part of the money, and with their small resources they have done a good deal. It was wonderful how their little wild Japanese ponies had been trained in a few days to draw their guns. After the review, we took a ride to the top of a hill, from whence we had a very fine prospect. It is a much more fertile district than this, beautifully cultivated; and the houses better than I have seen anywhere else in China. The people seemed very comfortable, and their relations with the French are satisfactory, as we may infer from the abundant supplies brought to market. On all these points, however, I have no doubt that the *Times* will supply details. On my return from a longish ride, I dined with the Admiral (Charner). Next day I remained on board, and then dined with another French Admiral (Page). On the following morning the English Admiral and General arrived. They had their interview with the French authorities, and settled that on the 26th the fleets should sail from Talien-Whan and Chefoo respectively to the rendezvous, somewhere opposite Taku. From that point the admirals and generals are to proceed on a further exploration, and to effect a disembarkation on the earliest possible day. So the matter stands for the present. The state of Europe is very awkward, and an additional reason for finishing this affair. For if Russia and France unite against us, not only will they have a pretty large force here, but they will get news *via* Russia sooner than we do, which may be inconvenient.

July 22*d.—Sunday:* the thirteenth since we parted. It seems like as many months or years. Some one said to-day at breakfast that it is the last quiet one we are likely to have for a while. In one sense, I hope this may turn out to be true. . . . To-morrow our cavalry and artillery are to be embarked. This takes place on the other side of this bay, and I intend to go over to see the operation. I went there also last evening with the General, and saw some of the preparations.

July 24*th.*—To-morrow we are to make up our letters, and on the 26th the mail leaves for the South, and we start for our rendezvous opposite the Peiho. We commence operations thus on the day three months after our parting. It is now much hotter, and I fear it must be very bad in that way at Shanghae. I must write, and urge F. to come up, if he is suffering from it. The embarkation yesterday was very well done, though not quite so rapidly as I had expected. I refer you again to the *Times* for details. It simplifies correspondence a good deal to have " Our Own " on board. Yesterday, a brother of L.'s, and Lord R. G. arrived from Japan. They speak of it most favourably; praise the people as much as we did, and report still more favourably of its trade. We underrated its capabilities in this respect. . . .

July 25*th.*—Baron Gros arrived this morning. . . . I hope our next mail will take some intelligence of interest to you. . . .

July 26*th.—Noon.*—I am now starting (having witnessed the departure of the fleet) for the scene of action in the Gulf of Pecheli. The sight of this forenoon has been a very striking one; just enough breeze to enable the vessels to spread their sails. We have about 180 miles to go to the point of rendezvous. . . . Meanwhile, one has as usual one's crop of small troubles. The servants threatened to strike yesterday, but they were soon brought to reason. . . .

July 27*th.—Ten* A.M.—We have reached our destination after a most smooth passage, during which we have followed close in the wake of the Admiral. . . . I am reading the *Lettres édifiantes et curieuses,* which are the reports of the Jesuit missionaries who were established in China at the commencement of the last century. They are very interesting, and the writers seem to have been good and zealous people. At the same time one cannot help being struck by their puerility on many points. The doctrine of baptismal regeneration pushed to its extreme logical conclusions, as it is by them, leads to rather strange practical consequences. Starting from the principle that all unbaptized children are certainly eternally lost, and all baptized (if they die immediately) as certainly saved, they naturally infer that they do more for the kingdom of heaven by baptizing dying children than by any other work of conversion in which they can be engaged. The sums which they expend in sending people about the streets, to administer this sacrament to all the moribund children they can find; the arts which they employ to perform this office secretly on children in this state whom they are asked to treat medically; and the glee with which they record the success of their tricks, are certainly remarkable. From some passages I infer that in the Roman Catholic view of the case, the rite of baptism may be administered even by an unbeliever. . . . It is a great deal hotter to-day, whether owing to our change of locality or to a change in the season I cannot tell. *Two* P.M.—Hope Grant has been on board. He tells me that the mouth of the Pey-tang is not staked, and that the Actæon's boat went three miles up the river. This river is seven or eight miles from the Peiho, and the Chinese have had a year to prepare to resist us. It appears that there is nothing to prevent the gunboats from going up that river. . . . Gros has also been to see me, and is as amiable as usual.

July 28*th*.—*Eleven* A.M.—The earlier part of last night was very hot, . . . and I got feverish and could not sleep. Towards morning—the good luck of the leaders in this expedition came again into play—a breeze sprang up from the right quarter, so that the whole of the sailing ships have been helped marvellously on their way. When I went on deck the whole line of the French fleet—it consists almost exclusively of steamers—was coming gallantly on, Gros at the head. He is quite cutting me out this time. The farther distance was filled by our sailing transports, scudding before the wind. They have been filing past us ever since, dropping into their places, which are rather difficult to find, as the Admiral has changed all his dispositions since his arrival here. The captain of the Actæon dined here yesterday. He told me he had gone a mile or two up the Pey-tang river, been allowed to land, seen the Fort, which is quite open behind, and contains about a hundred men. Thirty thousand English (fleet and army) and ten thousand French ought to be a match for so far-sighted an enemy. However, I suppose we must not crow till we see what the Tartar warriors are. *Three* P.M.—The French Admiral has just been here. He tells me that we are to move from the anchorage to a place nearer Pey-tang on Monday, and that on Tuesday a *reconnaissance* in force is to be made on that place, with the intention, I presume, of taking it. . . .

August 2*d*.—There have been a few days' interval since I wrote, and I now date from Pey-tang, and from the General's ship the Granada, a Peninsular and Oriental steamer; for I owe it to him that I am here. I need hardly tell you the events that have occurred—public events I mean—since the 28th, as they will all be recorded by " Our Own." We moved on the 29th to a different anchorage, some five miles nearer Pey-tang. . . . There we found the Russian and American ministers; and our Admiral had an opportunity of showing that he would not recognise their flags any more than Baron Gros' or mine. All the evidence was to the effect that the Pey-tang Forts were undefended, at least that there were no barricades in the river, and therefore that the best way of taking them would be to pass them in the gunboats as we did the Peiho Forts in 1858, and as we also passed Nankin that year, but, to please the French, who have very few gunboats, and our own Admiral, it was resolved that we should land a quantity of men in the mud about a mile and a half below them. This was to have taken place on the 30th, and those of my gentlemen who intended to leave me as better fun was to be found elsewhere, kept up a tremendous bustle and noise from about four A.M. However, at about six, they were informed that the orders for landing were countermanded, on the plea that there was too much sea to admit of the horses being transferred from the vessels to the gunboats. Next day, the 31st, was raining, and the sea seemed rougher in the morning. However, at about nine, the gunboats began to move. The General had agreed that I should have his ship, and that I should move either over the bar or as near to it as I could manage. . . . I anchored the Granada outside the bar, and as I did not choose to lose the sight of the landing, I got into my row-boat and came in to the place of debarkation. My incognito was respected for a considerable time. At last the Flag Captain came very near me, and I asked him where I had better go to see what was taking place. . . . It ended in my going at last on board the Coromandel, the Admiral's ship. . . . The landing went on merrily enough. It was a lovely, rather calm evening. We were within a long-range shot of the Forts; and if shot or shell had dropped among the boats and men who were muddled up on the edge of the mud-bank, it would have been inconvenient. Our enemy, however, had no notion of doing anything so ungenerous, so the landing went on uninterruptedly; the French carrying almost all they wanted on their backs,--our men employing coolies, etc., for that purpose. We saw nothing of the enemy except the movements of a few Tartar horsemen out of and into the town, galloping along the narrow causeway on which our troops were to march. At midnight eight gunboats—six English and two French—steamed past the forts. It was a moment of some excitement, because we did not know whether or not they would be fired at. However, nothing of the kind took place, and about an hour after they had started, three rockets that soared and burst over the village intimated that they had reached the place appointed to them. Having witnessed this part of the proceedings I lay down on the deck with my great-coat over me, but not for long, for at half-past two, Captain Dew (my old friend) arrived with the announcement that having been on an errand to the lines of the troops, he had met a party of French soldiers who were obliging some Chinese to carry a wooden gun which they had captured in the fort, declaring that they had entered it, found it deserted, and possessed of no defences but two wooden guns. It turned out that they had not entered first, but that an English party, headed by Mr. Parkes, had preceded them. This rather promised to diminish the interest of the attack on the forts which had been fixed for half-past four in the morning. But there was another fort on the opposite side of the river, perhaps there might be some resistance there. Alas! vain hope! Three shots were fired at it from the gunboats which had passed through during the night, and some twenty labourers walked out of it to seek a more secure field for their industry in some neighbouring village. Afterwards our troops went in and found it empty as the other—so ended the capture of Pey-tang. . . . I was rather tired, and having no means of retiring or dressing myself, I said to the Admiral that he had had, I thought, enough of me, and that I proposed to return to the Granada. He then told me he intended to send his flag-captain in a small gunboat, which might take me and my party if I chose, and that the Granada was to cross the bar in the afternoon. I took advantage of the offer, and started after seeing the two Generals—English and French. We came over the bar in the evening, and I went to see Hope Grant at the captured fort where he has fixed his abode. While there we discovered a strongish body of Tartar cavalry at a distance of about four miles along the causeway which leads from this to Tientsin and Taku. I urged the General to send out a party to see what these gentry were doing, lest they should be breaking up the causeway or doing any other mischief, and I heard from him this morning that he had arranged with General Montauban to do so, and that a party of 2000 men started on that errand early. The Tartars seem to be in greater force than was supposed. The officer in command (rightly or wrongly I know not which) resolved to consider the expedition merely a reconnaissance, and to retire after staying on the ground a short time. Of course the Tartars will consider this a victory, and will be elated by it, but perhaps this is a good thing, as it may induce them to face us on the open. The ground on which they were found is firm and fit for cavalry, and is about four miles from the Peiho Forts. This is a very nasty place, and just the sort of theme on which a correspondent of a paper loves to dilate. The country around is all under water, and it is impossible to get through it except by moving along the one or two causeways that intersect it. The military are therefore glad to find sound footing at no great distance. Gros came up yesterday, but he returns to-night. His vessel went aground, and he does not, I fancy, find himself very comfortable in a gunboat which he shares with his Admiral. . . . We are anxiously expecting the mail from England. . . .

August 6th.—The mail arrived last night. . . . You had not yet heard of our shipwreck. . . .

August 7th.—It was dreadfully hot yesterday, but at about seven P.M. I strolled to the General's quarter. I did not find him, but I learnt that there was a desire on the part of the French to postpone operations. Our delays on their account have already cost us the best of the season and at least a million of money. I was very much annoyed, and I went off to see him again this morning, to do my best to urge him forward. There is to be a conference to-day at twelve. He will call on me afterwards, and tell me the result. This alliance, what will it not have cost us before we have done with it! The French by their exactions and misconduct have already stirred to resistance the peaceful population of Chusan. They are cautious enough when armed enemies (even Chinese) are in question, but indisputably valorous against defenceless villagers and small-footed women. It is alleged that they hardly receive any rations, and that they have little to live on except what they rob. Our own coolie corps is, I am told, even worse than the French.

August 9th.—My diplomacy began yesterday, for I received in the morning a communication from the Governor-General of the Province, not frankly conceding our demands, but making tolerably plausible proposals for the sake of occasioning delay. I have refused to stay the march of the military on such overtures; but the great slowness of our operations is likely to lead me into diplomatic difficulties. The Chinese authorities, if they become frightened, are clever enough to advance propositions which it may be impossible to accede to without compromising the main objects of this costly expedition, and by refusing which I shall, nevertheless, expose myself to great animadversion. There was a reconnaissance again this morning, and I hope from the report of C. (who accompanied it, and who is doing very well), that the enemy will prove quite as little formidable as I have always expected. The serious advance was positively to have taken place to-morrow, but I almost fear there will be another delay to please the French. I am anxious to conclude peace as soon as possible after the capture of the Peiho Forts, because, from what I have seen of the conduct of the French here, I am sure that they will commit all manner of atrocities, and make foreigners detested in every town and village they enter. Of course, their presence makes it very difficult to maintain discipline among our own people. . . . I went off to see Gros in the Gulf yesterday, and got several duckings, we shipped so many seas. I went with the Admiral, who made himself very agreeable. To-day Ignatieff has been here. . . .

August 10*th*.—The Admiral has sent unexpectedly for my letters. It is raining, and there are doubts as to the troops advancing. It is very sad, but I cannot help it. May I have more progress to report to you by the next mail ! . . .

Tangkow.—*August* 23*d*.—The former part of this letter is on board of the "Granada." . . . Grant has been marvellously favoured by the weather, for the rain, which arrests all movements here, stopped the day before he moved out of Pey-tang, and began again about an hour after he had taken the Taku Fort, which led to the surrender of the whole. I must also say that the result entirely justified the selection which he made of his point of attack, and as this was against the written opinion of the French General, it is a feather in Grant's cap. The Chinese are just the same as they were when I knew them formerly. They fired the cannons with quite as little accuracy; but there was one point of difference in their proceedings. On previous occasions we have always found their forts open on one side; so that, when they were turned, the troops left them and escaped. In this instance they were enclosed with ditches, palisades, stakes, etc., so that the poor fellows had nothing for it but to remain in them till they were pushed out by bayonets. Almost all our casualties occurred during the escalade. I went through the hospitals yesterday, and found very few who had been struck by round shot. A very small portion of the force was engaged, so that my opinion of its unnecessary magnitude is not shaken. I need not describe the action for you, as you will no doubt see elsewhere a highly-coloured and detailed account of it. My own personal history will not be indifferent to you. I left the "Granada" at about 5.30 P.M. on the 20th (Monday). Found some dinner and a tent at the Camp at Sinho. Started next morning at about 5.30 A.M.; rode into Tangkow, where I now am, and mounted to the top of the Head-quarters' House, whence I had a very good view of the operations. I was dislodged after a while, because a battery opened fire at about fifteen hundred yards from us, and some of the balls fell so near, that we began to think they were perhaps firing at me. On being dislodged from my Belvedere, I took some breakfast to console myself; and soon after, seeing the British flag on the fort which we had been attacking, I rode over to it. We met a good many of our own wounded, and all round the fort were numbers of the poor Chinamen, staked and massacred in all sorts of ways. I found the two generals there, and soon after the Admiral came up from his ship under a flag of truce. Two letters came to me from the Chinese, but, true to my policy of letting the fighting men have all the prestige of taking the forts, I would not have anything to say to them. The messengers were told that they must give up the forts to the commanders-in-chief before I would listen to them, and that, in the meantime, the army would proceed with its operations. They moved on accordingly, and I returned to my post of observation at Tangkow. I had hardly reached it when the rain began, and in about an hour the roads had become absolutely impassable for artillery, and nearly so for everything else. The troops met with no resistance at the second fort, and the indefatigable Parkes having gone over to the unfortunate Governor-General, extorted from him a surrender of the whole, which he brought to the commanders-in-chief on the morning of the 22d, having, I believe, dictated its terms. Of course, Grant's triumph is complete, and deservedly so. . . . The system of our army involves such an enormous transportation of provisions, etc., that we make, however, but slow progress. I have, therefore, urged the Admiral, who has got through the barriers at the mouth of the Peiho (and who is not unwilling to go ahead), to proceed up the river with his gunboats: if he meets with any obstructions which are serious, he can stop his progress, and await the arrival of troops. If he meets none, he will soon reach Tientsin. I have sent Parkes with him, who is in himself a host.—*Ten* A.M. I am just told that the Granada is at hand, having been brought round from the Pey-tang river. I ought to have told you that I am now inhabiting a room in a joss-house, surrounded by a guard of hideous idols. Grant occupies a similar one immediately opposite. All our Staffs, not to mention that of Sir Robert Napier, and one or two wounded officers, are huddled up together in the same building. . . . We have not yet heard of the mail from home, which is extraordinary.—*Two* P.M. There is a rumour of a severe typhoon on the coast, so perhaps the mail-steamer may have been lost. It would be an extraordinary coincidence, as it brings the *contrecoup* of the loss of the Malabar. There is also a rumour that the Rebels are menacing the settlement at Shanghae.

August 24*th.*—I have torn up the earlier part of this letter, because it is needless to place on record the anxieties I felt at that time. . . . This morning at about four, Grant awoke me with a letter from the Admiral, saying that he had experienced in going up the river exactly what we did in 1858. The poor people coming down in crowds to offer submission and provisions, and no opposition of any kind. He wrote from ten miles below Tientsin, which place he was going to occupy with his small gunboat force. The General has agreed to despatch a body of infantry in gunboats, and to make his cavalry march by land; and I am only awaiting the return of the Admiral to move on. So all is going on well. Grant has also agreed to send a regiment to Shanghae in case there should be trouble there. To revert to the portion of my history which was included in the part of my letter that I have destroyed, I must tell you that it was on the 12th that the troops first moved out of Pey-tang. I saw them defile past, and in the afternoon rode out to the camp, but was turned back by a large body of Tartar cavalry, who menaced my flank, and as some of my people had just discovered, in the apartment of the Tartar-General at Sinho, a letter stating that they were determined to capture the "big barbarian himself" this time, I thought it better to retrace my steps. The second action took place on the 14th, and on the 15th I rode out to see the General, and had a conference with him. On the 17th, I went to the Gulf to see Gros. I have had dozens of letters from the Chinese authorities, and I have answered some of them, not in a way to give them much pleasure. All these details were given at full length in my annihilated letter, but already they seem out of date. . . . It really looks now as if my absence would not be protracted much beyond the time we used to speak of before I started. . . . At the same time, I do not like to be too confident. . . .

August 25th.—Noon.—High and dry at about fifteen miles below Tientsin. This must remind you of some of my letters from the Yangtze, two years ago. We started this morning at 6.30 in the Granada: the General and I, with both our Staffs. We had gone on famously to this point, scraping through the mud occasionally with success. In rounding a corner, however, at which a French gunboat had already stuck before us, we have run upon a bank. It is very strange to me to be going up the Peiho river again. The fertility of the plain through which it runs, strikes me more than it did formerly. The harvest is at hand, and the crops clothe it luxuriantly. The poor people in the villages do not appear to fear us much. We treated them well before, and they expect similar treatment again. The Admiral did his work of occupying Tientsin well. . . . He has great qualities. Still without news of the mail of June 26th, and I suppose this letter must be despatched to you to-morrow.

Lord J. Hay has just been telling me that he wishes to go *via* Japan to Vancouver's Island, after this affair is over, and I have told him (half in joke) that if he does so I should like to take that trip with him *en route* for England! . . . *Two* P.M.—We remained aground for an hour; and now, at 3.30, we have again stuck fast for the night. I still hope to despatch my letter from Tientsin, which is only some seven miles from this.

Tientsin.—Sunday, August 26*th*.—We reached this place about midnight. It was about the most nervous operation at which I ever assisted, going round the sharp turns with this long ship by moonlight. I had a moment of painful *saisisse- ment* when I felt almost certain that we should run into my dear colleague Gros, who had grounded in a little gunboat at one of the worst bends of the river. We only saved him by dropping an anchor from the stern, and going backwards full speed. The Yangtze was bad enough, but we never used to go on at night, and there was no danger of collisions. This ship looks also as if she would go head over heels much more easily than the Furious. I am waiting for Parkes and the General before I decide as to landing, etc. Is it not strange to be here? Immediately ahead of us is the yamun where Gros and I spent the eventful weeks in 1858, which preceded the signature of the Treaties of Tientsin! *Two* P.M.—We are to have the yamun in which Reed and Putiatine were lodged in 1858. A much better quarter than our old one; and the General, Gros, and I are all to lodge in it together. . . . *Five* P.M.—No mail yet! How strange and sad! . . . May I not begin to hope that we shall soon meet again! . . .

Tientsin.—August 27*th*.—I had a very bad headache after I had sent off the mail yesterday. . . . Our ship had, moreover, got aground, and was lying over so much on one side that it seemed possible that she might topple over altogether. Under these circumstances, and having the prospect of a very noisy night on board, I determined to land and sleep in my yamun. The portion of it dedicated to me, consists of a regular Chinese garden, with rockwork and bridges, and ponds full of lotus leaves, and flowerpots of all dimensions with shrubs and flowers in them, surrounded on two sides by wooden buildings, containing rooms with carved woodwork and other Chinese neatnesses. It is the only house of a Chinese gentleman I have ever inhabited, for when I was here before I dwelt in a temple. The mosquitoes were a little troublesome at first, but I got my net up, and slept tolerably, better than I should have done here; for the iron ships get so heated by the sun during the day that they are never cool, however fresh the night air may be. Indeed, I shall not be sorry to leave the Granada, for my life on board her has been like living in a tap. There is only one saloon, and as the ship is the common property of my Embassy and the General's Staff, while I am writing despatches at one end, eating and drinking go on at the other. Not strictly a dignified proceeding; but still she has been a great convenience to me, as the Admiral was not prepared to give me another ship which could cross the Pey-tang and Peiho bars. I am now sending off a somewhat—

August 29*th.*—Here I was interrupted by some one coming on business. I intended to have told you that I was sending a stiff letter to my old friend Kweiliang; but, in fact, it has taken some time and consultation with Gros to settle its terms, and it is only now being translated. Yesterday afternoon the long expected mail arrived. . . . Shall I really eat my Christmas dinner with you? Really many things are more improbable than that. I hoped at one time that this letter might be despatched from Pekin; but as we have to meet Commissioners here, and to make a kind of Supplementary Treaty before proceeding thither, it is doubtful whether we shall accomplish this. I am not sure that I like my present domicile as well as I did my domicile here in 1858, because, although it is a great deal more *orné*, it is proportionably hotter, being surrounded by walls which we cannot see over. It is a great place, with an infinite number of courts and rooms of all sizes. I should think several families must live in it, unless the establishment of a Chinese gentleman is very large indeed. If Kweiliang and Co. come into our terms, my present intention is to send at once to F. officially, and request him to come on to Pekin. . . . He has been having some very troublesome work at Shanghae with the Rebels; indeed, there is at present work enough for both of us in China. . . .

September 1*st.*—Kweiliang arrived last night, and sent me a hint that he intended to call on me to-day. I sent one in return, to say that I would not see him until he had answered my letter. I fear a little more bullying will be necessary before we bring this stupid Government up to the mark. Both yesterday and to-day I took a ride in the morning with Grant. I rode a horse of his, a very nice one. The sun becomes powerful very early, but it is a charming climate now. The abundance of all things wonderful: beef and mutton at about threepence a pound; peaches, grapes, and all sorts of vegetables in plenty; ice in profusion. I daresay, however, that in six weeks' time it may be very cold.

September 3*d.*—I was regularly laid up yesterday with a sort of attack which is common in this climate. To my great surprise, moreover, the mail arrived with your letters to the 10th July, hardly a week after the last. . . . I am getting on pretty well with my business. About this day week I hope to start for Pekin. . . .

September 8*th*.—I am at war again! My idiotical Chinamen have taken to playing tricks, which give me an excellent excuse for carrying the army on to Pekin. It would be a long affair to tell you all the ins and outs, but I am sure from what has come to pass during the last few days, that we must get nearer Pekin before the Government there comes to its senses. The blockheads have gone on negotiating with me just long enough to enable Grant to bring all his army up to this point. Here we are, then, with our base established in the heart of the country, in a capital climate, with abundance around us, our army in excellent health, and these stupid people give me a snub, which obliges me to break with them. No one knows whether our progress is to be a fight or an ovation, for in this country nothing can be foreseen. I think it better that the olive-branch should advance with the sword. I am afraid that this change in the programme,—a hostile instead of a peaceful march on Pekin, will keep me longer here, because I cannot send for F. till peace is made, and I cannot, I suppose, leave Pekin till he arrives there. We start to-morrow, but I hope to have an opportunity of writing to you after our second or third day's march. I was interrupted by C., who brought me a book full of photographs by a man of the name of Beato, who accompanies us. They are very good, and interesting. . . .

Sunday, September 9*th*.- - I have just returned from the balcony, where I have seen the carts with our baggage file off. It is a terribly long train, and I have had some trouble in keeping my numbers even to what they are. I set off with the General at four P.M. We encamp for the night about eleven miles off. Kweiliang and Co. wanted very much to call on me yesterday, but I would not receive them. The junior Commissioner, who was at Canton with Parkes, and knows him well, told him that, in fact, the people here had been urging them to make an effort to prevent war, saying : " If we were sure that the foreigners would have the best of it, we should not care ; but if they are worsted they will fall back on us, and wreak their vengeance upon us." This does not seem a very formidable state of mind as far as we are concerned. We have behaved well to the people, except at Pey-tang and Sinho, and the consequence is, that we can move through the country with comparative ease. If the people tried to cut off our baggage, and refused us supplies, we should find it very difficult to get on. . . . *Noon*.—I have just returned from a service on board the Granada, where the clergyman administered the sacrament to a small congregation. At four we march to the wars ; but as I go to bear the olive, it is not so bad a Sunday's work. I hope to be able to write later; but I leave this letter here to be sent by the next mail. You may very likely hear through Siberia of the result of our march before you receive this letter announcing that it is to take place. I shall not, therefore, speculate upon it. . . .

Yang-tsun, about twenty miles from Tientsin.—*September* 10*th.* —*Two* P.M.—We have accomplished the second day's march on Pekin. I started yesterday with the General at 4.30 P.M. We rode pretty fast, but did not arrive till 7.30. So I consider the march as nearer fifteen than ten miles. It was very hot; and I was by no means well in the night. . . . This morning we started at about five, and reached this encampment soon after seven. A very nice ride, cool, and through a succession of crops of millet; a stiff reedy stem, some twelve or fourteen feet high, with a tuft on the top, is the physiognomy of the millet stalk. It would puzzle the Tartar cavalry to charge us through this crop. As it is, we have seen no enemy; and Mr. Parkes has induced the inhabitants to sell us a good many sheep and oxen. Our tents were not pitched till near noon; so I sat during most of the forenoon under the shade of a hedge. There has been thunder since, and a considerable fall of rain. I hope it will not make the roads impassable; but if it fills the river a little it will do us good, for we may then use it for the transport of our supplies, and it is now too low. We do not know much what is ahead of us; but we hear of Tartar troops farther on, and at Tung-chow it is said that a large army is collected under San-ko-lin-sin himself (their great general). I am now enjoying the life of a camp; writing to you seated on my portmanteau, with my desk on my only chair. It is perhaps better than my hothouse at Tientsin.

September 11*th.*—*Six* A.M.—Parkes and Wade have just been in my tent with a letter from two new plenipotentiaries—really some of the highest personages in the empire—stating that they are under orders to come to Tientsin to settle everything, and deprecating a forward movement. I shall of course stick by my programme, and decline to have anything to say to them till I reach Tung-chow. Of course this proceeding on their part augurs well for peace. It poured all last evening, and the General determined not to march this morning; but as it is fine now, I think we may start at noon, and make out our allotted march. It is cooler this morning, and I think it not improbable that the thunder of yesterday may close the hot season. However, the sun is coming out in his strength, so one cannot say what the day may bring forth. *Ten* A.M.—All our cart-drivers, with their animals, disappeared during last night, leaving the carts behind them. Probably they got a hint from the

Chinese authorities. I am sorry for it, for if we begin to resort to measures of violence to supply ourselves, we may entirely alter the footing on which we have hitherto stood with the people. We are putting all our surplus goods into junks, in order to reduce our baggage. I must now send off this letter. . . .

Nan-tsai-tsun.—September 12*th.*—Where will this letter be sent from? It is begun at a small town on the close of our march of to-day, which ought to have been our march of yesterday. It was a very mild one—about eight miles—through a nice country, more wooded than former marches, and with bright sunshine, and a fresh, almost frosty air. The sunshine we had not at first, for we started before the sun had appeared on the horizon. Instead of trusting to our tents, we have this day taken up our abode in the house of a Chinese gentleman-farmer, the owner of about 1000 acres. It is nearly as large as the house I occupied at Tientsin; at least it has nearly as many courts. The gentleman has a good library, in which I have established myself, and he seems, poor man, very anxious to accommodate us, though his appearance is not that of a man entirely at his ease. As I was starting this morning I got a second letter from the new Plenipotentiaries, rather more defiant in its tone, and saying that there are troops at our next station with whom we shall come into collision if we advance with an army. Parkes is gone on with an escort, and we shall soon know from him what the state of the case really is.

September 14*th.—Ho-see-woo.*—We had a charming march to this place yesterday morning. The country much more beautiful than before, and hills in the distance. All around us the most luxuriant crops, and hamlets embosomed in clumps of willows. The temperature was delicious. Almost too cold at starting, but later, a fresh breeze in our faces, gave the requisite coolness and no more. Our march was about twelve miles, and on reaching its close I was conducted to a temple where I now am. It is a monastery, with very nice apartments; and quantities of stabling, grain, agricultural implements, etc., all indicative of a very prosperous community. I have seen no *bonzerie* on anything like so comfortable a scale. I had a second letter from my Commissioners in the evening of the last day on which I wrote a page of this journal, more humble in its tone than the preceding one, and as my General was getting uneasy about his supplies, etc., I thought it necessary to make a kind of proposition for an arrangement. . . . Our soldiers do so little for themselves, and their necessities are so great, that we move but slowly. Our present party consists of about 1500 fighting men; but we count about 4000 mouths, and all must have abundantly of the best. The French (I admit that they take more out of the country, and sometimes perhaps by rougher methods) carry on their backs several days' provisions. They work in all sorts of ways for the army. The contrast is, I must say, very striking. . . . I therefore thought it better to send Wade and Parkes to the new Imperial Commissioners, to see whether they intended to resist or not, and to make a proposal to test this. They set out last night, and I have just heard from them, that as they did not find the Commissioners at the place they expected (Matan), they are gone on to Tung-chow, the place where I intend to sign the Convention. Parkes is one of the most remarkable men I ever met; for energy, courage, and ability combined, I do not know where I could find his match; and this, joined to a facility of speaking Chinese, which he shares only with Lay, makes him at present *the* man of the situation.

Sunday, 16*th September.*—We have had service in my temple. The General and Staff attended. . . . Wade and Parkes did good work at Tung-chow. It is arranged now that the General and bulk of the force proceed to-morrow on their way to the point at which (if the Chinese Plenipotentiaries come into all our terms) we are to stay the progress of the main body, going on from that point with an escort of 1000 men. This place is about five miles from Tung-chow, and twenty from Pekin; and so I hope to effect my pacific entry into Pekin. . . . This place has been, I am sorry to say, much maltreated, for the people ran away, and when that takes place, it is impossible to prevent plundering. The present plan is, that I remain here till the army has taken up its new position, and all is arranged for my reception at Pekin and Tung-chow, when I shall move on. Gros is here. He has just been with me, and is in a great state because our soldiers, in their zeal to drive away all Chinese robbers, have driven away all his coolies! . . .

September 17*th.*—I rode out very early this morning to see my General before he started, and to give him a hint about the *looting,* which has been bad here. He disapproves of it as much as I do. . . . Parkes went off again this morning to Tung-chow, with another missive from me to my *Prince* (the new Plenipotentiary), rather stiff and plain-spoken; and Loch is gone with him to get carts, etc., as I have no means of conveying my goods and chattels. I shall probably hear to-morrow whether there is any hitch; but even if all be right, I hardly expect to get on before Thursday, for want of transport. . . .

September 18*th.*—*Noon.*—There is firing in front of us, and I have a letter from Parkes from Tung-chow, stating that the Prince and his colleagues made great difficulties about an *audience* with the Emperor. If I was sure that Parkes and Co. were well out of Tung-chow, and that we should push on well, I should not regret the firing. *Five* P.M.— M. de B., Gros' Secretary, has just returned from Tung-chow. He reports that the Tartars this morning were in possession of the ground on which, according to the understanding entered into with the Prince and Co., we were to have encamped. He had to ride through their army, to his no small alarm; but he met Parkes (who knows not what fear is) riding back to Tung-chow to tell the Prince, etc., of the position of the Tartar army, and that they should be held responsible for the consequences. Loch was with the General. I wonder he is not come to inform me of what has happened.

September 23d.—I have had a very busy time since I last wrote in this journal. I have, moreover, been separated from it, and from all my effects. At midnight on the 18th, I received a letter from the General; answered it at 3.30 A.M., and started at five A.M. to ride twenty miles to rejoin him. On the 21st, we had another battle with the Tartars. I accompanied the army, and saw it all. Considering that the Tartars are so wretchedly armed and led, they did pretty well. We are now about six miles from Pekin, but I believe the Generals will not move for a week. We learn that Parkes and his companions, viz., Loch, De Norman, Bowlby, Captain Brabazon, Lieutenant Anderson, nineteen Sikhs, and one of the Dragoon Guards, are in Pekin, but we have had no communication with them yet. . . . Perhaps I may have an opportunity of writing to you again for this mail. . . .

Pali-chiao.—September 27th.—I closed my last letter somewhat in haste, for I had been separated for three days from it and my desk, and when we met again, I was busy with my despatches, etc. The arrest of Parkes and the others is a very disagreeable incident, and we do not yet know what it may lead to. I sent word yesterday to the Emperor's brother, who is now named to treat with me, that unless they are returned to the camp within three days' time, and a pledge is given that the Convention I drew up at Tientsin is signed, Pekin will be assaulted. We are anxious, until we receive an answer to this ultimatum. It was a reply to a letter from the Prince to me, in which he coolly stated that the prisoners should be returned when our army and fleet had retired from the country. . . . Meantime we have an army in excellent health, abundantly supplied, and which, in five actions with the enemy, has lost some twenty killed ! . . . I think I told you at the close of my last letter, that at midnight on the 18th, I received a note in pencil from the General, telling me what had led to the conflict of that day. At 3.30 A.M. I sent an answer by C., and at five set off with an escort of thirty Irregulars, to ride about twenty miles to the General's camp. We then agreed that the Commanders-in-chief should send a notification to the chief mandarin of Tung-chow, to the effect that, unless our countrymen were forthwith restored, Pekin would be assaulted. No notice was taken of this. So on the 21st we advanced, and attacked a large body of Tartars, encamped between Tung-chow and Pekin. I accompanied the infantry and artillery during the day's proceedings. We encamped after the battle, where we now are, among some trees. We sleep in tents, but we have a house where we mess. I am living with the General, as my establishment has not yet been brought up from Ho-see-woo. The weather is getting cold at night, though the days are still hot, and I have caught a slight cold. I rode over yesterday to see the Russian Minister, who with his sixteen Cossacks is occupying the village, or rather town, of Chin-kia-wan, which was taken after the affair of the 18th. It is a sad scene of desolation. General Ignatieff was very obliging and friendly, as I have indeed found him to be throughout. He and I entirely agree as to how the Chinese should be fought. . . . At Chin-kia-wan, I received your letters to July 26th. . . . I may be very near the close of this China business, or I may be at the commencement of a new series of difficulties. All is very uncertain at present. . . . The climate is pleasant here, were it not for the quantity of dust, which is overwhelming. We have abundance of grapes, and some other good fruit. . . .

September 29*th*.—At midnight of the 27th I was roused by Wade, who brought me a letter from Prince Kung (the Emperor's brother), a good deal milder than the last, but still implying that Parkes, etc., were not to be returned until the Treaty, etc., was signed. The comparative mildness of the tone of this communication was clearly attributable to the firmness of my last letter, and I therefore induced those with whom I act to agree to my adhering to it in my reply. I accordingly wrote to say that the army would advance unless the prisoners should return in the course of to-day,—but that I do not intend to add to the Convention which I have already furnished to the Chinese Plenipotentiaries, and that I will sign that at once, and close the war, if they choose. I hardly expect to see our friends to-day. The Generals will not advance to-morrow, but they say they will on Monday. Meanwhile it is raining—a sort of English rain—not tropical, and if we have not too much of it, it will do good. . . . I am sitting in a greatcoat; but my cold is better. . . . I have been making more inquiries about the route home through Siberia, but the result is not encouraging, at least for a winter trip. Upwards of a thousand miles through Mongolia to begin with, intense cold, no roads, resting-places, or water; and even on the Russian side, an officer who had made the journey told C. that he travelled for a month, day and night, without having an opportunity of changing his shirt. I asked whether this was from want of time or linen, but the answer was not quite clear on this point.

October 1st.—Yesterday morning came another letter, proposing that the army should retire to Chin-kia-wan, and that then the Treaty should be signed and the prisoners restored. This was clearly inadmissible, as the Chinese would infer from it that whenever they had a difficulty with us they had only to kidnap some of our people to bring us to terms. So we have again handed the matter over to the Generals, from whose hands indeed it would not now have been taken if they had not urged me to make this last overture to Prince Kung. I do not know when they will advance. . . . Then, while I have these uncertainties in front, the Admiral keeps writing from the rear to suggest that Pekin should be held for the winter, that an attack should be made to the north of the Great Wall, etc. etc. . . . But it is impossible to saddle these professional gentlemen with the share of responsibility which really belongs to them,—for a measure which I decide upon diplomatically may be a complete success if it be carried out in one way, and a complete failure if carried out in another, yet if I hazard an opinion as to how it ought to be carried out, I tread upon ground on which, as a non-professional, I have no right to tread.

October 3d.—We have moved about two miles, and are now lodged in a mosque,—a nice building, a good deal ornamented, which is for the nonce turned to profane uses. I would just as soon live in my tent, but it saves trouble, so I take a room. The army was to have advanced to attack San-ko-lin-sin's force to-morrow, but now I am told the French are not ready. . . . These delays give the Chinese fresh heart, and they are beginning to send people to fire on our convoys, etc., coming up from Tientsin. . . . There was a letter sent to me yesterday by Prince Kung, signed by Loch and Parkes. Loch managed in his signature to convey to us in Hindostanee that the letter was written under compulsion. As it was in Chinese the information was hardly necessary. It said that *they two* were well treated, complimented Prince Kung, and asked for some clothes. We have heard nothing about the others who are missing. . . . It will be very hard if nothing is settled about the prisoners and the Treaty before this mail goes,—and all because of the delays. . . .

October 5th.—We left our mosque this morning at about

seven. The whole army was drawn up in contiguous columns of regiments, and had a good appearance. The cavalry on the right, then the artillery, and then the infantry. The French were on our left. In this way we advanced about four miles, when we reached a place from which we saw one of the gates of Pekin at about a mile and a half distance. We met with no enemy, but we heard of him about three miles farther on. However, the French declined to go any farther, so here we remain for the night, and we have got into a joss-house, which is lucky, for we have no tents with us. Only a very light kit and three days' provisions for each person. We hear that the Emperor has left for Tartary, which is very probable. We might have stopped him if we had marched on immediately after the 21st ultimo, but that was, in the judgment of the Generals, impossible. . . . To my great surprise and delight, your letters, up to August 9th, arrived at this place soon after we reached it. . . . I am writing under considerable difficulties now. Our ink has run out, and it is nearly pitch dark, so I must stop. . . .

October 6th.—*Five* P.M.—We are lodged in a *Lamaserie* in the north-west suburb of Pekin. Our move began at seven. We streamed along narrow roads in a long line. I got a scolding from the General for outflanking the skirmishers, which I did to get out of the dust. At about nine we reached a brick-kiln from whence we had a view of Pekin, and of a mound, behind which, as we were assured, San-ko-lin-sin and his army were encamped. We halted for some time and then advanced; we on the right, the French on the left towards these supposed camps. The French were to attack in front, we were to take the enemy in flank. I was with the second division of our force. When we arrived abreast of the entrenchment we could see nothing of an enemy. After a while I rode to the top of the mound at the corner of the entrenchment, and found the French General and Staff. The Tartars had all decamped the night before. I then rejoined our army and advanced with it to this point. With the exception of a few shots exchanged with a picket of the enemy, we know of no fighting which has taken place to-day; but strange to say, our cavalry which went off far to the right in the morning has not been heard of yet, and we cannot discover what has become of the French. It is a nice country, covered with clumps of trees and suburban villas. The temperature of the air cool, but the sun was very hot all day.

Sunday, October 7th.—We hear this morning that the French and our cavalry have captured the Summer Palace of the Emperor. All the big-wigs have fled, nothing remains but a portion of the household. We are told that the *prisoners* are all in Pekin. . . . Five P.M.—I have just returned from the Summer Palace. It is really a fine thing, like an English park. Numberless buildings with handsome rooms, and filled with Chinese *curios*, and handsome clocks, bronzes, etc. But alas! such a scene of desolation. The French General came up full of protestations. He had prevented *looting* in order that all the plunder might be divided between the armies, etc. etc. There was not a room that I saw in which half the things had not been taken away or broken to pieces. I tried to get a regiment of ours sent to guard the place, and then sell the things by auction; but it is difficult to get things done by system in such a case, so some officers are left who are to fill two or three carts with treasures which are to be sold. . . . Plundering and devastating a place like this is bad enough, but what is much worse is the waste and breakage. Out of £1,000,000 worth of property, I daresay £50,000 will not be realized. French soldiers were destroying in every way the most beautiful silks, breaking the jade ornaments and porcelain, etc. War is a hateful business. The more one sees of it, the more one detests it. . . .

October 9th.—Yesterday at four P.M., Parkes, Loch, and one of Fane's Irregulars arrived. With them were four French soldiers and M. d'Escayrac (the head of a scientific commission). The hands and wrists of the latter were in a sad condition, they had been so hurt by the cords tied round them. Bowlby, De Norman, and the rest, do not seem to be in Pekin as we had hoped. Parkes and Loch were very badly treated for the first ten days; since then, conciliation has been the order of the day, and I have no doubt, because I stood firm. If I had wavered, they would have been lost; because the Chinese, finding they had a lever with which they could move us, would have used their advantage unsparingly. Parkes and Loch have behaved very well under circumstances of great danger. The narrative of their adventures is very interesting, but I cannot attempt to give it in this letter. They seem to be in good health notwithstanding the hardships they have gone through. I must close this, though I may possibly write again for this mail. . . .

Camp near Pekin.—October 14th.—We have dreadful news respecting the fate of some of our captured friends. It is an atrocious crime, and, not for vengeance, but for future security, ought to be severely dealt with. . . .

Camp near Pekin.—October 26th.—This will be one of the shortest letters which you have received from me since we parted, and yet perhaps it will not be the one which you will welcome the least, because it will convey to you the news that

I have signed my Treaty, and that the specific object for which I came out is therefore accomplished. I have not written my daily journal lately, because it would have been filled with my difficulties in getting things done as I wished. . . . However, I have succeeded at last in a sort of way. . . . I have held my own, and have done what I thought it right to do. . . . Loch is going home with the Treaty, and will make a point of seeing you, and giving you all our news. . . . I cannot decide as to my own return until I see F. . . . The deaths of poor Bowlby, and the others who were with him, were very sad! Loch's escape was most providential. With 5000 men led on without delay, as ought to be done in China, nothing of this kind would have occurred. I told Palmerston so before I started, but the delays incident to conveying so large an army as ours, without risking anything, have nearly made the whole thing break down. . . .

October 27th.—Nine A.M.—Loch tells me he must be off, so I must end my brief epistle. I take up my abode in Pekin to-day, in the palace of the Prince of I., who played me false at Tung-chow.

Pekin.—Prince of I.'s Palace.—October 30th.— . . . I sent off a very shabby letter by the hands of Loch, but since his departure, a note from the Admiral informs me that he intends to despatch a steamer direct to Hong-kong, to meet the mail there. This enables me to write again. I have been in bed for two days with an attack of influenza, but I am better to-day, though by way of not going out. It is lucky I took to my bed here, instead of at the Head-quarters, where the General and I occupied what looked like the same room, everybody going to see him passing through mine, which was separated from his by a curtain only. Here we are occupying a great enclosure containing a series of one-storied wooden buildings with covered passages and verandahs. There is a good deal of aristocratic seclusion about the place, as it is surrounded by walls, and entirely cut off from the world without; but there is little appearance of luxury and comfort about it. It rained yesterday and the day before, and I had considerable difficulty in reading in my bed, as my paper windows, which keep out the cold pretty well, keep out also a good deal of light. They are not transparent, so the view through them is not lively. To-day there is a beautiful sunshine, and I have been walking about a little in the court before my room door. The present arrangement is that we remain here till the 8th. I had some difficulty in obtaining this; but it is of great importance that before the army goes, I should get a decree from the Emperor sanctioning the publication of the Treaty all over the Empire. . . . The French General will not, however, consent to remain. . . .

October 31*st*.—Another fine day; but I have not left the house, partly from consideration for the remains of my cold, and partly because I have had letters to finish. I have had visits from both my colleagues, Gros and Ignatieff. The latter and I are always very good friends. Perhaps he takes advantage of my simplicity; but at any rate we always seem to agree remarkably. He is wide awake to the Jesuit intrigues here. By the way, I should mention that the French had a wonderful funeral on Sunday, in honour of the murdered captives. I could not attend, being in bed at the time. Several speeches in bad taste were delivered, and a remarkable series of performances took place. Among other things, each soldier (this is, I believe, the French practice on such occasions) fired his musket *into* the grave; so that the coffins were covered with cartridges. The Chinese say that it was because they were not sure whether the occupants were really dead. But the incident which created the most sensation, was when our General was presented with the—(I forget the name of the implement) to sprinkle holy water over the graves. He could not refuse, but the look of horror with which he performed the office, was, I am told, very striking. On the day following, they inaugurated the old Jesuit cathedral, which they have recovered from the Chinese Government, and the bishop who preached, in order to make amends for the omission of all reference to us at the ceremony of the funeral, complimented Queen Victoria and her *digne représentant* for having come to China to set up the Roman Catholic cathedral in Pekin. This reflection will comfort Spooner when he comes to vote next year the balance of the £10,000,000 spent. I have no news of F. yet; so I am no further advanced with my own plans than I was when Loch left me. . . .

November 1*st*.—A fine, cold morning. My cold much better. . . .

Pekin.—November 2*d*.—Yesterday, after the mail had left, I mounted on horseback, and with an escort, and Parkes, and C., proceeded to the Imperial City, within which is the Imperial Palace. We obtained access to two enclosures, forming part of the Imperial Palace appendages. Both elevated places, the one ascended by a pathway in regular Chinese rock-work on a large scale, and really striking in its way; and the other being a well wooded park-like eminence, crowned by temples with images of Buddha. The view from both was magnificent. Pekin is so full of trees, and the houses are so low, that it hardly had the effect of looking down on a great city. Here and there temples or high gateways rose above the trees, but the general impression was rather that of a rich plain densely peopled. In the distance the view was bounded by a lofty chain of mountains, snow-capped. From the park-like eminence we looked down upon the Imperial Palace—a large enclosure crowded with yellow-roofed buildings, generally low, and a few trees dotted among them. It is difficult to imagine how the unfortunates shut up there can ever have any exercise. I don't wonder that the Emperor preferred "Yuen-ming-yuen." The yellow roofs, interspersed here and there with very deep blue ones, had, however, a very brilliant effect in the sunshine. After enjoying these views I went to the Russian Minister's, and found him installed in a house got up à l'Européenne, and looking very comfortable, with his national stoves. He showed me his chapel also. This morning I got a letter from Gros telling me that, in opposition to my advice, he had been to see Prince Kung. I told him he ought to let the Prince come to him first, —but the Jesuits think that they can curry favour with the Chinese by making him *condescend*. They are quite wrong, as I am sure the result will prove. The Prince came to see me to-day before returning Gros' visit, which goes for something in this land of ceremony. I received the Prince with all honour, and had a good deal of talk with him through the interpreters, in a style which reminded me of the dialogue at the commencement of *Eöthen*. I have, I believe, secured the edict for which we have been waiting; so I have done everything except see the Emperor, which I am not likely to do, as he is at Zehol. We ended by photographing the Prince, a proceeding which I do not think he much liked. . . .

November 7th.— . . . There has not been much to report since the 2d. I returned Kung's visit the next day, and we had a more *coulant* conversation than I have before had with any Chinese authority. It is something to get at men who are so high placed that they are not afraid,—or at any rate are less afraid, of being denounced if they listen to foreigners. I dined the night before with the Russian Minister, who was very hospitable. He made all my escort drunk, and it was not for want of encouragement if I was not the same. On Sunday I went to see two temples in the Chinese city, the one being that to which the Emperor goes four times a year to offer sacrifices to Heaven, the other the temple of agriculture.

November 10th.—I had got so far when a note from F. reached me, saying that he had started at one A.M. on the 6th from Tientsin, to ride to Pekin, and had been obliged, by fatigue, to rest at Ho-see-woo. We were to have left Pekin on the 8th, so I was obliged to send to beg one day's respite from the General. It was impossible to make F. start back to Tientsin on the very day following his arrival. At about noon he reached Pekin. It was a great relief to me, because I had been choosing a house for him, and there were other matters concerning which it was most important that he should be consulted. I found him very well disposed to stay on at Pekin, but on finding that both Gros and Ignatieff were opposed to leaving their legations there for the moment, we both agreed that it would be better to act as they had resolved to do. I therefore wrote to Prince Kung acknowledging the good faith which he had shown about the Emperor's edict and the publication of the Treaty (both of which things have been done in the most complete manner), and adding that the English army would, in accordance with the terms of the Convention, retire at once from Pekin. I went on to inform him that I proposed to call on him to take leave, and at the same time to introduce to him Mr. Bruce, who had just arrived at Pekin. We proceeded, accordingly, to his palace, at four P.M. on the 8th, with an imposing military escort. After we had conversed some time together, I told Parkes to explain to the Prince that in England the individual who represents the sovereign, whatever his personal rank, always takes precedence of all others,—that, as my task in China was completed, Mr. Bruce would henceforward occupy that position, and that, therefore, with the Prince's permission, I would give up to him the seat of honour on which I was placed and take his seat instead. I then rose and changed seats with F. This little bit of acting answered very well. It put F. into direct relations with the Prince, and did away with the impression (if it existed) of my having superior rank to him. The Prince was civil, and said, rather neatly, that he hoped they would conduct business satisfactorily, not only because he was British Minister, but brother to Lord Elgin, with whom he had had such pleasant relations. On the following day (the 9th), before we started, he came to our abode to return our visit. I made F. receive him, telling the interpreters to say that I had no business to speak of, but that I should come into the room before he left the house to take leave of him. The consequence was that F. had a long, and to all appearance satisfactory conversation with him. After this interview we set out for Tung-chow. We had to wait there all night, as our boats were not ready, and we are now (10*th November, noon*) gliding down the river, each in a *chop* boat (a little boat with a very convenient cabin, in which one can sleep, read, write, etc.), on a lovely autumn day, low temperature, and bright sunshine. I think that this wind-up at Pekin was very promising. It is probable that there may be some reaction when the Emperor and the bad advisers whom he has about him return, and even Ignatieff did not choose to remain at Pekin during that moment of reaction. At the same time, it is evident that Kung, who is his brother, has committed himself to the peace policy, and that his intercourse with us has been much more satisfactory to him than he at one time expected. It is probable that the Emperor will for once hear something of the truth. Kung will claim credit for having induced us to remove from Pekin to Tientsin, while the fact that we are still as near as Tientsin will be an *in terrorem* argument in support of his policy of conciliation. If Kung weathers the difficult moment which he will have to traverse when the Emperor returns, I have hopes that all the benefit which I have expected to derive from our minister's residence at Pekin will be achieved. Our *Sinologues* are fine fellows. It is refreshing to see their spirit and pluck. Both Wade, Parkes, and Morrison, put their services at our disposal, and offered to remain alone at Pekin. My choice, however, fell on a younger man, of whom I have a very good opinion, and who has been with me as assistant-interpreter. I thought it better, for many reasons, to leave a person who had smaller pretensions than any of those I have named. The gossip is that the Emperor is occupying his time at Zehol by marrying a fourth wife (a rather expensive proceeding) and getting tipsy. I am afraid he is not much worth; although, if the papers in the vermilion pencil, which we found in the Summer Palace, are his writing, he is not such a fool as people suppose. On Tuesday, I went to see the palace in Pekin. I had understood that I was to be shown the hall of audience, but after we had passed through three courts we were told it was impossible for us to go farther. We saw enough to discover that it is on rather a grand scale, but in wretched condition. . . . F. brought with him your letters to September 10th. . . . I pray that you may now be rejoicing in the belief that B. is getting on well and happily at school. . . .

Sunday 11*th.*—*Seven* P.M.—We travelled all last night; not a very quiet proceeding, and rather cold towards morning. I have a stove, but I do not keep it alight at night. It is still as fine weather. We expect to reach Tientsin to-morrow.

Tientsin.—*November* 14*th.*—Here I am again in the house which I occupied two and a half months ago, and which is by far the nicest Chinese house I have seen, and its exposure to the sun is now most agreeable. The climate is at present charming. If nothing else had been done by these recent proceedings, the fact of placing our troops and embassy here, instead of in the south of China, would have been almost worth the trouble. It is also a much drier climate than that of Shanghae. We have had about seven days of rain in all, since I left Shanghae in July. F. had nineteen days consecutively just before he left Shanghae. He was not well himself then, but he is all right now. His ride to Pekin—eighty miles in thirty hours—set him up again. I found the Admiral very cordial. . . . Gros is not yet come, and I do not like to depart from here without seeing him.

November 17*th.*—My letter goes from here after all. I find a good many things to do, and I think I shall not now get off till the next home-mail has arrived here. I intended to have cut both Shanghae and Hong-kong; but I may have to go to both. . . .

Ferooz.—Gulf of Pecheli.—November 27*th.*—So far on my way home. I left Tientsin on the 25th at about seven A.M. We had to plough our way through ice until we reached the Taku Forts, at 8.30 P.M. We found the Admiral in the Coromandel. He was very civil, and would have given me accommodation for the night; but I had so many people with me, that I thought it better to push on. So at about midnight we crossed the bar of the Peiho river. There was so much broken ice on the inner side of it, that it reminded one of some of the pictures of the Arctic voyages. We forced our vessel through—a little Indian river-boat—and found on the outside enough sea to make us very glad when we reached the Ferooz at 2.30 A.M. It was about four A.M. when I was able to lie down to rest. Since then we have been waiting for Parkes, who stayed at Tientsin for a letter from Pekin about the opening of the Yangtze river; which I am anxious to take with me to Shanghae. . . . Yesterday was a lovely day; a bright sun, and the air frosty enough to stimulate one to walk briskly. This morning there was a strong gale from the northwest, but it subsided after mid-day. I had a very satisfactory time at Tientsin. We got through a good deal of business; and what is most pleasant to me, F. seems perfectly satisfied with the whole affair, and the part I have taken in it. . . . The Admiral, who is very strong in support of me, had given orders that the whole fleet should be illuminated with blue-lights, if I reached the Ferooz at night. This I did not know, or I should not have chosen so unseasonable an hour. The consequence was that the illumination was not complete, but it had a fine effect so far as it went. Scores of transports have taken their departure, which is a great blessing, for they have been costing fabulous sums. Too many troops are still left; but I hope soon to get them reduced.

November 28*th.*—*Two* P.M.—We are off. All the vessels in the English fleet here manned yards and saluted as we passed; and when we reached the French fleet all the yards were manned, and the Admiral saluted. I thought we could not do less than return the latter. It was all a very fine sight, the day being favourable. Parkes arrived last night while we were at dinner, but without the letter which he had waited for. The latter, however, reached me this morning, and is very satisfactory; so that I shall have accomplished the great object of opening the Yangtze to trade. . . . My cabin is much more comfortable than it was. I have a door and a stove. After Hong-kong I shall not, at least for a time, need the latter, but at present it is almost a necessity, for the cold is considerable.

November 29th.—We did not get on fast during the night, which was, however, lovely; a full moon, and calm till morning. We are only now (two P.M.) passing the Meautau Islands. . . . The wind is south, which is rather unusual at this season. The temperature is already much higher. . . .

Sunday, December 2d.—Three P.M.—We have just descried the lighthouse off the Yangtze, which we have been hunting for in a mist. It has been lovely weather, and I have already discarded my fire. . . . This ship is certainly a most splendid yacht. Such a fine deck, and quieter than a Royal Navy vessel; and now I am shut in to my cabin, I appreciate her better than I did. . . .

Shanghae.—December 4th.—We reached this place at three P.M. yesterday. I have received your letters to October 9th. . . . How I grieve for your anxiety about B.'s illness! . . . How glad I am he is near the S.'s! He could not be watched over by kinder friends. . . .

December 5th.—Soon after writing the above, I descried the Granada, with Hope Grant and Co., coming up the river. He came to see me. . . . After he left, I landed to establish myself in the house of Mr. Whittal, Jardine's representative here. . . . We have a French cook, and my room is very comfortable.

December 6th.— . . . I shall send this off to-day, as it is doubtful whether I could catch the mail at Hong-kong myself. The opening of the river Yangtze is a very serious matter, and requires much consultation and consideration. . . . I have been asking for kites for the children, but my informant told me: "Piecey kite muchee bettee Nankin side." I hardly suppose you wish me to go there to get them! . . .

Shanghae.—December 14th.—I am a good deal puzzled about my departure. The opening of the Yangtze and the Rebel question are serious matters, and I do not like to leave them unsettled; on the other hand, I can hardly, even if I were so inclined, remain here till they are settled. I think it will end in my staying till the next mail comes in from the North. When I get away from here, I do not think there will be anything more to delay my progress homewards. . . . I propose this time to take the Trieste route, instead of that by Marseilles, if I can. . . .

December 16*th.—Eight* A.M.—*Sunday.*—The mornings are lovely here now; a bright sun, rising about half-past six; and not exactly frost, but a mere hint of its presence in the air. I take walks, and have just returned from one; generally the tour of the race ground, which is the only walk here. While I humbly pace along, the clerks of the *Hongs*—such of them at least as are careful of their healths, and moderate in their supper arrangements—flaunt past me on their chargers. I march on, thinking whether it would not in a new existence be advisable to begin life as a tea-taster. . . .

December 21*st.*—The wind has changed to the north, and my walk this morning was a colder one. Yesterday I made a tour of the town of Shanghae, and find that the French, by way of protecting it, burnt down about one-half of the suburbs during the summer. They have destroyed it to a greater extent than we destroyed Canton in 1857 by our bombardment. " Save me from my friends," the poor Chinaman may well say. The French have some method in their madness, for they want the ground of the burnt district, and they insist on having it now at the cost of the land, " as there are no houses upon it." At Canton, in the same way, they have seized land in the most unjustifiable way, to build churches on. Meanwhile, here they are, General, Admiral, fleet, and army (our General is gone to Japan). . . . The French say they expect orders from home by the next mail respecting the destination of their army, as an aide-de-camp was sent to Paris to ask for them, after the capture of the Taku Forts. This is a shabby letter, but I have no news yet from the North. . . . I fear this date will disappoint you. I hope my next will be posted at some point nearer home. . . .

Shanghae.—Christmas Day.— . . . We were together last Christmas day, and on this so far sundered! . . . I heard yesterday from the Admiral from the North. He is to be soon here, but I do not think I shall wait for him. . . .

December 31*st.*—I hope to start as soon as the mail from Hong-kong has arrived. Yesterday was a torrent of rain, and I never left the house. As I have a comfortable room, and no great interruptions, I get through a good deal of my reading. . . . There was a fortnight of the *Times* to begin with. The Reviews. . . . Trollope's novel of *Dr. Thorne; Aurora Leigh* (which I admire greatly); then Sir Robert Wilson's *Russian Campaign*, which contains some curious revelations; Darwin's *Origin of Species*, which is audacious, etc. etc. In short, you will allow that I have not been quite idle during the fortnight. . . .

January 1*st*, 1861.—This is the first time I sign the new year. May it bring much happiness to you! . . . It was introduced here by dancing. But I was not in a lively humour, and retired as soon as I could. . . . No mail yet, and I would start without it, were it not that I expect three mails by it. . . .

January 3d.—Two mails arrived yesterday. The earliest has not yet reached me, with your letters of September 26th. . . . I am packed up and ready for my start, which takes place at two P.M. . . . The Government has agreed to my suggestion that F. should have the rank of ambassador, if he takes up his abode permanently at Pekin. . . .

January 4th.—*Ferooz, at Sea.*—Hurrah! I am off at last! with a fair wind. . . . We anchored last night, there being a thick fog. . . .

January 5th.—Going on smoothly. There never certainly was an easier ship than this, and the temperature is pleasant. . . .

Sunday, January 6th.—We have more wind, and fair, but this ship, with all her merits, is not fast. . . .

Hong-kong, Government House.—*January 9th.*—I reached this place yesterday, and to-day your missing letters of September 26th arrived, from I hardly know where. . . . There are some little matters to arrange here, but not much to detain me. One or two things about Canton, and Kowloon to take over. I am a guest with Sir Hercules and Lady Robinson, who are very kind. Another home-mail will be here to-morrow, but I do not expect my letters, as I fear they will have been detained at Galle. . . .

January 10th.—I presume, from the apologetic tone of a speech (very civil in itself) made by Lord John Russell in the city, and quoted in the *Home News*, that I was being well abused in England when the mail left. . . . It is all miserable enough, but I had rather that it had blown over before I reach home, as I might seem to reflect on others if I defended myself, and you say truly that we have had enough of that kind of thing. . . .

January 12th.—I am on my way to Canton, to remain there a couple of days. . . . I then return to Hong-kong, and start for home after taking possession of Kowloon. . . . I intend to take the route of Manila, and perhaps Batavia, as a change. I do not think it will interfere with my writing for each mail; but if it should do so, you must not be surprised.

Canton.—*Sunday, January 13th.*—I arrived this forenoon, and am lodged with Brigadier-General Crawford and his wife. It is a very cold raw day. I return to Hong-kong on Tuesday, and hope to sail again on Saturday. . . . May we soon meet after you receive this! . . .

Hong kong.—January 11*th.*—We reached this place half an hour ago, and I find the mail detained, so I can add a postscript. The weather was really cold at Canton, so I could walk comfortably all about the town. I find that the new Factory site, about which I had such a fight with the merchants last time, is a great success. Its merit is now acknowledged by the blindest. . . . *Noon.*—I have no more to add, but I hope all my business here will be finished by the end of the week. . . .

Hong-kong.—January 21*st.*—I have only time to say that I am off homewards *viâ* Manila. I have had so much to do to-day that I am not able to write more. . . .

At Sea, near Manila.—January 24*th.*—I wrote a very shabby line to you as I was leaving Hong-kong, but it may not perhaps be an unwelcome one, as it informed you I had started. We have had rough weather, and I take up my pen to-day for the first time. We are now under the lee of some of the Philippines, so we get less of the great swell which has been rolling down from the north-east, and of the gale which blows during this monsoon down the channel that separates the island of Formosa from the Philippines as through a funnel. . . . We had a sort of ceremonial on Saturday. I went to Kowloon, and proclaimed formally the annexation of that territory to the dominions of the Queen. This acquisition, the good site at Canton, and the opening up of the North of China and Japan, have added at least twenty per cent. to the value of European life in China. I do not expect any news or letters till I reach Galle. The route by Manila and Batavia makes little difference in point of distance, and gives me something new to see. . . .

Off Manila.—January 25*th.*—I have a longer letter on the stocks, but lest it should not catch the mail, I send a short one. We reached Manila, after a quick but rough passage, early this morning. I am to land at four P.M. But I arrive at a bad time, for a new Governor-General is hourly expected. This will probably abridge my visit. The Consul has been on board. . . . If I had been on shore, I might have sent you a pocket-handkerchief that would not weigh a penny stamp, but that must wait for another time. . . .

Manila.—January 26*th.—Eight* A.M.—I sent off a few lines to you yesterday, to tell you of my very inopportune arrival off this town, at a moment when all the world, functionaries, etc., are on tiptoe expecting a new Captain-General to make his appearance at any hour. However, Castilian hospitality is not to be taken in default, and at four P.M. we landed with great ceremony, and after being conducted to the Palace, and exchanging a few glances with the acting Governor, who cannot speak a word of any language known to me, I was shown a magnificent suite of apartments destined for me and my following, and then conveyed for a drive in one of the carriages-and-four (*vide* Sir J. Bowring's book), escorted by a guard of lancers. It is very curious to see a state of things so different from ours. Such a number of troops; gens-d'armes on horseback; not a person meeting us (the Governor-General was with me) who did not take off his hat. At dinner I sat next the Admiral, who also speaks nothing but Spanish; so we passed our time in looking at each other unutterable things. . . . *Ten* A.M.—I have just got rid of my uniform, in which I thought it proper to attire myself in order to receive all the officers, naval and military, who came at nine o'clock to pay their respects. I had strolled out much earlier *incognito*, and wandered into several churches. They abound here, as do monks of all orders. The decorations seemed tinselly enough, but *there* was the Catholic ritual, with its sublime suggestions and trivial forms, repeating itself under the equator in the extreme East, as it repeats itself at Paris or Madrid, and under Arctic or Antarctic circles. And *here*, as *there*, at these early morning services, were a few solitary women assisting; some of them commonplace-looking enough, but others, no doubt, with a load of troubles to deposit at the altar, or in the ear of the monk in the box, heavy enough to furnish the burden of many such romances as those which thrill the public sensibilities in our days. After all, when the horrors which have brought about the result are past and forgotten, there *is* something gained by that truculent Spanish system which forces the faith upon all who come within its reach. *Fais-toi chrétienner ou je t'arrache l'âme*, as Charlemagne (not a Spaniard, by the way, so there my illustration halts), said to the Paladins, his enemies. There is something, I say, gained by it when the origin is forgotten, because the bond of a common creed *does* do a little towards drawing these different races together. They are not separated from each other by that impassable barrier of mutual contempt, suspicion, and antipathy, which alienates us from the unhappy natives in those lands where we settle ourselves among inferior orders of men. An administrative net of a not very flexible nature encloses all, and keeps each member of the body politic pretty closely to the post allotted to him; but the belief in a common humanity, drawn perhaps rather from the traditions of the early, than from the practice of the modern church, runs like a silken thread through the iron tissue. One feels a little softened and sublimated when one passes from Hong-kong where the devil is worshipped in his naked deformity, to this place where he displays at least some of the feathers which he wore before he fell. So you must pardon me, if my letter reflects in some measure the phase through which my mind is passing. *Eleven* A.M.—I found next me at breakfast the Chief of the *Secrétariat*, an intelligent man, speaking French. He confirmed a good many of the impressions which my own observations had led me to form respecting the state of affairs here. The army is composed of natives; officers and non-commissioned officers Spanish. The artillery, or a portion of it, also Spanish. The native Indians pay a capitation tax of $1 a head; half-castes double; Chinese $50, $30, or $12. As usual, my poor Chinamen are hated and squeezed. They are not obliged to become Catholics, but the native Indian women $\begin{Bmatrix} can \\ will \end{Bmatrix}$ not marry them unless they are, and they are not allowed to make public profession of any other religion. . . . After breakfast came in an English merchant, who made the passage from Suez to Singapore with me in 1857. He says foreigners are very well treated here, but they have some difficulties about customs duties, which I have asked him to state in writing, to me, that I may say a word about them if occasion offers. The greater part of the trade here is in English hands. No matter what the Yankees may say, we are incontestably a "great people." To pass from the higher thoughts which suggested themselves when I visited the churches this morning, I may tell you that I saw some of the devout Indian women when they left the churches on their return. They were generally very plain, to say the least of it. Round their waists and over their under-dress they pass a piece of silk, which is wrapped tight round the person. The result is as nearly as possible the opposite to the effect produced by a crinoline. . . . *Three* P.M.—I have returned from a very hot drive to visit a sugar refinery and a cigar manufactory. I saw little to interest at the former, except the process of making chocolate by mixing cocoa, cinnamon, and sugar. At the latter, some 8000 girls were employed, not very pretty, but cheerful-looking. A skilful worker can make 200 a day, so that these young ladies can poison mankind to the tune of 1,600,000 cigars a day. . . .

Sunday, January 27*th.—Ten* A.M.—In my early morning's walk I again visited the churches, which were in greater activity than yesterday. In the cathedral I came in for a sermon which began "Illustrissimo Señor," so I suppose the Archbishop was present, and probably had me in his eye. I could understand very little, so I did not stay it out. It was delivered without notes (having evidently been learnt by heart), in rather a monotonous way; with a sort of little action, all confined to a slight movement of the hands and flipping of the fingers. . . . The Archbishop is, I am told, very bigoted. He did not come to dinner yesterday (a grand full-dress dinner given in my honour), and some say it was because of my being a heretic. I take it I was in error yesterday, in speaking of the Spanish system of compelling conformity of belief as necessarily beginning in harshness. I fancy the monks have won over the simple Indians here to a great extent by gentle methods. They protect them, and manage their affairs, and know all their secrets through the confessional, and amuse them with no end of feast-days, and gew-gaws, and puerile ceremonies. The natives seem to have a great deal of our dear old French Canadian *habitans* about them, only in a more sublime stage of infantine simplicity. The new Captain-General is not yet arrived, and I have settled to start as soon as the Ferooz is ready for sea, unless his appearance obliges me to change my plans. . . .

January 28*th*.—Nothing yet of the Captain-General. My departure stands for to-morrow. News from Hong-kong of the arrival of another mail from England, to December 10th, when Parkes' and Loch's release was known. . . . I drove this morning to a village pueblo about seven miles off, starting at 5.30. The weather nice and cool. The country very rich. The cottages of bamboo and leaves, and all raised on bamboo-posts of about ten feet in height, seemed very comfortable. I never saw a more cheerful-looking rural population. All nicely and modestly dressed. The women completely emancipated from all eastern seclusion. I visited in this pueblo another great cigar manufactory; 8000 girls employed. I must say that this colony appears to be a great success, as far as the natives are concerned, and I almost regret that I am not going to see something more of the interior. C. has been through the barracks, which he says are in admirable condition. The native soldiers appear to be very well treated. We dined yesterday with the Admiral. Grease and garlic somewhat plentiful; and as I was rather disposed to fast, I had a good opportunity to do so. Just before we set out for this dinner, a procession was announced, and I went to the balcony to see it. The students of a college, some 350 in number, were escorting about two spangled and sparkling images of the Virgin, and a variety of flags. Each carried a lighted torch, and they lined both sides of the road, the interval between their rows being occupied by the images, three or four bands of music, the flags, etc. As all the bands played at once, and as loud as they possibly could, the noise was tremendous, and the cathedral bell helped, by tolling its deepest tone as the procession passed. These processions are the great religious stimulant here, and they form another point of resemblance with the French part of Canada.

January 30*th*.—*Ferooz, at Sea.*—I embarked yesterday at

about noon. All honours paid in profusion. The Captain-General not yet heard of. We have a dead calm, wind if any from the south, which is unusual at this season. It is pretty hot, but quite bearable, at least at this hour (six P.M.). . . .

February 1st.—We have just (nine A.M.) had our first heavy shower, the sign of our approximation to the Line. Yesterday a pleasant breeze, fresh and fair, pushed us through the difficulties of this navigation, and kept us somewhat cool. . . . We need not however expect to be really cool again till we get near Suez. On the other side of the Line we shall find midsummer. I shall pass near Sarawak, but I do not intend to call there. I cannot afford the time, and I do not think the Government would approve of my doing so. . . . When I reach Galle I shall find four mails! Two months of news. I always feel nervous as to what so long an interval may bring forth!

February 4th.—We are now off Sarawak. We had to anchor for some hours last night, as we could get no sights during the day, and our captain was not sure of his way in the dark, and we rolled a great deal. Now there is a nice breeze, and we are going on merrily. . . . I think it will probably be Thursday before we reach Batavia. Am I to bring this letter myself? I think it is not unlikely, if I do not catch a mail at Galle. . . .

February 6th.—A fine morning, and we are going through the Gaspa Strait in about 2° 30' south, not very far from where Lord Amherst was wrecked in the Alceste. We anchored again last night, but in a calm. Yesterday morning Neptune made his appearance, and those of us who had not passed the Line had to pay the penalty. I compounded for his claims on me, and the crew had a good lark in shaving with tar and ducking some other novices. We are now in midsummer, having passed at a bound from mid-winter. There is little difference however, in these latitudes, between one part of the year and another. The principal difference consists in the rainy and dry seasons, and as near the Line as this there is I suppose always more or less rain. *Two P.M.*—I went on deck this morning at eight, after writing, to discover why we were stopping, and I found that a squall had closed in all around us, and hid the land. It lasted only about an hour, when we set off again, passing through a great many little islets all covered with trees, so different from the barren Pulo Lapata and Pulo Condor which we pass on the route between Singapore and Hong-kong! The weather is delicious, and I am confirmed in my doctrine, that if you are compelled to be in or in the vicinity of the Tropics, the nearer the Line the better. You have not the interminably long summer days which you have at more remote points, and constant showers veil the sun and cool the air. This makes Singapore comparatively so bearable, and I suppose Sarawak has some of the same advantages. I wonder what Batavia is like? We expect to reach it before twelve to-morrow. . . .

Java.—February 8th.—Three P.M.—Here I am looking out from my window upon a piece of park-like scenery,—a sheet of water, drooping trees, and deer feeding among them. The only drawback is that it is raining, and this is not an unqualified evil, because the rain cools the air. The place I am at is the residence of the Governor-General of Java (or of the Indies, I believe his title is), about forty miles from Batavia the chief-town, at which I landed yesterday at five P.M., with much honour in the way of salutes, etc. We were conveyed in carriages-and-six, with an escort, to the Governor's town palace, which I was told to consider placed at my disposal. It consists chiefly of a very spacious room on the ground floor, paved in marble, and looking very brilliant, lit up with wax candles in chandeliers. Some of the high officials came to dinner, and we were waited on by black servants in state liveries and bare feet, who moved noiselessly over the marble floor. The original town of Batavia is unhealthy for Europeans, so they live in villas which extend from the town for some miles, on both sides of the main road into the interior. The villas looked very nice, and white women seemed to abound in them. It was hinted to me that the Governor-General would like to see me at his residence, so I set out for this place at about seven this morning, performing thirty-six miles in two hours and fifty minutes, in a comfortable carriage drawn by six ponies, changed every five miles. I need hardly say that we always went at full gallop. The country was not very interesting, being chiefly low and rice-bearing, nor did I see the cheerful firm-looking maidens who struck me so much at Manila. This island is *exploité* entirely for the Government and dominant race, and with no little success, for I am told that the surplus revenue last year was £6,000,000, £4,000,000 of which was remitted to Holland. I shall end by thinking that we are the worst colonizers in the Eastern world, as we neither make ourselves rich nor the governed happy. The household here consists of the Governor-General, a widower, and his daughter, a widow. He appears as yet rather stiff in manner, but he is very bountiful in giving me the means of going about and seeing whatever I choose. . . . The mail, with news to the 26th December from England, arrived at Batavia at the same time that I did, and it was then known by telegraph that peace was concluded at Pekin. . . .

February 9th.—I took a drive at six this morning, and then a walk through the botanic garden, which is attached to this house and has a great reputation. I am no judge, as you know, but everything seems in beautiful order, and it is of great extent. After a light repast I got a carriage to take me down to a spacious swimming-bath, paved with marble and shaded by magnificent trees, in which I felt rather tempted to spend the day. I should mention that before dinner yesterday, when the rain slackened, I went into the garden, and was arrested as I wandered along the paths musingly, by a monument with an English inscription. It is to the wife of Sir Stamford Raffles, who died here in 1814, while the colony was in our hands; died *here*, that is, at Buitenzong, for this inscription has taught me the name of the place, which I had not been able to catch before. I see little of my host. We dined at half-past six; nobody but his staff and daughter and my rather numerous following, who are not I fear all as well dressed as he approves of; a short *séance* after dinner, and then to our private apartments. To-day we met in the same stiff way at twelve, for breakfast. I have not seen a book or a paper in the house, but that may be because I am not admitted to the parts of the mansion where they are to be found. An expedition has been organized for me, and I start to-morrow morning. It will occupy four days, but it would be absurd to come to such a place as this, and to leave it without seeing anything. The Governor-General has spent thirty-one years of his life here, but for a time (six years) he was Colonial Minister in Holland. His daughter's husband was killed by a native running *a'muck* (this is a Javanese expression) some years ago. She seems a gentle person, and has a daughter eight years old. We all speak French, which is an improvement on my Manila experiences.

February 11*th.—Bantong.*—About 120 miles from Batavia, on a plain about 3000 feet above the level of the sea. The weather comparatively cool, though this is the hot season. I have just (ten P.M.) returned from a Javanese *soirée*. The Regent (a sort of native Lord-Lieutenant) invited me to his house to see some dancing. This Regent is very rich, about £12,000 a year, which he receives from a tithe paid to him by all producers in his regency. The dancing was performed by four girls wearing strange helmet-shaped head-dresses, and garments of a close-fitting stiff character reaching to the ground. They swayed their bodies to and fro in a melancholy way to a very monotonous plaintive sort of music, but their chief art consisted in the wonderful success with which they twisted their arms and fingers. In a second dance they carried bows and arrows, and went through a kind of pantomimic fight. After this was over, as I had expressed a wish to see more of his house, I was taken across a court to another ground-floor room, and was startled by finding myself suddenly introduced to *Madame la Régente*, an odd little woman with a wizened face, and mouth and teeth blackened by betel nut. I was rather put into a difficulty in finding conversation for her, for I did not know whether she would like being complimented on the ballet we had just seen. I then went to look at the musicians and their instruments, the latter consisting chiefly of coffee canes struck by a sort of gong-sticks. The sound at a distance was bell-like and not unpleasing. I was informed that the Regent had paid £500 for his set of instruments. After this I returned to my inn in my carriage. How I got to this place I shall tell later. I must now go to bed as we start at five A.M. on an expedition to see an active crater.

February 12*th.--Six* P.M.—We started nearly as early as was proposed. Two hours of carriage work along a road made heavy by rain, and about two hours more of riding up a steep mountain side, covered with tall trees sinking under a load of creepers and orchideous plants, not so wild and bold as the mountain scenery of Jamaica, but with somewhat of the same character. We ascended about 4300 feet from our starting-point, so that when we reached our goal we were 6500 feet above the sea. Our goal was a covered shed overlooking a crater, not in a very active state, but puffing sulphureous smoke from numerous chinks and chasms. Beyond this first crater was a second, very similar to it; and beyond both, far below, the plain of Bantong, where we now are, lay green and smiling. We could not see a great extent of it, for the heavy clouds were already mustering for the rain which at this season falls always in the afternoon. (It is now pouring, with thunder and lightning.) But the scene was very striking, and the clouds added to the mystery. We returned through a quinine plantation which is an experiment, and promises to be a successful one, and then through a coffee plantation, different, and much prettier to look at than those of Ceylon and Jamaica, for here the bushes are allowed to grow to their full height (about twenty feet), and have a graceful pyramid-like shape; whereas *there*, they are all pruned down to about five feet in height. There are also here some large trees left to give shade to the coffee bushes. I can conceive nothing more lovely than these plantations must be at the time of flowering. We got back to our hotel at two P.M., since when I have had breakfast, bath, and reading, and am now preparing for dinner. *Ten* P.M.---Another Javanese *soirée*. No ladies this time. To begin with: two kinds of marionettes; the first behind a kind of crape screen,—strange figures cut very beautifully out of buffalo hide, and jumping about to a very noisy vocal and instrumental accompaniment. The second, something like Italian marionettes, worked by a man's fingers, but without any attempt to conceal the operator. Both sets, I believe, represented historical subjects. When we had had enough of these, we went into another room, where were assembled a priest, and a whole lot of followers from a mosque. The amusement here consisted in seeing boys from the mosque stick into their cheeks, etc., daggers and pointed weapons, which the priest blessed, and which were therefore innocuous, a milder specimen of the supernatural I certainly never witnessed. All took place at the Regent's palace, from which I have just returned. His son, a boy of about fourteen, was present to-night and last night. A rather nice-looking boy. He never came near his father without crouching on his heels or knees, and putting his hands up to his face in an attitude of submission, if spoken to by him.

February 13*th.* --*Ten* P.M.-- *Chipana.*--(The place we slept at on the night of the 10th.) On this, as on the former occasion, the population make a sort of festival of my visit, and turn out to perform dances, etc. The performances are not so refined as at the Regent's, but they are more picturesque and lively. The ladies move about in the same dreamy way about lamps, or rather torches, but here they have partners to dance with them. The noise is tremendous, and has not yet ceased, although I have retired, on the understanding that the entertainment is to come to an end, as we again start to-morrow at six A.M. To-night, all the dancing has been in the open air. It was a wild, barbarous-looking scene; but I do not know that I should much care to see it again. We started this morning at six, and travelled, as we have always done, at full gallop on the level or down hill, and with the aid of four buffaloes in front of our six ponies when we came to mount steep hills, of which there are many. The roads are excellent. They are made by forced labour, and, what seems rather hard, the natives with their carts, etc., are not allowed to use them. I found here a bath formed by a hot iron or sulphur spring, into which I plunged before dinner. These Javanese seem the most timorous of mankind. All, men and women, crouch on their heels or knees when our carriage approaches, and they do this, I believe, to all white people, as well as to their own chiefs. But it is not only this crouching, they have, moreover (especially the women), a way of turning their heads aside, as if they were afraid to look at one. The natives of the eastern part of the island are said not to be so timid.

Ferooz, at Sea.—*February* 16*th.*—*One* P.M.—We are entering the Strait of Sunda, which separates Java and Sumatra. When through it we have a clear sea-way to Galle. *Two* P.M.—We have just passed the high land which forms the north-western point of Java, and is called Cape St. Nicholas. It is beautifully rich-looking; the bright green of its grass and crops, embroidered over by the darker green of the clumps of trees which are scattered upon it. Farther down to the south, on the same side, is the flat promontory known as Angen Point. On the other side we have the coast of Sumatra, wooded and broken, with mountains in the background, and green islets tossed out from it upon the ocean, in the foreground. And a sailing ship moving along it in the same direction with ourselves, her sails flapping idly in the calm. . . . It is too hot for much writing. . . .

Sunday, February 24th.—We have just had service on deck, under a double awning. A little fanning breeze from the north-east seemed to say that we are at last getting back into the region of that monsoon, which we left when we went to the south of the Line. I have been some days without writing, for there has been nothing to tell, and we have had a good deal of bad weather, rain, and rolling and pitching; but we must not complain, as it was more convenient to have it here in the open sea, than if we had encountered it in a narrow passage such as we have passed through. We expect to reach Galle in three days, and I cannot but feel a little nervous as to the news I may find there. We are in God's hands, and this sort of doubt makes us feel the more that we are so. . . . I find that there are some gaps in the narrative of my proceedings in Java, which I ought to fill up. On the evening of the 9th, when I entered the reception-room where we assembled before dinner, I was informed that the Governor-General could not make his appearance; and his daughter explained that he was subject to nervous headaches, which completely upset him for the time. She sat out the dinner, and then retired immediately. We started next morning at six, in three carriages-and-six, and reached, in two days' journey, Bantong, which I have already mentioned. At Chipana, where we slept the first night, we were to have ascended a mountain 9000 feet high, but were prevented by the rain. On our return we left Chipana at six A.M., and reached Buitenzong at ten A.M., and had time to dress and prepare for the stiff breakfast at twelve. Our host seemed more lively. As I have said, he always spoke French to us, but his daughter told me that he spoke English so well, that he was sometimes taken for an Englishman: "Partly," she added, in a sort of hesitating way, "because his manner is so like that of an Englishman." At two P.M. we set off again for Batavia, travelling as usual. I must observe that the population of this part of the island are much less humble in their manner than those on the upper plateau which I visited; probably because they see more Europeans. We reached the Batavian palace at five P.M., and some grandees came to dine with me at seven. Next morning I took a walk; went to inspect a museum of Javanese curiosities, and embarked at four, and sailed at five A.M. on Saturday the 16th. Altogether, I was much interested by Java. As I have said, it is ruled entirely for the interest of the governing race. No attempt is made to raise the natives. I *believe* that the missionaries are not allowed to visit the interior. I asked about schools, and ascertained that in the province of which the Regency of Bantong forms a part, and which contains some 600,000 inhabitants, there were five; not, I suspect, much attended. It was clear from the tone of the officials that there was no wish to educate the natives. There is a kind of forced labour. They pay a tithe of the produce of their rice-fields; are obliged (in certain districts) to plant coffee, and to sell the produce at a rate fixed by the Government; in others, to work on sugar estates, and in all, to make roads. Nevertheless, I am not satisfied that they are unhappy, or that the system can be called a failure. In those districts which I visited, there was no appearance of their being overworked; and I was assured that on the sugar estates, the proprietors have no power of punishing those who do not work; that it rests with the officials exclusively to do so. The tone of the officials on the subject is, that no punishment is necessary, because—although they are so lazy that if they had the choice they would never do anything they do not make any difficulty about working when they are told to do so. Economically it is a success. The fertility of the island is very great, so that the labour of the natives leaves a large surplus after their own subsistence is provided for. There are twenty provinces, in each of which the chief officer is the President—a Dutchman; but the native Chief (Regent) has the more direct relations with the people, arranges about their labour, etc. The Dutch officials look after him, and see that he does not abuse his power.

February 26*th.*—*Noon.*—No observation taken to-day. The wind has been against us again, and neither yesterday nor to-day have we been able to see the sun at midday. This did not matter yesterday in the open sea, but we are now approaching Ceylon, and it is important that we should ascertain our exact position, to prevent delay. It is wonderfully cool for the latitude, and the rain poured during the night in torrents. . . .

February 27*th.*—*Noon.*—Ceylon is in sight. A fine day. . . .

Ceylon.—*March* 2*d.*—I found here your letters to January 10th, and am relieved. . . . I sail to-day for Aden, and the mail only leaves this to-morrow, but as it will probably beat me, I send this letter by it. . . . Where is our meeting to be? You must settle this. ... If I can, I shall take the Trieste route, but it leads, I believe, equally through Paris. ...

Ferooz, at Sea.—March 4th.—I left behind me at Galle a long letter for you. Will you receive it or me first? ... We sailed with a fair wind, and I hoped that we were to have the monsoon with us to Aden, but it soon left us, and we have since had light winds from all quarters. It is smooth, however, and not very hot, though the sky has a little of the burnished brass look about it, which warms one. ...

Sunday, March 10th.—We have just had service on deck. It was pretty hot, as the little wind there is is astern. Weather charming, and we have made about 200 miles a day. ... I have been reading all I could lay my hands on. ... The only incident since I wrote last has been the appearance of a large steamer—probably the mail from England. ...

March 11th.—Passed Cape Guardafui this morning, and we are now running along an arid-looking hilly coast, with a fair wind filling all our sails. ...

Sunday, March 17th.—We reached Aden on the night of the 12th, but the Bengal, with the mail, had made a very rapid passage from Galle, and was already off for Suez before we arrived. We coaled rapidly too, and started to follow her on the evening of the 13th. ... On that morning, I breakfasted with the Peninsular and Oriental Agent, and afterwards accompanied the Deputy-Resident, Captain Playfair, to the cantonment, and spent the day there. Revisited the tanks, which are in much greater order than when I first saw them four years ago; passed through the fortifications, which seem to be very strong; and re-embarked at six P.M., when we set sail. ... I am told there is now (noon) a large steamer in sight. ... *Three* P.M.—The steamer turned out to be the mail-packet for Bombay. T. went on board, and brought off a couple of weekly papers. ... At Aden I found two mails. ... After some pleasant weather, we have a strong wind against us, which will, I suppose, last till Suez is reached. ... This letter will not be with you, I presume, sooner than I am. ...

March 20th.—Noon.—We are now in the Gulf of Suez. On the right side a row of arid mountains with serrated crests, and a margin of flat dry sand at the base, and behind them what is reputed to be Mount Sinai. Only a glimpse of the latter can, however, be caught at one point, where there is a depression in the nearer range. On the left there are mountains of a similar character, overtopped by one 10,000 feet high. The sea is deeply blue and the sun scorching, but the air cool—almost cold. We have had a good deal of wind and sea against us for the last three days; but we passed the Straits of Jubal early this morning, and hope to be at Suez during the night. . . .

Sunday, 24th March.—On board H. M. S. Terrible.—Here is a change of scene! The last words of this journal were written in the Gulf of Suez, on board the Ferooz. I now write from the Mediterranean, off the island of Candia, whose snow-capped mountains are looking down upon us; very different from the parched ranges of hills wrapped in perpetual heat haze, which I described to you four days ago. . . . As we neared Suez, we met the steamer with the English mails of March 10th. We communicated, but she had no letters for me. On arriving at Suez I found yours of February 25th. . . . And I also got a note from Lord John Russell, saying that he had ordered a man-of-war to be ready to take me from Alexandria to Trieste, etc. . . . I remained one night at Cairo, and received your letters of the 2d and 9th of March. Next morning we proceeded to Alexandria, and weighed anchor at about four P.M. on the 22d. This is a very fine vessel, but we have the wind contrary, and have not made more than nine knots. . . .

March 26th.—Seven A.M.—I have been about two hours on deck. A beautiful morning, and smooth sea. On our right the coast of Albania, hilly and wooded. On our left the land is low, and covered apparently with olive-trees. Before us the southern end of Corfu, which we are approaching. Farther on, the channel along which we are gliding seems to be closed in as a lake; the Corfu mountains and those of Greece overlapping each other. The snow-covered crests of some of the latter gleam in the sunshine. It is a lovely scene. Yesterday we passed Cape Matapan, Zante, etc., all on our right; but there was a good deal of wind and sea, and an unusual amount of motion for the Terrible. Navarino, too, we passed; but I did not know it at the time. We propose to call in at Corfu, take in coal, and see what can be seen during the day. But I hope to be off for Trieste to-morrow morning. I calculate that you will hear to-day of my having left Galle. . . .

March 27th.—We found at Corfu three line-of-battle ships, and Admiral Dacres, who came on board to see me. I landed at eleven A.M., and went to the Government House, where I found Sir H. Storks. He took me a drive of about thirteen miles, to the top of a pass in the mountains called Pantaleone, from which there is a very extensive view. It is a beautiful island. The day bright and sunny. Nothing can be more picturesque than the town. The people, too, seem to me very handsome. I saw this morning the captain of a sloop-of-war who has been visiting various ports in the Adriatic. He was received at Ancona with a *furore* of enthusiasm, and exceedingly well treated at Venice, Trieste, etc., by the Austrians, who are burning to revenge themselves on the French, and anxious to ally themselves with us for that purpose. I sent off telegrams to England from Corfu. . . . We have been steaming through a narrow channel, with the snow-covered mountains of Albania on our right; but we are now emerging into the open Adriatic.

March 28*th.*—A great deal of rolling yesterday, and a contrary wind; but this morning, to my surprise, I found our square sails set, and we are going on fast, and hope to reach Trieste to-morrow evening. But the Adriatic is not much to be relied on. . . .

March 29*th.*—*Eight* A.M.—A calm sea and thick atmosphere. Probably we may reach Trieste by about one P.M., in which case I hope to start for Vienna to-night. . . .

March 31*st.*—*Vienna.*—I have just received your note of the 27th. . . . If you meet me at Paris, you may come on Friday, and I shall arrive early on Saturday. . . .

VICEROYALTY OF INDIA.
1862.

Paris.—January 29*th*, 1862.—I am arrived thus far, after a pretty fair passage. We have breakfasted, and are ready for the Lyons train. It would be all well, if it were not carrying me away from you and the darlings. I think I see B., with his deep eyes looking into yours, and trying to comfort you. But even he will be taken from you to-morrow, to return to school. You will still have L. . . .

H.M.S. Banshee.—Marseilles.—January 30*th.*—I write one line from on board. The weather promises to be calm; but I have little faith in the promises of the Mediterranean. . . . I shall direct this to Dalmahoy. . . . Tell R. I wish he was with me in this ship. . . .

Marseilles.—January 31*st.*—Only think of my writing again from Marseilles! I was breakfasting yesterday, when there was a cry of "A man overboard!" We went on deck. After a while, the man—who had enormous water-boots on, but who was fortunately a good swimmer—appeared on the surface, caught hold of a life-preserver which had been thrown out to him, was picked up by a boat, and hoisted on board. After a bumper of brandy, he seemed none the worse. But in the meantime we had sprung our *rudder-head* (the same sort of accident as befell the Great Eastern). It must have been bad, or it could not have gone as it did. The captain said to me: "We may go on for a few hours, and see what we can do, and then return if necessary." I did not see the fun of this plan, and suggested that we had better at once find out what was the matter. We returned to port, and, after a long deliberation, a scheme of patching was resolved upon. . . . It is most vexatious to be doing nothing, when my moments have been of late so precious and so hurried. We took a long walk, dined at a café, and assisted at the Gymnase at a kind of pantomime— very good of its kind— . . . and slept at the hotel. I am expecting the captain of the Banshee to report progress. . . .

February 1*st.*--We are told that the ship is ready now, so we must start. . . .

H.M.S. Banshee.—February 3*d.—Off Sicily.—*We are to reach Malta, I am told, to-morrow early. It blew hard from the north on the 1st, and the night following. On Sunday the 2d, we reached the Straits of Bonifacio, and getting under the lee of Sardinia, have had smoother water since. I thought of you, on this desolate Sunday, the first after our separation. . . . I slept badly, and awoke with a headache at three A.M. . . . I am now better. I rather regret that I did not take the route of Messina instead of Malta. . . . This ship is not as comfortable as the Caradoc was. No cabin on deck, and no awning, so the soot and coal-dust are most annoying. The weather is now fine; the sun rather overpowering even at this season. . . .

February 4*th.—-Three* P.M.—Just off from Malta.

H.M.S. Banshee, at Sea.—February 5*th.—Noon.—*I sent a letter to you from Malta. . . . We reached it at four A.M., and from that hour till seven A.M. there was a row like that of a general action over my head. I went ashore to breakfast at the hotel, and before that was over Sir G. le Marchant arrived, and asked me to lunch with him. I visited Lady le M. soon after, and he then took me to the cathedral, which I had not before seen, and which is most magnificent. The marble floors covered with designs in marbles of various colours, and the monuments to the different Grand Masters of the Order, are very beautiful, not to speak of the proportions of the edifice itself. Sir G. has done a good deal to restore the Palace, where he lives, etc. etc. . . . I met at his house General W., who was private secretary to Lord Hardinge. He gave me a gloomy picture of my prospects. The badness of the climate of Calcutta, the utterly overwhelming amount of work, etc. etc. . . . We re-embarked at three P.M., and the sea has been calm since, and the temperature delightful.

February 6*th.—*It was roughish during the night; otherwise the weather continues favourable. . . . I have just finished a long despatch to the Foreign Office, in answer to the one which arrived while we were discussing our farewell meal in London. I hope that it may be of use to F. I intend to work moderately, but not very hard, while I am on my voyage, as it is better to reserve my strength for what awaits me on my arrival. . . .

February 7*th.—*Smoother to-day. Indeed, I was so far taken in by the appearance of calm, that before I got up I opened the scuttle which is beside my bed, in the hope of getting a whiff of fresh air. I had hardly done so, however, when we gave a lurch, and a magnificent green wave rolled up to the aperture, and poured itself in the most deliberate way over my couch.

We hope to reach Alexandria to-morrow morning, for we are now going fast—which this ship, from the ingenious way in which she is trimmed, never does until almost all her coal has been consumed. ...

February 8th.—*Ten* A.M.—*Alexandria.*—The Consul-General is coming off. ... I have asked for a special train. *Noon.*—I am starting. The Pacha is at or near Cairo. I shall call on him if he is in the town, if not, hurry on to Suez. I hear the Ferooz has been waiting there three weeks. ...

Ferooz.—*February 9th.*—When I got on board this morning my heart smote me a little for having discouraged your coming out with me, for nothing can be more comfortable than this ship has been made, with a view to the accommodation of poor Lady C. and you. Perhaps the contrast with the Banshee enhances her merits. ... Our journey through Egypt was very rough, the road being in many places in indifferent repair. A truck off the rails detained us an hour; so, leaving Alexandria at one P.M., we reached Suez at 9.15 P.M.; slept at the hotel, which is very much improved, and embarked this morning at seven, and with some difficulty got our horses safely on board. ... I find no less than eight native servants on board, sent by Lord C.,—dressed in flowing scarlet robes. ... The weather is still delightful, and rather cold in the morning. ... *Eight* P.M.—It is very lonely to be spending this Sunday evening by myself, after the many happy ones I have enjoyed with you and the children during the past three months; and yet I would not forego the recollection of these happy days though it deepens the gloom of the present. Surely, whatever may happen to us all, it is something gained to have this retrospect in store. ...

February 10*th.*—Another beautiful day,—warmer, but not unpleasantly so. We passed the Strait of Jubal this morning, and are now going at full speed, which we did not do before, not wishing to reach this dangerous place during the night. ... The horses are very comfortable, and objects of great interest to the sailors.

February 12*th.*—Going on as smoothly as ever. ... I have been reading over some old manuscript books, written from twenty to twenty-five years ago, and containing a record of my thoughts and doings at that remote time. It is very interesting and useful to look back. I was working very hard during these years, searching after truth and right, with no positive occupation but that of managing the Broomhall affairs, and riding at a sort of single anchor with politics. Would it have been better for me if I had had more engrossing positive work? There is something to be said on both sides in answering that question. However, these books will not be again read by me, for I shall consign them to the Red Sea. . . . The temperature has changed from 50° at Suez, in the morning, to from 75° to 80° here (opposite Jeddah). I do not, however, suffer from it as yet. . . . *Three* P.M.—The mail-steamer in sight. I hope to send this letter by her.

Ferooz.—Red Sea.—February 12*th.—Eight* P.M.—I went on deck after bringing my last letter to a hasty close, and descried a steamer altering its course in order to approach us. When nearer we put out a boat with my letters, and she did so likewise. It turned out that Mr. Parkes, from China, was on board, and he came off to see me. He was in very good spirits, and returned after talking to me for half an hour on China matters. I was surprised at the Peninsular and Oriental steamer remaining so long, but I found that she is two days before her time, and hardly knows how to waste it. The passengers will have to wait in Egypt for the Marseilles boat, and this is expensive and inconvenient to many. . . . By this lucky accident you will have a letter about the 27th. . . .

February 13*th.*—The breeze is freshening and dead ahead. . . . I have been thinking of the past, and remembering that just twenty years ago, at this same season, I set out on my first visit to the Tropics. What a strange career it has been! How grateful I should be to Providence for the protection I have enjoyed! How wild it seems, to be about, at the close of twenty years, to begin again. At any rate, if this does not answer to me personally, I hope that it may enable me to put the children in a better position. . . . I shall leave this at Aden ; . . . but you will probably have to wait longer for the next letter, as there is little chance of meeting a mail-packet on the wide ocean. . . .

Sunday, February 16*th.*—A bad time since I last wrote. We have had a very strong gale. . . . There is less motion to-day, probably because we are under the lee of the Arabian coast. I could not wish that you had been with me while we were undergoing this misery ; and we have made slow progress, but may reach Aden to-morrow. It has been a sad time. . . . I could not read, and have been lying down, thinking over so many things ! . . . But there may, please God, be a good time beyond. I have been thinking of the little party in your room on this day, and endeavouring to join with you all. . . .

Aden.—February 17*th.*—We reached this place at four P.M. I am at Captain Playfair's ; and the climate is really very charming here now. We hope to sail to-morrow at two P.M.

Ferooz, at Sea.—February 18*th.—Four* P.M.—We have just rounded the peninsula of Aden. Wind still against us, but not the same amount of sea as before we reached Aden,—when we are supposed to have encountered, in the Red Sea, the strongest gale which has been experienced in these localities this year. ... I have sent a message to Canning (*viâ* Bombay) to say that I will give up Madras if he telegraphs to Galle asking me to do so. And now I expect to pass some ten monotonous days, without even a chance of posting a letter to you. We have a hundred tons of coal on deck, and shall be very dirty until we burn it all up. ...

February 19*th*.—*Seven* A.M.—I have just had my first walk on deck for this day. It is fine, and the head wind keeps up a cool draught of air for us. The night was pleasant and cool, and I spent an hour before I went to bed, walking up and down the bridge, between the paddle-boxes, looking at a great moon, a little past the full, climbing up the heavens before us, and (as Coleridge says, I think in the notes to the *Ancient Mariner*, of the stars) entering unannounced among the groups of stars as a guest certainly expected,—and yet there is a silent joy on her arrival. ... If this sort of weather would last!—but Calcutta! ...

February 20*th*.—*Noon*.—Yesterday, at about three P.M., we were aroused by the report of a steamer in sight, and made out that she came from the Mauritius. She stopped to communicate with us, as her passengers were anxious to know whether we were at war with America. I sent a note to you by her. ... We have a light breeze now, and more on our beam, which enables us to set our fore and aft sails; the temperature delicious. ... I have committed the last of my old note-books to the sea, after gleaning from them some recollections of myself in earlier days, which, strange to say, one is apt to lose. I was working pretty hard then, between the end of Oxford and the beginning of active political life, perhaps in rather too desultory a way, but acquiring large views of men and things, which were afterwards not without their use.

February 22*d*.—A little more motion yesterday; but still delightfully cool. ... I am reading Elphinstone's *History of India*, which is pretty dry; and a good many odds and ends of papers on India. I am also writing a monster letter to F., which I intend to post at Galle, as I do not know when I may have time to write to him again. ... We are a very quiet party as compared with former occasions, and I have little to write about. ...

Sunday, February 23*d*.—We had service to-day. ... Our fourth Sunday. But the first was a rough day in the Banshee; the second, the day we left Suez; the third, a storm in the Red sea. So this is the first Sunday quiet enough for service. ... The wind is ahead, and we go on slowly; ... but if it were not for Canning, I should not care for the long passage. I have no great object to gain by arriving; very different from when I was looking forward last year to my return home! . . . I spend almost all day in my cabin, as it is protected from the sun, and I have enough to occupy me. . . .

February 25*th.*—The wind is a little fairer. . . .

February 26*th.*—We are getting on so much better, that we now speak of the 29th as the probable day of our arrival at Galle. . . . The heat is increasing. . . .

February 27*th.*—According to the account of our captain, who hails from Bombay, the Governor there must be very well off as regards climate. He has the sea air at Bombay itself; 2000 feet of elevation at Poonah; and 5000 on a mountain accessible in two days from Bombay. So that his family may always live in a cool climate, and he can join them when business permits. Perhaps at some future time the convenience of the situation of Bombay, its greater vicinity to England, etc., may place the Governor-General there; but this will not happen in our time. As I went into my cabin yesterday before dinner, I observed a swarm of white flies with long wings, by the side of one of my open ports. I found out that they were white ants which had burst through the wood-work, and which seem to be provided with wings under such circumstances, in order that they may migrate. The wood-work inside near the place from which they burst out, was completely destroyed by them, and reduced to a pulp. It appears that there are quantities of these creatures in this ship. It is believed that they are only in the scantling or upper wood-work. It is to be hoped that this may be so; for they devour timber with wonderful rapidity, and ships have been lost by their eating away portions under water. . . . It is sensibly hotter.

Galle.—March 2*d.—Sunday.*—I have been at the Galle Church. The last time I was there was on the Sunday after our shipwreck! Canning has telegraphed to say I need not hurry; so I shall call at Madras. I am on Mr. F.'s hill, which is always cool and pleasant. We found here yesterday on our arrival Lord J. Hay in the Odin, with the Japanese ambassadors. They number with their suite thirty-seven; so it is rather a large party, and I am glad it was not my fate to succeed them in the Odin, as was once reported. I find no news here, either from home or from India. . . .

March 3*d.—Seven* A.M.—I am to be on board the Ferooz by half-past eight. It is a two or three days' passage from here to Madras. . . .

Ferooz, at Sea.—March 3*d.*—I hope that you will receive in due time the letter which I left this morning at Galle, to be sent to you by the first opportunity. . . . We are going on much as we did before reaching Galle. A light head wind, and the coast of Ceylon still in sight on our left. . . . With Madras begins the serious part of my duties. I have had an easy time as yet, although I have been getting up as well as I can a variety of subjects. . . . The mail of the 10th of February from England will probably catch us up at Madras.

March 4th.—We have not seen the home-bound steamer, though her lights were supposed to have been perceived about midnight; so this letter must be with me till I leave Madras. We stopped to sound several times during the night, and there was a great noise each time of steam escaping, but we are going on smoothly to-day. . . .

March 5th.—In all probability we shall reach Madras to-morrow morning. . . . Canning stayed there ten days. . . . I do not think I shall remain beyond Monday the 10th at the farthest; but time will show. . . .

March 6th.—Ten A.M.—Last night we again stopped often to sound, and the wind blew so strongly through my ports, that I actually pulled the blanket over me! When I went on deck at six A.M. I saw land, but we did not well know where we were. A low, flat coast, without landmarks; but now we have sighted the Madras lighthouse, and may expect to arrive by noon. . . .

Eleven A.M.—The lighthouse turns out not to be the one at Madras at all, but about forty miles above! so we have put about, and are going with all speed backwards. . . .

March 7th.—Madras. — In consequence of our blunder in missing Madras, we only reached the anchorage at 4.30 P.M. We soon got into one of the country boats made for landing in the surf (without nails, and all the planks sewn together). We were hoisted by the waves upon the beach, and found there a considerable crowd, with the Governor, Sir W. Denison; Sir H. Grant, etc., and a guard of honour, to receive us; Sir W. D. drove me out to this place, Guindy, which is about eight miles from the town, and consists of a charming airy house, in a large park. There was a full-dress dinner party and reception last night. . . . I have decided to proceed to Calcutta to-morrow. . . .

March 8th.—Seven A.M.—Sir W. and I have had our morning walk, in which Lady D. joined us. . . . It is a great comfort to live in a park out of town. One cannot stroll out in this free and easy way at Calcutta. I am to have a levee this afternoon before I start. . . .

Ferooz.—March 9th.—Sunday.—It was very hot during the service under the awning. But you and the little ones were remembered on this sweltering Bengal sea. . . . My visit to

Madras was pleasant, and an agreeable change. . . . And I collected there papers and official documents enough to keep me going till I reach Calcutta. . . .

March 10*th*.—We have made 250 miles in the last twenty-four hours, which is a great run for this ship. . . .

March 11*th*.—The home-going steamer passed us at one A.M., and we did not communicate, so you will receive by it only the letter left at Madras. At about ten A.M. we took a pilot at the Sandheads, and are now (*Noon*) near the bar at the entrance of the river Hoogly. . . .

March 12*th*.—I spent last night at the same anchorage (Diamond Harbour) at which I spent the night of the 8th of August 1857. To my surprise the air was cool and pleasant, and there were no mosquitoes. I telegraphed to Canning, to say that I would arrive at Calcutta at one P.M. to-day; but I received a reply begging me not to reach that place till 4.30 P.M. We therefore started later, and had just passed over the famous shoal *James and Mary*, when a small steamer met us with C.'s military secretary and two aides-de-camp. I received from them the programme of the ceremony of reception, and they brought with them your letters to the 1st of February. . . .

Calcutta.—*March* 13*th*.—Yesterday evening brought me another and later letter from you. . . . The ceremony of installation went off well. Canning is very kind. I do not think him looking so ill as I expected. But those about him say he is far from right in health. I hardly know yet what my labours are to be. The climate is more tolerable than I expected to find it at this season. . . . My room is comfortable. It has an enclosure of mosquito-net fixed in a frame, large enough to hold a bed, writing-table, etc., and reaching up to the ceiling, with a punkah inside it, which is kept in motion all night. . . .

March 14*th*—There was a great dinner yesterday (of about seventy). Canning entertains me till Friday, when I take the house, etc., over. He embarks, I believe, on Tuesday. . . .

March 15*th*.—A great reception was held here last night, at which, I suppose, some 800 or 900 people walked past. The mixture of costumes, military uniforms, and native attire, was very effective. The rooms, too, are very handsome, and the night was cool. . . . I took a short ride this morning. . . .

Sunday, March 16*th*.—My first in Calcutta as Governor-General. . . . Another dinner of eighty people yesterday. . . .

March 17*th*.—I was at the Cathedral yesterday. The Bishop preached, and it was not so hot as I expected, the punkahs kept the air in motion. Canning goes to Barrackpore to-day, and embarks to-morrow. . . .

March 18*th*.— . . . I do not yet find it too hot to take some exercise in the morning. The garden here is a place one can walk in without being much seen, so I go out before the sun rises, and stroll about till a little after six, when I come in and have my coffee. This was my practice in the West Indies. ...

March 19*th.*—Your letters to February 17th have just reached me. ... I must close this. ...

Calcutta.—March 19*th.*—This will probably be a short letter, though I begin it so soon, as the intervals are very unequal here between the despatch of the mails *viâ* Bombay and those from Calcutta. ... I have just taken a drive for the first time along the public drive, where all the world congregates at sunset, in my barouche with four horses and postilions, and an escort of the mounted body-guard. I remained a very short time, and ended with half an hour's walk in the garden.

March 20*th.*—On Saturday I am to receive the Rajah of Puttiala at a public durbar, which is a grand ceremonial. It is still cool for the season. This morning at sunrise it was almost chilly. ...

March 21*st.*—I have consulted Dr. Macrae, as I felt a little out of sorts, and I am all right again. ...

March 22*d.*—The days are very uniform in their round of occupations, so I have little to record that is interesting. As long as one has health, it is easy to do a good deal of work here, because for twelve hours in the day (from six A.M. to six P.M.) there is no inducement to leave the house. I have hitherto had a little exercise before and after those hours. I rush into the garden when I awake, and return when the sun appears, glowing and angry, above the horizon. ...

March 23*d.*—I woke this morning at four, and went out at five. It was then close and muggy, a white mist hanging over everything. It became a little fresher just before six, but the sun is only now (seven A.M.) beginning to appear. In the afternoon I held a durbar, of which I enclose the programme for the amusement of the children. ... You must see from my letters what wonderful care I am taking of myself! ...

Calcutta.—March 24*th.*—I sent off a letter to you yesterday, and afterwards I attended the funeral of one of my councillors, Ritchie by name; a very excellent man, and I shall feel his loss very much, I fear. ... I had my walk this morning, which was a clear one. As usual, while I was taking my rounds, a dark figure wrapped in a white sheet (the gardener) rushed out of the shrubbery, and with force "salaams" presented me with a bouquet most artistically arranged. ...

March 25*th.*—This is to be a ceremonial day, a levee, and a return visit to the Rajah of Puttiala. ...

March 26*th.*—My levee went off well. My visit to the Rajah was a dusty drive along a bad road to his residence, and while the presents were being set out, we were entertained by a Nautch girl, who wailed a harsh ditty through her nose, and then moved in a melancholy way about the room, twisting her hands about as they did in Java, to the music of a hurdygurdy.

March 27*th.*—I intend to have one large formal dinner a week, and three or four guests every other day. I shall in this way get acquainted with people, and suck their brains. . . .

March 29*th.*—We have just had a north-wester, accompanied by a hailstorm, with hail as big as lumps of ice. It has cooled the air, but it is not quite over yet. . . . A telegram from Bombay brought news yesterday, a week later than what we had heard the day before through Galle. . . . My chief councillor, Sir B. Frere, is named Governor of Bombay. This will be a loss to me here. . . . I had a grand dinner of some sixty people on Thursday, and my usual small one yesterday. . . .

March 30*th.*—*Sunday.*—The storm continued till about ten P.M. yesterday. A constant growl of thunder, and lightning scoring the black clouds in all manner of zigzags. It had a wonderful effect on the temperature. Indeed, I was very chilly at dinner. These changes are, I suspect, very trying. I have been to a church nearer than the cathedral.

March 21*st.*—A pleasant morning. March has been much more lamb-like than I anticipated, but I am told it has been a singularly cool one. . . .

April 1*st.*—This promises to be a busy day. Two addresses, and a public and private durbar to end with. It is getting hotter again, as we lose the influence of the recent storm. We shall go on accumulating electricity and heat for several days, when another disturbance of the elements will take place. This appears to be the order of proceeding during our hot months. It is better than I fancied, for I did not know that the continuity of our heat was ever interrupted. The thermometer was at 65° two mornings ago, when I came in at sunrise, but I do not expect to see it so low again for several months. . . .

April 4*th.*—I have received your letters of February 25th and March 2d within one day of each other! . . .

Sunday, April 6*th.*—This is a hot day, and I have not gone to church. . . . Shut up in my room, and with a punkah going; the heat is, however, by no means unbearable. I heard a splashing of water in my bedroom yesterday, and on going into it I found that one of my windows had been opened, and a matting of scented grass put up in its place, which a " Bheestie" drenches every now and then with cold water, and through which the air penetrates into the room, causing a cooling evaporation to take place. This matting is called a " tattie."

April 8th.—Yesterday was really hot, but my room was comparatively so cool, that when I went out to ride at six P.M., it seemed like going into a vapour-bath. . . .

April 9th.—I sent off a letter to you an hour ago, and now I begin another, although ten days will, I suppose, elapse before it is despatched. . . .

April 12th.—I received another address of the usual kind yesterday. . . . These little incidents are the only variations in my existence here, which is of the most monotonous description. . . . I still think this mode of life, and no exposure to the sun, is the best on the whole for health, and as it is very conducive to the despatch of business, I shall probably continue it, not even going to Barrackpore, as yet. . . . Just about a year has elapsed since I met you at Paris on my last return from China. How many things have passed since then! The stay in London; the offer of India; the pleasant days in Scotland; the parting; the long voyage; and now I am already Viceroy of India of one month's standing! I can hardly believe that all this has occupied only a year. . . .

Sunday.—April 13th.— . . . I am going to afternoon church at the Fort, at 6.30 P.M., in the cool of the evening. . . . I am anxious for letters. . . .

April 14th.—I hope for letters to-morrow. . . . There is a register kept of the state of the thermometer at all the principal electric telegraph stations, and transmitted here daily. Calcutta heads the list in point of heat, 94° being the latest figure given. In my room it has seldom been much above 80° yet. . . . The *tattie* keeps down the temperature, and being made of scented grass, conveys a pleasant perfume as well as coolness. . . .

Good Friday.—I have received four letters from you nearly at once. . . . This is a reward for my waiting. . . . The last was finished on the 17th of March, and I received it on April the 16th. But this is by the Bombay route, by which we gain several days both ways. It was very hot at the church in Fort-William. . . .

Easter-Day.—I have just returned from church. . . . I found a telegram with news to the 26th March, which seems menacing news enough, in so far as the peace of the world is concerned; the letters of the same date will not arrive here for a week, and after I have despatched this letter to you. I see that the telegraphic wire is laid to Jubal in the Red Sea, so that we ought to be able to receive intelligence from England in about twelve days *via* Bombay! . . . I find that Dalhousie was hardly ever in Calcutta—about two seasons out of eight—the others he passed in hill stations; Simla, the Neilgherries, etc. Canning, on the contrary, was almost always here. Indeed I believe he liked the climate of Calcutta better than the hills. What am I to do? . . . For the present I shall remain as much as possible at Calcutta, so as to have my hands as free as may be afterwards. . . .

April 23*d.*—This goes to-day. We had rain last night, which has rather cooled the air. . . . I enclose an address which I received yesterday. . . . Mr. Laing has been told by his doctor that he must not remain here after the beginning of June. So that I shall soon have lost all Canning's councillors except one. . . .

April 24*th.*—After the departure of yesterday's mail, which carried off Sir J. Grant, I had a special meeting of Council to swear in Mr. Beadon as his successor, and Mr. Grey, as inheritor of Mr. Beadon's seat in Council. Both appointments were duly notified by salutes from the fort. . . . It is very important that I should see the northern parts of India as soon as possible. I believe that the whole tour cannot be accomplished in less than two seasons; and that the most convenient way would be to do half of it in one winter, pass the summer at Simla, and do the other half in the second winter in the way down to Calcutta. But it is very difficult to lay down plans. I have an entirely new council, etc. etc.; and besides, there is the *imprévu*, which plays so large a part in Indian affairs. Even now there is a movement of Persia on our northern frontier which may give us trouble, and upset the best-laid schemes. . . .

April 25*th.*—Before my ride was over yesterday, a violent wind came on, ending in rain; so I got the first ducking I have had since my arrival. . . .

April 28*th.*—Yesterday brought me home-letters. . . .

May 2*d.*— . . . I am distressed to find that on the 2d of April you had not received the letter which I left for you at Galle a month before. I have telegraphed to know if it was duly forwarded. . . .

May 4*th.*—*Sunday.*—I have just returned from church, where it was rather cooler than last time, and I must send off this letter.

May 6*th.*— . . . The season is still, they say, remarkably cool. Constant thunder-storms of late, which have cooled the air. This morning the whole *Maidan* is a sheet of water. Probably we shall pay for these early rains in some way or other. . . . It appears that there has been a hurricane here once in ten years—in 1832, 1842, and 1852, and now it is looked for again. There is a general massacre of the crows on such occasions; they are to be found lying dead in heaps on the Maidan. It is described as terrific.

May 7*th.*—Lady Franklin has suddenly made her appearance

here *en route* from China to England. I have asked her to dine with me to-day. She called on me at my mountain cottage in Jamaica seventeen years ago! She was travelling then, as now, with a niece. . . .

May 8th.—Lady Franklin informs me that she left London, soon after I met her at Sir R. Murchison's, in 1859, I think. She went to New York, thence by Cape Horn to San Francisco; from that to British Columbia and back; then to the Sandwich Islands and back; then from San Francisco to Japan, Shanghae, Hong-kong, Calcutta! She is a wonderful traveller, and puts me to shame. She describes the King of the Sandwich Islands as a very enlightened gentleman. He gave them a state dinner, served *à la Russe*. She starts for England to-morrow. . . .

May 11th.—I am expecting letters in two days. I trust they will tell me that you have received the missing letter. . . . No incident of any kind has happened lately. . . . Laing is likely, I find, not to return again. . . . I am to assist at a lecture which he is to deliver to-morrow. . . .

May 13th.— . . . My uniform life was broken in upon yesterday to the extent of dining half an hour earlier, and going to a public meeting to hear Mr. Laing's lecture. He looked ill and worn. . . . His lecture was a good one, though somewhat dry in part, which is more than I was, for I had an arm-chair out of the draught, and the punkah was rather high over my head. I proposed a vote of thanks to him at the close, which was well taken. . . .

May 15th.—Letters arrived yesterday evening, which were telegraphed as in the river the day before, but they remain frequently for about thirty hours within about as many miles of Calcutta. . . . It now appears that my missing letter was sent from Galle, by some mistake, *viâ* Southampton instead of *viâ* Marseilles. . . . However, it is a relief to know this, for I began to fear for my other letters. . . . The homeward mails start earlier now, because of the adverse monsoon. . . .

May 19th.—After dinner, yesterday, I started to pay my first visit to Barrackpore, with the intention of remaining till this evening. I found it, however, so much hotter there that I resolved to come back this morning. It is hotter here, too, than it was. . . . But apart from the heat of the house, which is more slightly built than this one, nothing could be more charming than the place. I did not admire it as much in 1857. The park contains beautiful trees, and has much of the character of an English park. Then there is the magnificent river which runs just under the house, with a broad terrace-walk above it, which terminates near the enclosure where Lady Canning lies, overlooking what was a favourite view. . . .

May 21st.—Mr. and Mrs. Laing dined a farewell dinner with me yesterday. They start the day after to-morrow. . . . It is very hot during the day now, but we have more or less rain every evening. . . . I am obliged to go out in the morning, before five generally, in order to escape the sun. . . .

May 22d.—This letter goes to-night. I have little to communicate, but it is well that it should be so, for it shows that things are going on smoothly. . . .

Sunday, May 25th.— . . . The telegraph brings news so quickly that one gets into a complete confusion about dates. As to public events of importance, they are all anticipated long before newspapers arrive, so that what they tell is quite stale. Mr. Laing has taken his departure. I have assumed his office, but I do not as yet find the work too much. On the contrary, time would be heavy on hand if I had not enough to do to fill it. . . .

May 27th.—I went to my first evening party yesterday. It was given by the new Lieutenant-Governor of Bengal,—Mr. Beadon, and a good many natives were invited as well as the European society. It was a kind of imitation of the Bath House reunions,—electric telegraphs, steam-engines, photographs, etc., dispersed about the rooms. It was very successful. As there was no moon, we drove in the open carriage with uncovered heads. We had about three miles to go, and I should not have been sorry if it had been twice as far. The day had been very hot, but a storm at about six cooled the air. . . . As I stepped on to my verandah just now, to see if the riding horses were at the door, the air felt like the blast of a furnace. In my own room the thermometer is 85°.

Sunday.—June 1st.— . . . Three days ago I received your letters to April 25th. . . . There was a very nice note from B., who was with you for his Easter holidays, which were less merry than they ought to have been,—"because mamma was so ill!" Dear fellow! he seems to be working hard, and trying to please us. On Wednesday (4th of June) I am to have an Eton dinner, which was Canning's practice. I believe we shall muster from fifteen to twenty. For the last few days it has been *very* hot,—quite as hot, they say, as it ever is. . . . I am longing for the rains, which are to cool us, I am told. . . .

June 4th.—I have received the mail of the 3d of May. . . . I am too anxious to write much until I hear again. . . .

Sunday, June 8th.—I could not begin my letter till I heard from or about you; and by some extraordinary Providence, contradicting the adage about bad news, the mail bringing your note, dated 9th of May, has made the quickest passage on record! It has reached Calcutta, *rid* Galle, two days within the month, from London! So I can at once answer it. . . . A. has been so kind, I must write and thank her with all my heart. . . .

June 9th.—A very short letter, but I could not continue my journal after the last mail. . . .

Sunday, June 15th.—I have not taken my rides for a few days in consequence of a trifling accident, so I have taken advantage of my carriage drives to visit some parts of the neighbourhood. In fact, I had never gone beyond the Maidan (our Hyde Park) in my rides. One day I drove to a place called Garden reach, on the bank of the river. It used to be a favourite site for villas, etc., but the ex-king of Oude is now established there, buying up all the houses, and enclosing them with high walls, within which he keeps his ninety wives, and an army of ragamuffins of all descriptions. It is a great nuisance, but I do not know how to abate it. All sorts of stories are told of his intriguing, etc., but I do not believe them, though some of the people about him may wish to make mischief. The dust on these roads used to be suffocating, while the Maidan is watered. The rains have, however, now commenced, so that one can drive in the country with comparative comfort. As yet the rains are very mild; not much more than one good shower a day, and the temperature of the air is sensibly lower. . . . Next Friday I am to give a ball. There will be a variety of costumes, for many natives are asked. . . .

June 17th.— . . . I took a notion yesterday that I would start at once for Delhi; the soldiers there are working themselves into a panic, and doing all manner of mischief. I might perhaps stop it by going to the place. . . . *Three P.M.*—A telegram from Bombay; much later than usual, but no reason given. It is pouring. The rains are fairly set in, I suppose. . . . It is rather dull to stay in the house all day, without even one's hour of riding. I shall not now hear of you for a long week. May my news be good! . . .

June 19th. . . . It poured all yesterday, with a good deal of wind. The consequence was, that my windows were open all day, and I was tolerably cool. I daresay many exhausted East Indians would complain of the chilliness, but I did not. The thermometer was at 80° during the greater part of the day.

Sunday, June 22d.— . . . This letter must be posted tonight, but I have nothing further yet from you. . . . Till I get another report, I do not feel inclined to say much. . . . I have abandoned for the present my notion of going to Delhi. The foolish panic which led me to entertain it has subsided, and its authors are, I hope, rather ashamed of their work. My ball on the 20th went off as well as such things generally do, and the variety of dress gave it a gay look. I did not get to bed till nearly three, and have not yet quite recovered from the effects of this unusual dissipation, three A.M. being generally much nearer the hour of my rising than of my retiring. The room was not nearly so hot, at least for non-dancers, as a London ball-room. . . . I am in distress at this moment, because all kinds of pressure are being brought to bear on me to induce me to reprieve an Englishman, who has been sentenced to be executed to-morrow for the murder of a native. These cases are always very painful, and especially so here from the rivalry of race. . . .

Calcutta.—June 28*th.*—I have received your letters of May 18th and 26th. . . . You know the disinclination I always feel to settling things long beforehand. I believe that this arises in a great measure from the many changes that I have gone through, and the practical conviction of the uncertainty of human schemes which these changes and vicissitudes have impressed upon me. However, all arrangements here must be made long beforehand, so I have set to work to look the question steadily in the face since I received your letter. . . . I very much doubt if you could stand the temperature we are now enduring, and the worst is, I fear, yet to come. The heavy, dull, damp, calm heat between the falls of rain is most trying. . . . Altogether, this is very much my original plan. . . .

Sunday, July 6*th.*—Is it indeed true? Three batches of news reached me to-day: first, letters up to June 3d, *via* Bombay; next, a telegram from Galle with intelligence to June 10th; and lastly, a telegram to June 19th, saying that Canning died on the 18th! The last rumour of the kind was the report of my death, when I was mistaken for Eglinton; but this time I fear it is only too true! It will add to the alarm which India inspires. But poor Canning certainly never gave himself a good chance; at least not during the last year or two of his reign here. He took no exercise, and not even such relaxation of the mind as was procurable, though that is not much in the situation of Governor-General. When I told him that I should ask two or three people to dine with me daily, in order to get acquainted with all the persons I ought to know, and to talk matters over with them by candle-light, so as to save daylight for other work, he said: "I was always so tired by dinner-time that I could not speak." Perhaps he was only referring to his later experience; but still it was enough to break down any constitution, to wear one's-self out for ever by the same train of thought, and the same routine of business. I think there was more in all this than met the eye, for work alone could not have done it. We shall have no confirmation of this rumour in letters for a fortnight or more. . . . Poor Canning! He leaves behind him sincere friends, but no one who was much dependent on him. . . . I hope my last letter will have set you at rest as to L.'s coming out with you. I am satisfied that it may be done if the plan which I sketched can be carried out; and at any rate, if it cannot, I must devise some other, which, in so far as health is concerned, will do as well for you and her. . . .

July 8th.—I am sleeping rather badly; waking at two, three, four, and all sorts of unearthly hours. . . . I am going to Barrackpore to-night. Perhaps the change of air will do me good. . . .

Barrackpore.—Sunday, July 13th.—I have received your letter telling me of your safe arrival in London on the 10th of June, which gave me great joy. . . . I trust you may be able for your long journey when the time for it shall arrive. I came here on Tuesday last, bringing with me Sir R. Napier and his family, who remained till Friday, when we went into Calcutta for Council, and I returned yesterday, with Sir B. Peacock (the Chief-Justice) and his wife. They leave this to-morrow; but I think I shall stay, and only go into town to see councillors, etc. It is cooler here now than formerly, and I have slept better since I changed the air, though I have not been quite well of late. . . . This place looks wonderfully green. . . . At the end of the broad walk on which I am gazing from my window, is Lady Canning's grave; it is not yet properly finished. Who will attend to it now? . . . Meanwhile, it gives a melancholy character to the place, for the walk which it closes is literally the only private walk in the grounds. The flower garden, park, etc., are all open to the public. . . . Although Canning did not die at his post, I thought it right, as his death took place so soon after his departure from India, to recognise it officially, which I did by a public notification, and by directing a salute of minute guns to be fired. . . . I do not in the least believe that any man can win a name here unless there be some great events, such as the Mutiny, Dalhousie's Annexations, etc., to set his qualities on a pedestal. Nevertheless, for the sake of the country, we must say amen, with all fervour, to those who pray that we may have quiet in our time; and we must content ourselves with maturing peaceful measures of improvement and progress for the Secretary of State and his fifteen colleagues to peck at.

July 15th.—It is still cloudy and pleasant, and I again took a ride this morning. I go into Calcutta early to-morrow. . . .

Calcutta.—July 16th.—Eight A.M.—I had a cool drive from Barrackpore. Cloudy, and a little rain. I send off a mail to-day. . . .

Barrackpore.—July 20*th.*—I received yesterday yours of the 22d June, with the photographs of the children. . . . They reached me just in time to cheer me on this day; and the accounts sent by others of the dear boys are, as well as yours, delightful. . . . Will they get on as well without your tender care ? . . . The travelling with a camp is a very slow business, and not very fatiguing. There are two sets of tents. You leave your one house in the morning, travel about ten or twelve miles, and find your other house ready built for you when you reach your stopping-place. You may go in your carriage or on horseback as you prefer; and the climate is, I fancy, at that season (winter) delicious. The great inconvenience is the dust and confusion occasioned by the bodies of troops, baggage-wagons, elephants, camels, etc., which accompany the march. . . . I must stop now, for two men have just entered my room loaded with red boxes, and I must see what they contain. . . .

July 21*st.*—The telegram reports that Canning was buried in Westminster Abbey; so would poor Dalhousie have been if he had died as soon after his return. On what accidents such things hinge!

Barrackpore.—July 26*th.*—I went into Calcutta on the morning of the 23d, in time to write by the after packet; but I did not write, for I was met on my arrival by a telegraphic rumour, which quite overwhelmed me. . . . I should hardly have allowed myself to believe that the sad report could be true, had it not been for the account of R.'s illness, which your last letters had conveyed to me. . . . Next day another telegram by the Bombay mail of the 3d July left no doubt as to the name. . . . A week, however, must elapse before letters arrive with the intelligence. . . . I hurried over my business, and came back here yesterday evening. It is more quiet than Calcutta; and sad, with its *one* walk terminating (as I have told you) at Lady C.'s grave. Poor R., how little did I think when we parted that I was never to see him again ! How little at least, that he would be the defaulter ! He has left few equals behind him : so true, so upright, so steady in his principles, and so winning in his manners. Of late years we have been much apart, but for very many we were closely together, and perhaps no two brothers were ever more mutually helpful. Strange, that with F. and me, in these regions, he should have been carried off first, by a malady which belongs to them. . . . I write at random and confusedly, for I have nothing to guide me but that one word. And yet how much in that one word ! It tells me that I have lost a wise counsellor in difficulties; a stanch friend in prosperity and adversity ; one on whom, if anything had befallen myself, I could always have relied to care for those left behind me. It tells, too, of the dropping of a link of that family chain which has always been so strong and unbroken.

July 28*th.*—I went to church yesterday morning at seven A.M. It was close and hot, and I thought the clergyman would break down. He was obliged to go into the vestry at one time to refresh himself. Later in the day it rained hard, and became cooler. We are now approaching what is, I suppose, our worst season. I know something of it, as I experienced it in 1857. . . .

July 29*th.*—Last night came your letters to June 26th. You were all anxious. . . . But you did not seem to anticipate what was so near at hand. . . .

August 2*d.*—Yesterday, I received your letter, with all the sad details. . . . It was truly a lovely death, in harmony with the life that preceded it. Poor K.! . . . I have written a few lines to her, which I enclose for you to forward. . . . It is indeed a heavy blow to all. . . . This is a sad letter, but my heart is heavy. It is difficult to make plans, with such a break-down of human hopes in possession of all my thoughts. . . .

Calcutta.—*August* 8*th.*—It is now dreadfully hot. . . . In search of something to stay my gasping. I mounted on to the roof of the house this morning, to take my walk there, instead of in my close garden, where there are low shrubs which give no shade, but exclude the breeze. I made nothing, however, by my motion, for no air was stirring even there. I had a solitary and ghastly stroll on the leads, surrounded by the *adjutants,*—a sort of hideous and filthy vulture. They do the work of scavengers in Calcutta, and are ready to treat one as a nuisance, if they had a chance. . . . There is much sickness here now. . . .

August 9*th.*— . . . The Ferooz will not reach Suez till about the middle of November, so you had better not arrive there till after that time. You will have the best season for the voyage, and time to rest here before we go up the country . . .

Calcutta.—*August* 17*th.*— . . . I told you that I was feeling the weather. . . . I am going to-morrow for change of air, to a place about 300 miles from Calcutta, on the railway. It is not cooler, but drier, and the doctor strongly recommends the change. This is our worst season, and I suppose we may expect six weeks more of it. If this change is not enough, I may perhaps try and get a steamer, and go over to Burmah. But there is some difficulty in this at present. . . .

Bhagulpore.—*August* 19*th.*—We made out our journey to this place very well yesterday. The morning was cloudy, with drizzling rain, and much cooler than usual, and we had the great advantage of little sun and no dust all day. At the station of

Burdwan, the inhabitants of the station, some of them ladies; met us, and in a very polite manner presented flowers. We kept our time pretty well in our special train, and reached our abode at about seven P.M. The air here is sensibly fresher than at Calcutta. . . . The house is a regular bungalow, a cottage,— all on the ground-floor. It is situated on a mound overlooking the Ganges. There is no garden about it, but a grass field, with a few trees here and there. Between the window at which I am writing and the river is an open shed, in which two elephants are switching their tails, and knocking about the hay which has been given them for their breakfast. This is a much more quiet and rural place than any which I have visited since I have been in India; for Barrackpore is a great military station, and the park, etc., there are quite public. Here there are not altogether above five or six European families. . . . We have a train twice a day from Calcutta, so I can get my boxes as regularly as I do there. . . .

August 21st.— . . . The chief people here are Mr. and Mrs. M. She took me a drive on Tuesday in her carriage, and he carried me yesterday in his gig to a house on a mound with a very fine view, which they want Government to buy as a retreat for the Governor-General when at Calcutta. I do not think the change sufficiently great to warrant a permanent arrangement of this nature, as no doubt cooler places will soon be made accessible by railway; also, I doubt the Governor-General's being much at Calcutta during the summer. Then there is Barrackpore. . . . This letter must leave this place to-morrow at seven A.M. . . .

Bhagulpore.—*August 25th.*—On Saturday, we made an expedition to a place called Monghyr, about forty-five miles from here, where there is a hot spring, and something like *hills.* (I am told also, that on a particularly clear day I can see from here the highest mountain in the world.) We did not leave this till three P.M., and were back again by eight P.M., having travelled some ninety miles by rail, and driven in carriages about ten or twelve more,—the fastest thing, I should think, ever done in India. There has been a good deal of rain, and I still feel well here, but I suppose on the 29th I must return to the Calcutta steam-bath. This forenoon I paid a visit to a school, one of the Government schools. The boys (upwards of 200) are not of the lowest class. They all read English very well, and when asked the meaning of words, gave synonymes or explanatory phrases with remarkable readiness. During their early years, I should certainly say that they are quicker than English children. They fall off when they get older.

August 26*th*.—Home letters arrived last night. . . . You have anticipated my wishes respecting B.'s examination. I shall be anxious to hear the result, meanwhile his trials at Glenalmond have been most satisfactory. . . . I dined yesterday with Mr. M., the Commissioner here. We had all the society, about five ladies, and twice as many men. . . . For the last two days it has been really cool. I am standing at my writing desk now (four P.M.) with my coat off and all the windows open, and really comfortable,

August 31*st.—Calcutta.*—We returned to this place on Thursday. It is cooler than when I left, but I fear we have not done with the heat yet. All agree that September is about the worst month in the year here. . . .

September 2*d*.—Your letters to the beginning of August just received. . . . The report of dear B.'s examination is very satisfactory, and I quite approve of his going to Eton at Christmas. . . . If one lives through this heavy hot month, I shall begin to breathe again, and to hope for your coming. . . .

Calcutta.—September 8*th.*—I do not think that Dr. M. is particularly proud of the way in which I am bearing up against this oppressive and depressing season. . . . I wish that we were going to the Neilgherries instead of to Simla. The climate is, I believe, better, and the place more agreeable, but it is entirely out of the way of business for me now, whereas Simla is a natural stage to the most important part of my government. . . .

September 13*th.*—. . . The climate continues to be very trying, and I have had some idea of running away for two or three weeks during what are called the Holidays, when all offices here are shut up. The great difficulty is to find a place to go to. I am told that Burmah is hotter than Calcutta during the month of October. I have half a mind to offer a week's visit to Sir W. Denison, who is now at the Neilgherries. . . .

September 17*th.*—This letter goes to-day. . . . I have given up my morning walks. It is now always sultry before sunrise, and the dulness of pacing up and down my garden at that hour is intolerable. So I walk till daylight in my verandah. . . .

September 19*th.*—I have been driven in from my ride two evenings following by a pour of rain, and I am trying to write a few lines by candle-light, which is not my usual practice. It has almost been cool, the last few days. . . .

September 23*d*.—. . . It seems strange to think that this is one of the last letters which you will receive from me in England, but yet it is still a long time before I can hope to see you here. The poor boys! You will be preparing to part from them, and all will be sad. Give them my love and blessing. . . .

September 30th.—. . . For several reasons I have abandon‹ my intention of visiting Sir W. Denison on the Neilgherries. .

October 2d.—This letter must go to-day. May it find y‹ hearty and able to bear up against the fatigues of the voya‹ . . . and I trust that the difficulties of the transit may dimini‹ as you approach them. . . .

Calcutta.—October 19th.—. . . I believe that Sir B. Frere h made all needful arrangements for your comfort on board t‹ Ferooz, and I understand that he has written to advise you n to go beyond Cairo until you hear that the Ferooz is actually Suez. . . .

October 23d.—My last letter I sent under cover to the Gove nor of Malta. . . . I send this to the care of the Consul Alexandria. . . . I am getting a mosquito-net enclosure, and fire-place put up in your apartments. The weather is becomi‹ somewhat cooler. The thermometer marks 76° to-day, but it a pour of rain. . . .

Barrackpore.—November 23d.—I send this to Galle. . . . O weather is very pleasant now, and I am well, except that sleep badly. . . .

Calcutta.—December 9th.—Admiral Hope, who has been wi me here for a week, sails to-day for England, and I give hi this note for you, to tell you that all is ready for you here. . This is the second letter you will find at Galle. I shall course hear of your arrival by telegraph when you reach th point. . . .

www.ingramcontent.com/pod-product-compliance
Lightning Source LLC
Chambersburg PA
CBHW031950230426
43672CB00010B/2108